G000256164

Bloomsbury Keys
Adjectives

BLOOMSBURY

First published by Bloomsbury Publishing Plc, 2 Soho Square, London W1V 6HB.
Copyright © 1995 by Bloomsbury Publishing Limited.
British Library Cataloguing in Publication Data. A CIP record for this book is available from the British Library
ISBN 0 7475 1882 3

Compiled and prepared for typesetting by
Market House Books Ltd, Aylesbury.

Printed in Great Britain by
HarperCollins Manufacturing, Glasgow.

Introduction

This book contains a list of adjectives, both common and unusual, arranged alphabetically. Under each entry, a selection is given of alternatives that may be used in place of the headword or that are associated with the headword. Where appropriate, these synonyms have been divided (using semicolons) into related groups. The book also contains cross references to related headwords.

True synonyms – i.e. words that have exactly the same meaning under all circumstances – are rare, and the entries contain a wide range of words that express the meaning in the headword. The book is intended for those who are searching for an alternative adjective, either to express their ideas more clearly or to avoid repetition. We hope that the user will find it both useful and informative.

KEY ADJECTIVES

A

abducent centrifugal, repelling, diamagnetic.

able competent, proficient, fit, capable, accomplished, skilled.

abnegating relinquishing, self-sacrificing, self-renunciatory, self-denying.

abnormal anomalous, unnatural, deviant, aberrant, mutant, variant, irregular, odd, queer.

abominable disgusting, obnoxious, loathsome, foul, horrible, repulsive.

abrasives harsh, rough, grating; sharp, caustic, cutting, biting.

abrupt curt, brusque, gruff, rude, irascible, short-tempered.

absent not present, nonattendant, unavailable, nonexistent, inexistent, unreal, nonoccurrent, null, void. *See also* away, truant, missing, vacant, unoccupied.

absent-minded daydreaming, woolgathering, stargazing.

absolute total, utter, entire, unrestricted, pure; definite, sure, precise; authoritative, autocratic, tyrannical, dictatorial.

absorbent absorptive, adsorbent, sorbent, assimilative, ingestive, imbibitory, blotting, spongy.

abstaining abstinent, ascetic, dry, shunning, temperate, moderate.

absurd ludicrous, ridiculous, crazy, preposterous, senseless, silly.

abundant plentiful, ample, lavish, copious, overflowing, profuse, superabundant.

abusive violent, harmful, injurious, forceful, offensive, damaging, evil, exploitative, oppressive, fraudulent, extravagant, wasteful, barbarous, solecistic, outrageous, impious, profane.

academic scholarly, erudite, learned, intellectual, bookish; theoretical, abstract, conjectural, hypothetical.

accelerating quickening, speeding-up, getaway, overtaking, passing, lapping.

acceptable tolerable, satisfactory, admissible, so-so; pleasing, agreeable, welcome.

accepted approved, acknowledged, authorized, customary, conventional, traditional, established.

accessible through, connecting, communicating, linked, bridged, flyover, spanned, arched, main, arterial, trunk, paved, cobbled, skidproof, sign-posted, signalled, well-lit, floodlit, well-used, busy,

accidental unlucky, unfortunate, infelicitous, disastrous, calamitous, fatal.

crowded, beaten, trodden, bumper-to-bumper.

acclamatory applauding, clapping, cheering.

accompanied attended, escorted, chaperoned, protected, guarded.

accompanying concomitant, attending, attendant, belonging, complementary, accessory, collateral, incidental, background, contextual. *See also* concurrent, associated, accompanied.

accomplished done, won, completed.

accountable liable, responsible, answerable, obliged.

accounted audited, balanced, tallied, registered, recorded, credited, debited, deposited, saved, received, spent, invoiced, billed, costed, settled, carried forward.

accounting book-keeping, reckoning, computing, calculating, accountable, fiscal, financial, economic, commercial, statistical, actuarial, bursarial, budgetary, inventorial, itemized. *See also* accounted.

accurate precise, exact, perfect, word-perfect, definitive, meticulous, pinpoint, detailed, particularized, defined, microscopic, correct, right, apt, rigorous, faultless, absolute, flawless, punctilious, mathematical, scientific, documented, fine, squared, trued, set, trimmed, delicate, refined, nice, subtle, faithful, straight, dead-on (Inf) bang-on (Inf), spot-on (Inf). *See also* correct.

accursed cursed, damned, doomed, ill-fated, wretched.

accusatory accusing, accused, imputative, charged, countercharged, blamed, denounced, alleged, under suspicion, cited, summoned, arrested, booked, prosecuted, impeached, indicted, incriminated. *See also* perjurious.

acid sharp, sour, tangy, tart, pungent, acerbic, acidulous, lemony, vinegary, unripe, green, immature, unsweetened, dry, acrid, biting, bitter. *See also* unpalatable, splenetic.

acknowledged recognized, accepted, avowed, professed; answered, accepted, recognized.

acquainted aware of, informed, cognizant of, privy to, conscious of, conversant, knowledgeable.

acquisitional collective, accumulative, cumulative, mountainous, augmentative, expansive, gaining, widening, inflationary, improvable, improved.

acquitted absolved, pardoned, exonerated, excused, let off, spared, clear, discharged, released, liberated.

acrimonious bitter, sharp, cutting, sarcastic, spiteful, caustic.

acting doing, happening, performing, working, in action, in operation, in harness, operative, industrious, busy, active, creative, artistic, dramatic, militant, brave, heroic. *See also* effective.

active interactive, sociable, activated, moving, going, running, working, operative, in action, incessant, unceasing, expeditious, able, strong, quick, fast, speedy, brisk, spry, nimble, agile, smart, keen, vigorous, strenuous, energetic, forceful, dynamic, thrusting, pushing, enterprising, lively, sprightly, frisky, dashing, spirited, alive, animated, vivacious, eager. *See also* busy, industrious, meddling.

actual definite, true, certain, positive, indisputable; existent, present, prevailing, current.

adapted to drought xerophilous, xerophytic, xeromorphic.

adaptive adaptable, resilient, buoyant, flexible, adjustable, responsive, lively, compliant, accommodating, yielding.

addicted drug-dependent, hooked (Sl).

addictive narcotic, hallucinogenic, psychedelic, mind-blowing (Sl).

additional added, included, interpolated, annexed, loaded, reinforced, additive, adjunctive, adjunct, attached, adjoined, inserted, prefixed, adventitious, supplementary, complementary, subsidiary, incremental, auxiliary, collateral, contributory, another, further, more; supplementary, appendant, suffixed, postpositive, postpositional, another. *See also* extra.

adept able, proficient, skilful, accomplished, clever.

adequate capable, fit, able, competent, suitable, apt, appropriate, up to.

adhesive adherent, cohesive, connective, sticky, gummy, tacky, gluey, viscous, colloidal, congealed, coagulated, concrete, inextricable, linked, bonded, cemented, close, side-by-side, shoulder-to-shoulder, cheek-by-jowl, close-fitting, close-packed, tight, clinging, figure-hugging, moulding, skintight. *See also* tenacious.

administrative divisional, governmental, departmental, congressional, constituent, metropolitan, municipal, provincial, rural, territorial, national.

admirable laudable, praiseworthy, commendable, fine, excellent.

admired respected, popular, in demand.

admissible permissible, allowed, permitted, lawful, justifiable, tolerable.

admissive admissible, acceptable, suitable, receivable, receptible. *See also* receptive, introductory, absorbent.

adolescent juvenile, young, teenage, youthful, boyish, girlish.

adoptive appropriating.

adorned decorated, embellished, gilded, beautified, enriched, garnished.

adult mature, senior, experienced, prepared, grown-up. *See also* ageing, middle-aged, aged.

advanced forward, progressive,

avant-garde, ahead, precocious, promoted.

advancing oncoming, approaching, connivent.

advantaged ahead, keen, sharp, acute, biting, pungent, effective, forceful, incisive, powerful.

advantageous beneficial, worthwhile, helpful, valuable; superior, dominant, favourable.

adventurous venturesome, game, foolhardy, rash, danger-loving.

adverse contrary, conflicting, opposing, hostile, antagonistic, troublesome, difficult, hard, bleak, dreadful, dire, ominous, bad, sinister, disastrous, destructive, ruinous, doomed, miserable, in trouble, unwell. *See also* unprosperous, unlucky.

advisable recommendable, prudent, wise, judicious, politic, sensible, practical, expedient.

advising advisory, counselling, consultative, deliberative, monitory, therapeutic, instructive, informative, moral, persuasive, encouraging, dissuasive, admonitory, cautionary. *See also* advisable.

aerial buoyant, inflated, blown-up, flatulent, pneumatic.

aerostatic aerodynamic, pneumatic.

affected precious, pretentious, mannered, self-conscious, conceited, artificial, unnatural, stilted, sanctimonious, euphemistic, showy, meretricious, theatrical, histrionic, puffed up, boastful, swanky, mouthy (Sl), specious, tongue-in-cheek (Inf).

affectionate loving, caring, warm, tender, friendly, fond.

affirmative affirming, affirmatory, assertive, supportive, declarative, annunciative, validatory, predicative, predicational. *See also* stated, vowed, supported, assertive, emphasized, definite.

afflicted troubled, plagued, depressed, distressed, miserable, grievous, grief-stricken, sorrowful, woeful, sad, hurt, in pain, sick, ill, unhealthy, sore, damaged, injured, wounded, tragic.

afraid scared, terrified, frightened, fearful, apprehensive.

afternoon postmeridian.

aged old, grown old, elderly, venerable, patriarchal, matriarchal, geriatric, well-preserved, white-haired, grey-haired, gaga (Sl).

ageing growing old, senescent, greying, getting crow's-feet, declining, weakening, waning, sinking, moribund.

agelong aeonian, millennial, immemorial.

aggravated worsened, not improved, exacerbated, intensified, heightened, deepened, increased, magnified, enhanced, enlarged. *See also* aggravating.

aggravating annoying, irritating, exasperating, provoking, vexing, vexatious.

aggressive antagonistic, repugnant, conflicting, contentious, clashing, opposing, quarrelsome, dissenting, belligerent, bellicose, militant, at loggerheads, at cross-purposes. *See also* militant, attacking, critical.

agile nimble, supple, quick, lithe, lively, sprightly.

agitated perturbed, troubled, disturbed, discomposed, embarrassed, nervous, nervy, edgy, uneasy, jittery, upset, unsteady, confused, ruffled, flurried, flustered, shaken, shaken up, shocked, stirred up, worked up, troublous (Arch). *See also* restless, turbulent, shaky, convulsive, flickering.

agreeable agreed, united, unanimous, solid, harmonious, peaceful, concordant; acceptable, unopposed, viable.

agreeing agreed, agreeable, concordant, accordant, concurrent, concurring, approving, approved, voted in, carried, consenting, affirmative, confirmative, blessed, willing, acquiescent, acquiescing, accepting, compliant, united, unanimous, in unison, in chorus, attuned, in tune, congenial, harmonious, in step, sympathetic, empathetic, reciprocal, cooperative, cordial, coexisting, friendly, like-minded, reconciliatory, peaceful, at peace. *See also* contractual, compatible, suitable.

agricultural agrarian, agronomic, agrological, agroecological, agrobiological, geoponic, farm, farming, farmhouse, rustic, rural, pastoral, peasant, bucolic, agrestic, praedial, georgic (Arch). *See also* farmable.

aimless purposeless, pointless, futile, vain, worthless, inconsequential.

airy aery, aerial, aeriform, aeriferous, airlike, ethereal, insubstantial, lighter-than-air, weightless, light, exposed, roomy, rare, rarified, thin. *See also* atmospheric, aerial, breezy, open-air, ventilated, bubbly.

alarming scaring, frightening, intimidating, distressing, ominous, startling.

alert on guard, watchful, vigilant, prepared, heedful; lively, quick, nimble, sprightly, agile.

alike similar, corresponding, equivalent, resembling, same.

alive living, quick (Arch), animate, conscious, breathing, incarnate, existent, extant, surviving, ongoing, long-lived, old, aged, ancient, lasting, lifelong, viable, vital, vivifying, life-giving, Promethean, enlivened, revived, restored, reborn. *See also* lively, biotic, born.

allied corporate, affiliated, associated, bonded, joint, conjoint, combined, combining, connected, linked, merged, contributing, coactive, synergic, colluding, conspiring, conspiratorial, collaborating, collaborative, fraternal, co-existing.

allocated allotted, assigned, apportioned, divided, shared out, distributed, dividable, divisible.

allowing no delay demanding,

all right
importunate, burning, imperative, exigent, urgent.

all right fine, fit, well, healthy, balanced, OK (Inf).

alone solitary, isolated, apart, separate, isolationist, unilateralist, detached, aloof, insular, withdrawn, reclusive, lonely, friendless, deserted, abandoned, forsaken.

aloof private, discrete, separate, independent, free, isolated, unassimilated, secluded, solitary, unsociable, antisocial.

alternating every other, antiphonal, cyclical.

altimetric topographic, orographic, hypsometric, hypsographic.

amazed awed, marvelling, admiring, impressed, astonished, astounded, stupefied, stunned, speechless, struck dumb, dumbfounded, thunderstruck, staggered, shocked, disconcerted, disappointed, flabbergasted (Inf), gobsmacked (Sl).

ambiguous equivocal, involved, complicated, complex, contorted.

amenable compliant, acquiescent, biddable, persuadable, pliable, pliant, tractable, manageable, obedient, docile.

amorous romantic, sentimental, emotional, tender, soft, adoring, melting, flirtatious, coquettish, seductive, coy, passionate, lustful, ardent, yearning, longing, moping, mooning, desirous, lascivious, capricious, ecstatic, excited, erotic, sexy, alluring, erogenous, ensnaring, possessive, jealous, randy (Inf), horny (Sl).

amphibian batrachian, apodan, salamandrian, newtlike, caudate, neotenous, froggy, toadish, anuran, salientian.

ample abundant, profuse, rife, plentiful, copious, bumper, in profusion, galore (Inf).

anachronistic misdated, parachronistic, prochronistic.

anaesthetic analgesic, deadening, numbing, hypnotic, narcotic, soporific, somnific.

anaesthetized etherized, frozen, hypnotized, insensible, numb, deadened, inured.

anarchic anarchical, disorganized, ungoverned, lawless, unofficial, wildcat, disobedient, insubordinate, seditious, disorderly, rampant, unruly, wild, riotous, chaotic, rebellious, revolutionary, mutinous, dog-eat-dog. *See also* anarchistic.

anarchistic nihilistic, antinomian, syndicalistic, ochlocratic, mobocratic.

ancient old, archaic, antiquated, prehistoric, old-fashioned, out-of-date.

angled scalene, triangular, square, right-angled, perpendicular, rectangular, quadrilateral, quadrangular, polygonal, pentagonal, rhomboidal, hexagonal, trilateral, cuneate, cuneiform, polyhedral, prismatic, pyramidal, faceted, diamond.

angry irate, ireful, cross, aggressive, belligerent, bellicose, wrathful, furious, infuriated, choleric, indignant, livid, enraged, raging, incensed, fuming, boiling, burning, smouldering, sulphurous, huffed, beside oneself, frenzied, foaming, rabid, berserk, hopping mad, stuttering, gnashing, growling, snapping, dangerous, violent, fierce, savage, rampaging, roaring, mad (Inf), apoplectic (Inf), sizzling (Inf), ratty (Inf), waxy (Sl).

angular cornered, pointed, bent, hooked, jointed, forked, bifurcate, L-shaped, V-shaped, A-framed, dog-legged, mitred. *See also* oblique, angled, biased.

animal-fearing, zoophobic.

animalian animal, animalic, animalistic, zoic, brutish, subhuman, dumb, brutal, bestial, beastly, beastlike, animal-like, zoomorphic, therianthropic, theriomorphic. *See also* of animals, zoological, animal-loving, animal-fearing.

animal-loving zoophilic.

annihilated destroyed, exterminated, eliminated, dissolved, liquidated, ruined, doomed, fated, destined.

anniversary commemorative, annual, yearly, centenary, sesquicentennial, bicentenary, tricentenary, Metonic, millennial, secular.

annotative glossarial, scholiastic, explanatory, critical, editorial, commentarial.

annoying irritating, irksome, exasperating, maddening, bothersome, infuriating.

anomalous abnormal, unusual, exceptional, odd, peculiar, irregular.

anonymous nameless, unknown, unidentified, incognito.

answerable responsible, liable, accountable, required, obliged, obligatory, under obligation, duty bound, beholden, dutiful.

answering replying, responsive, responding, respondent, acknowledged, confirmed, returned, retorted, backchatting, insolent. *See also* reactive, retaliatory, solved, correspondent, answerable.

antagonistic adverse, opposite, opposed, hostile, unfriendly, dissonant.

anthropological anthropographical, ethnological, ethnographic, ethnogenic, anthropogenic, ethnoscientific, anthropogeographic, demographic, palaeoanthropological, epigraphic, sociological, anatomical, anthropometric, anthropometrical, anthroposcopic, craniometric, craniometrical, craniological, osteometric. *See also* racial, societal.

antiquarian ancestral, antecedent, preceding, foregoing, outdated, outworn, outmoded, old hat, anachronistic, antiquated, fossilized, old-fashioned, obsolete, passé, stale, moth-eaten.

antisocial withdrawn, unfriendly, unsociable, retiring, reserved, hostile.

anxious worried, troubled, appre-

apart hensive, uneasy, nervous, concerned.

apart asunder, broken, shattered, split, schizoid, rent, riven, cloven, cleft, dispersed, scattered, fugitive, divergent, radiating, sundered (Arch).

apathetic indifferent, noncommittal, resigned, retired, withdrawn, aloof, absent, distant; unconcerned, uninterested, unemotional, listless, passive, torpid.

appalling terrible, dreadful, horrifying, dire, frightful, ghastly.

apparent surface, outward, ostensible, superficial, shallow, seeming, imaginal, impressional.

appealing emotional, moving, affecting, charming, attractive, gripping, fascinating, irresistible, charismatic, magnetic, mesmeric, hypnotic, compelling, inspirational, encouraging, motivating, suggestive, tempting, seductive, addictive, infectious, contagious.

appearing apparent, material, embodied, incarnate, realized, there, present, evident, patent, manifest, showing, visible, in sight, on show, on view, exposed, displayed, revealed, epiphanic, theophanic, prominent, spectacular, beginning, coming, arriving, entering, emergent, arising, developing, unfolding, waxing, recurring, repeated. *See also* outer, ostensible, aspectual.

appearing guilty shamefaced, ashamed, sheepish, blushing, stammering, hangdog, red-handed, contrite, conscience-stricken, remorseful, regretful, sorry.

appetizing delicious, mouthwatering, tasty, inviting, tempting.

appreciative grateful, thankful, indebted, obliged; admiring, respectful, aware, cognizant.

apprehensive anxious, worried, nervous, on edge, uneasy, concerned.

approaching impending, imminent, oncoming, advancing, coming, incoming, inbound, inward-bound, homeward, homeward-bound, nearing, terminal.

approvable satisfactory, acceptable, passable, permissible, worthwhile.

approved passed, tested, accepted, supported, backed, endorsed, favoured, recommended.

approving satisfied, content, appreciative, grateful, approbatory, respectful, well-inclined, favourable, complimentary, commendatory, laudatory, admiring, eulogistic, encomiastic, panegyric, acclamatory, fulsome, flattering, adulatory, idolatrous, lionizing, hero-worshipping. *See also* supporting, acclamatory, praiseworthy, approvable, approved, admired.

approximate rough, imprecise, estimated, relative; near, close.

arachnidan spidery, arachnoid, acarid, acaroid.

arboricultural silvicultural, dendrologic(al), dendrologous.

arched arcuated, arcuate, rounded, lancet, parabolic, segmental.

architectural edificial, architectonic, tectonic, structural. *See also* structural, arched, roofed, vaulted, columned.

ardent fervent, burning, passionate, eager, enthusiastic, vehement, fiery.

arduous difficult, onerous, hard, rigorous, laborious, burdensome.

arguable debatable, disputable, contentious, topical, controversial, questionable, doubtful, dubious, challenging, problematic, refutable, in question, moot, unsettled, undecided, misunderstood.

arguing quibbling, quarrelling, wrangling, squabbling, bickering, at odds, dissenting, rowing, scuffling, clashing, at loggerheads, scrapping (Inf). *See also* argumentative, hostile, arguable, logical.

argumentative quarrelsome, disagreeable, disputatious, litigious, dissentious, factious, querulous, peevish, irritable, contrary, testy, petulant, fractious, choleric, cross, irascible, cantankerous, grouchy (Inf).

arid dry, desert, parched, sterile; boring, uninteresting, dull.

aristocratic noble, blue blooded, thoroughbred, ennobled, titled, high-class, upper-class, U (Sl), gentlemanly, ladylike, well-bred, ducal, lordly, princely, well-born, highborn, patrician, baronial, high-caste,

classy (Inf), first-class, top-drawer (Inf).

arranged ordered, orderly, structured, ranged, arrayed, marshalled, disposed, placed, aligned, grouped; settled, negotiated, covenanted, contractual, pledged, promised. *See also* organized, organizational, rearranged, categorized, categorical, diagrammatic, tidied.

arriving incoming, immigrant, entering, emerging, appearing. *See also* approaching, welcoming.

arrogant lofty, haughty, uppish, uppity, pushy, proud, tyrannical, shameless, presumptuous, overweening; overconfident, bold, brazen.

artful crafty, clever, deceitful, cunning, ingenious, shrewd.

arthropodous arthropodal, chelicerate, arachnoid, spidery, insectile, crustacean, arachnological, entomological.

articulate clear, distinct, lucid, intelligible, eloquent, meaningful.

artificial synthetic, man-made, manufactured, imitation, sham, fake.

artistic painterly, decorative, picturesque, aesthetic, arty (Inf), arty-crafty (Inf), arty-farty (Inf).

ascending upward, uphill, climbing, scansorial, scandent, steep, uparching, upwith (Dial), upturned, upcast, uplifted, turned-up, retroussé. *See also* rising, leaping, ladder-like.

ashamed shamefaced, guilty, embarrassed, mortified, sheepish, sorry.

aspectual beautiful, attractive, sightly, decorative, well-dressed, fashionable, ugly, unattractive, homely, unsightly, plain, ill-dressed, unfashionable.

aspirant ambitious, go-getting, dreaming, wishful, desirous, longing, yearning.

assembled collected, heaped up, congregated, aggregated, amalgamated, merged, collective, conglomerate, associative, congregational. *See also* collected, cumulate, grouped, crowded.

assenting in agreement, concurring, concordant, unanimous, solid, like-minded, confirmative, affirmative, approving, consenting, supportive, sympathetic, cooperative, collaborating, willing, acquiescent, compliant. *See also* agreed.

assertive self-assertive, assertory, assured, confident, forceful, decisive, decided, incisive, outspoken, blunt, plain, thrustful, driven, insistent, dogmatic, peremptory, pontifical, vehement, emphatic, vigorous, positive, pushy (Inf).

associated partnered, coupled, paired, wedded, married, combined, joined, inseparable, hand-in-glove.

associating allied, affiliated, comradely, fraternal, friendly, concordant, harmonious, concurring, commensal, conniving, collusive, conspiratorial.

assorted mixed, chequered, miscellaneous, motley, dapple, omnifarious, multifarious, allotropic, kaleidoscopic, sundry, various, multipurpose, multifaceted, multiform, diversiform, polymorphous, heteromorphous, multicoloured, divers (Arch).

assumed false, fake, bogus, phoney, imitation, sham.

assured self-confident, composed, authoritative.

astonishing amazing, breathtaking, staggering, astounding, impressive, surprising.

astronomical astrophysical, cosmological, uranographic(al), cosmic, celestial, heavenly, universal, galactic, intergalactic, extragalactic, interstellar, stellar, sidereal, starry, astral, star-studded, solar, heliacal, interplanetary, planetary, Mercurian, Venusian, Martian, Jovian, Saturnian, Neptunian, Uraniun, Plutonian, extraterrestrial, extramundane, terrestrial, telluric, tellurian, synodic, lunar, asteroidal, cometary, meteoric, heliocentric, geocentric, telescopic, spectrometric, photometric, astronautic(al).

at a loss off course, disoriented, confused, bewildered, astonished, dumbstruck, astray, floundering, gobsmacked (Sl).

at ease easeful, relaxed, resting, casual, carefree, laid-back, content, eudemonic, comfortable, peaceful, quiet, tranquil, leisured, idle, lazy, leisurely, unhurried, sabbatical, postprandial, after-dinner. *See also* labour-saving.

athletic fit, able-bodied, energetic, strong, muscular, powerful.

atmospheric ambient, aural, situational; stratospheric, tropospheric.

atoning making amends, expiatory, reparatory, rectifying, redressing, compensatory, repaying, indemnificatory, restitutive, recompensing, righting, squaring, propitiatory, appeasing, satisfying, conciliatory, reconciliatory, pacifying, apologetic, sorry, regretting, penitent, repentant, contrite, lustral, purgative, cleansing, purifying, piacular, offering, oblatory, sacrificial.

atrocious horrible, monstrous, brutal, barbaric, cruel, abominable.

attacking assaulting, invading, storming, charging, boarding, fighting, striking, harrying, kicking, punching, flailing, cutting, slashing, destructive, violent, bloodthirsty, savage, brutal, cruel, barbarous, bloody, uncontrollable, overpowering, overwhelming, frenzied, raging, berserk.

attempting trying, essaying, seeking, striving, game, nothing daunted, daring, venturesome, ambitious, enterprising. *See also* tentative.

attendant participating, watching, witnessed, associated, accompanying, concomitant, companionable, sociable, regular, habituated.

attentive aware, heedful, alert, concentrating, watchful, studious.

attracting pulling, drawing, dragging, tugging, adductive, associative, adducent. *See also* attractive.

attractive seductive, enticing, tempting, charming, fascinating, captivating, charismatic, irresistable, alluring, fetching, appealing, good-looking, sexually attractive, sexy (Inf), dishy (Inf), hunky (Inf).

audacious bold, assured, brazenfaced, blatant, flagrant, precocious, obtrusive, familiar, unabashed.

aural auditory, acoustic, audio, radio, transmitted, telephone, audiovisual, audient, listening, attentive, musical, bugged (Inf). *See also* otological, hearable.

auspicious propitious, promising, encouraging, hopeful, potential, possible, likely, fortunate, favourable, optimistic, good, bright, fair, golden, rosy, cloudless.

authentic real, genuine, official, original, inimitable, unique, pure, unadulterated, sterling, hall-marked, valid, bona fide, legitimate, rightful, sound, solid, substantial, undoubted, unquestionable, unqualified, unrefuted, unconfuted, undenied, honest-to-goodness, pukka (Inf).

authoritarian domineering, autocratic, strict, severe, harsh, dictatorial.

authoritative official, definitive, ex officio, powerful, empowered, regal, royal, noble, leading, ruling, reigning, authoritarian, dominant, predominant, overbearing, high-handed, masterful, domineering, condescending, patronizing, imperative, imperious, arrogant, coercive, lordly, superior, supreme, senior, mighty, strong, potent, legitimate, legal, lawful, rightful, influential, preeminent, peremptory, overruling, confident, self-assertive, knowledgeable, puissant (Arch), bossy (Inf). *See also* elected, authorized, expert.

authorized certified, empowered, enabled, permitted, licensed, entitled, allowed, documented.

autocratic authoritarian, arbitrary, dictatorial.

automatic automated, mechanical, mechanized, push-button; habitual, routine, spontaneous, unconscious, involuntary.

autumn golden.

available plenty, sufficient, accessible, at hand, on, on tap, ready, handy, convenient, near, close, immediate, in view.

avant-garde advanced, trendy, fashionable, modish.

avaricious greedy, grasping, acquisitive, mean, stingy, covetous.

average usual, normal, par, typical, general, common, prevailing, current, popular, prevalent, predominant, sweeping, universal, generic, representative, characteristic, ordinary, everyday, familiar, household, routine, habitual, customary, accustomed, wonted, traditional, accepted, conventional, middlebrow, standard, stock, set, established, regular, classic, orthodox, normative, prescriptive. *See also* medium, mediocre.

averse opposed, hostile, loath, reluctant, unwilling, disinclined.

avian birdlike, birdy, struthious, goosy, anserine, anseriform, gallinaceous, rasorial, columbine, psittacine, hawkish, aquiline, vulturine, owlish, hirundine, passerine, oscine, fringilline, turdine, corvine. *See also* ornithological.

avid eager, enthusiastic, fervent, keen, passionate, ardent.

avoidable avertable, preventable, escapable, unsought, unattempted.

avoiding evasive, equivocal, elusive, slippery, untamed, wild, shy, flinching, blinking, blenching, shrinking, backward, reluctant, unwilling, noncooperative, noncommittal, unforthcoming, taciturn, passive, inert, inactive, not involved, apathetic, uncommitted, neutral, centrifugal, fugitive, escaped, runaway, hunted, hiding, skulking, cowering, hidden, latent, repressive, suppressive, preventive, censorial, defensive, fly-by-night (Inf). *See also* abstaining, avoidable.

aware conscious, mindful, knowing, apprised, alert, acquainted.

away out, gone, departed, dematerialized, missing, lost, disappeared, vanished, absconded, flown, fled, vamoosed (Inf), off (Inf).

bashful

awe-inspiring imposing, impressive, important, authoritative, august, sage, wise.

awesome overwhelming, astonishing, daunting, intimidating, magnificent, wondrous.

awkward clumsy, gauche, ungainly, inept, hamfisted, lumbering.

B

backward retrograde, retrogressive, retrocessive. *See also* receding, retroactive, reversed, resilient, returning.

bad nasty, obnoxious, objectionable, unpleasant, disagreeable, horrible, horrid, evil, base, gross, irredeemable, execrable, unspeakable, abominable, awful, horrific, horrendous, terrible, dreadful, gruesome, grim, onerous, tedious, distressing, vicious, villainous, wicked, heinous, depraved, sinful, dishonest, criminal, ghastly (Inf), beastly (Inf), crooked (Inf); poor, inferior, incompetent, lamentable, awful, terrible, clumsy, inept, hopeless (Inf), pathetic (Inf), ham-fisted (Inf), cack-handed (Inf).

badly behaved ill-bred, mischievous, naughty, bad, wicked, ill-mannered, ungracious, impolite, rude, discourteous, selfish, inconsiderate, obnoxious.

bad-mannered unchivalrous, badly behaved, rude, insolent, impudent, impertinent, saucy, churlish, truculent, abusive, cursing, obstreperous, forward, irascible, difficult, vulgar, offensive, injurious, coarse, boorish, caddish, gross, crude, loutish, ill-bred, unrefined, uncouth, uncultured, barbarian, savage, foul-mouthed, growling, grumbling, swearing, cheeky (Inf).

baked parched, sun-dried, sun-baked, burnt, scorched, bleached.

bald hairless, receding.

banal everyday, commonplace, trite, ordinary, pedestrian, stale.

banging crashing, slamming, bursting, exploding, booming, thundering, ear-splitting, deafening. *See also* crackling.

barbaric savage, primitive, wild, uncivilized, barbarous, brutal.

barbed prickly, scratchy, notched, hacked, hairy, unshorn, hirsute, shockheaded, bushy, woolly, flocculent, lanate, furry, matted, curly, frizzy, fuzzy, shaggy, bristly, barbellate, setiform, setose, strigose, hispid, unkempt, unshaven, stubbled, bearded, moustached.

bare nude, naked, undressed, stripped, shorn, exposed.

base ground, ground-level, supporting, underlying, basal, basilar, bottom, rock-bottom, bottommost, undermost, nethermost, lowest, basic, fundamental, essential, inherent, radical, rudimentary, vestigial.

baseless unfounded, groundless, unsupported.

bashful coy, prudish, shockable,

demure, chaste, pure, shamefaced, confused, chaste, virtuous.

basic fundamental, essential, necessary, vital, key, primary.

basted greased, oiled.

bathymetric bathometric, oceanographic, sounding, depth-sounding, probing, echolocating.

bearable tolerable, endurable, supportable.

beastly nasty, mean, loathsome, unpleasant, awful; brutal, cruel, bestial, barbarous, sadistic, savage.

beaten defeated, overcome, conquered, thwarted, cowed, vanquished; stirred, blended, mixed, whipped; trodden, trampled, worn.

beautified decorated, adorned, embellished, embroidered, trimmed, tricked out, decked out, improved, touched up.

beautiful lovely, lush (Sl), gorgeous, handsome, pretty, fine, good looking, attractive, fair, bright, comely, shapely, bonny, cute, sweet, winsome, exquisite, glamorous, pulchritudinous, gracile, well-built, manly, statuesque, Junoesque, aesthetically pleasing, tasteful, picturesque, scenic, ornamental. *See also* personable.

befitting fit, appropriate, right, proper, suitable.

beggarly mendicant, homeless, hungry, starving, barefoot, in rags, tatty, threadbare, shabby, scruffy, mean, seedy, squalid, dirty, slummy, dilapidated.

begging cadging, mendicant,

fund-raising, chain-letter, scrounging (Inf), sponging (Inf), freeloading (Sl), mooching (Sl).

beginning commencing, dawning, initial, inceptive, inaugural, introductory, first, newborn, debut. *See also* front, prime, embryonic, inventive, inaugural, rudimentary.

behaving ethological, tactical, strategical, political, statesmanlike, governmental, businesslike. *See also* well-behaved, badly behaved.

belated late, overdue, delayed, tardy.

beleaguered harrassed, beset, besieged, assailed, persecuted, vexed.

believable credible, creditable, tenable, plausible, reasonable, realistic, possible, probable, likely, convincing, persuasive, impressive, commanding, reliable, trustworthy.

believed undisputed, authoritative, accredited, doctrinal, creedal, received, accepted, putative, supposed, alleged, hypothetical.

believing assured, confident, convinced, sure, certain, positive, opinionated, dogmatic, trusting, unhesitating, unquestioning, undoubting, unsuspecting, faithful, conformist, orthodox, converted, born-again. *See also* gullible, believable, believed.

belonging appurtenant, part of, one of, essential, fundamental, intrinsic, inherent, integral, particular.

beloved cherished, adored, esteemed, revered, preferred, fancied, favourite, chosen, pet, darling, dear, admired, regarded, respected, well-liked.

bemused perplexed, muddled, stunned, confused, baffled, overwhelmed.

beneficial good, salutary, advantageous, favourable, propitious, expedient, profitable, gainful, valuable, remedial, therapeutic.

benevolent kind-hearted, warm-hearted, good, nice, benign, helpful, amiable, sociable, friendly, affectionate, loving, considerate, decent, thoughtful, attentive, solicitous, courteous, mindful, condolent, sympathetic, empathetic, good-natured, cordial, genial, affable, well-meaning, tolerant, compassionate, open-hearted, humane, forgiving, indulgent, soft-hearted, lax, lenient, obliging, accommodating, neighbourly, paternal, maternal. *See also* charitable.

benighted dismal, gloomy, cheerless, depressed, dejected, mournful, clouded, murky, wicked, evil, ominous, menacing, threatening, sinister, shadowy, shady, sombre, grim, forbidding, unenlightened, ignorant, blind, oblivious, obfuscated, obscure, cryptic, mysterious, enigmatic, mystic, inscrutable, secret, arcane, hidden, occult, esoteric.

bent crooked, twisted, stooped, hunched; determined, resolved, inclined, disposed.

berserk frenzied, manic, insane, raging, violent, rabid.

besotted doting, smitten, spellbound, infatuated; drunk, intoxicated, muddled, befuddled.

bespectacled long-sighted, far-sighted (US), short-sighted, near-sighted (US), four-eyed (Inf).

best greatest, supreme, superlative, crowning, cardinal, capital, matchless, peerless, unparalleled, unrivalled, unequalled, unapproachable, unsurpassed, inimitable, incomparable, unique, unbeatable, invincible, perfect, highest, maximal, utmost, topmost, tiptop, prime, dominant, preponderant, hegemonic, prevailing, paramount, foremost, main, chief, principal, central, focal, first, record, top-ranking, champion, gold-medal, victorious, winning, triumphant, world-beating, record-holding, A1, number-one, pre-eminent, supernormal, immortal, ultimate, transcendent, upmost (Inf), topnotch (Inf), chart-topping (Inf), chart-busting (Inf).

better greater, preferable, superior, finer, larger, surpassing, worthier.

between times interim, intermediate, intercalary, intercalated, intervallic, interwar, interglacial, interlunar.

bewildered confused, puzzled, confounded, mystified, perplexed, taken aback.

bewitched enchanted, spellbound, entranced, fascinated, hypnotized, mesmerized, hag-ridden, obsessed, possessed, bedevilled, cursed, hexed, jinxed, haunted, ghost-ridden, spooked (Inf).

biased slanted, angled toward.

big large, great, full-grown, full-blown, full-scale, large-scale, considerable, substantial, bumper, ample, generous, voluminous, baggy, capacious, spacious, roomy, family-size(d), economy-size(d), man-size(d), king-size(d), giant-size(d), record-size(d), huge, enormous, immense, massive, gigantic, colossal, titanic, monstrous, mammoth, monster, Gargantuan, towering, monumental, grand, imposing, epic, tremendous, stupendous, prodigious, megalithic, macroscopic, astronomical, bulky, mighty, broad, comprehensive, expansive, extensive, vast, limitless, infinite, tidy (Inf), healthy (Inf), jumbo (Inf), almighty (Inf), whopping (Inf), walloping (Inf), whacking (Inf), spanking (Inf), thumping (Sl), thundering (Sl), mega (Sl), ginormous (Sl).

bigger larger, extended, lengthened, drawn-out, stretched, spread-out, widespread, splayed, fanned out, dispersed, expanded, widened, broadened, flared, dilated, distended, swollen, bloated, tumid, turgid, incrassate, dropsical, oedematous, puffed-up, inflated, blown-up, pumped-up, stuffed, padded, fatter, overweight, increased, built-up, augmented, heightened, raised, magnified, amplified, developed, mature, fully fledged, full-blown, fully developed, hypertrophied,

overgrown. *See also* growing, enlargeable.

biological zoological, botanical, bacteriological virological, gnotobiotic, parasitological, anatomical, morphological, physiological, biochemical, endocrinological, immunological, histological, cytological, genetic, biotechnological, embryological, palaeontological, taxonomic, systematic, ecological, bionomic, biophysical, biometric, bionic. *See also* living, physiological, cellular, genetic, developmental, taxonomic.

biotic symbiotic, biological, biogenetic, protoplasmic, protoplastic, bioplastic.

black sable, raven, ebon, ebony, jet, jet-black, pitch-black, inky, sooty, fuliginous, coal-black, sloe-black, blackish, nigrescent, blue-black, grey-black, brown-black. *See also* dark, blackened, black-haired, black-hearted.

blackened singed, charred, tanned, suntanned, black-and-blue.

black-haired raven-haired, dark-haired, brunette, black-eyed, sloe-eyed.

black-hearted evil, wicked, nefarious, heinous, villainous, blackguardly.

blameless innocent, guiltless, faultless, in the clear, unblemished, virtuous.

blameworthy responsible, culpable, criminal, guilty, reprehensible, objectionable, impeachable.

blue

blaming accusatory, judgmental, condemning, damning, denunciatory, recriminative.

bland dull, boring, humdrum, insipid, tasteless, weak; amiable, agreeable, affable, congenial, courteous; mild, soft, soothing, gentle.

blank vacant, vacuous, empty-headed, absent-minded, forgetful, amnesic, Lethean, nirvanic.

blasphemous profane, impious, sacrilegious, irreverent, ungodly.

blatant flagrant, shameless, brazen, lurid, extravagant, sensational, obtrusive, vulgar, crude, public, screaming, camp.

bleak bare, desolate, windswept, open, chilly, raw.

bleeding haemorrhaging, blood-soaked, bloody, ecchymosed.

blemished flawed, masked, defective, deformed, defaced, disfigured, imperfect, spoiled, soiled, shop-soiled, damaged, polluted, cracked. *See also* marked, seedy.

blessed sacred, holy, adored, revered, divine; favoured, endowed, lucky, fortunate.

blighting rotting, decaying, mildewed, mouldy, baneful, pestilent, noisome, noxious, harmful, virulent, poisonous, venomous, toxic, malevolent, cursed, evil.

blind sightless, unseeing, eyeless, amaurotic, glaucomatous, registered blind, visionless, stone-blind, snow-blind. *See also* weak-sighted, blinded, blinding, blind to, hidden.

blinded snow-blind, dazzled, blindfold(ed), blinkered.

blinding dazzling, stunning, darkening, obscuring, hiding, masking, deceptive, misleading.

blind to imperceptive, unaware (of), unconcerned, oblivious (of), unconscious (of), thoughtless, inconsiderate, unobservant, unmindful, ignorant, unenlightened, blinkered, undiscerning, benighted.

blissful ecstatic, elated, euphoric, joyful, rapturous.

blithe joyful, carefree, merry, cheery, light-hearted, vivacious.

blocked barred, walled in, fenced in, restrained, anchored, curbed, shackled, chained, tethered, leashed, deterrent, interventional, inconvenient, bureaucratic, regulatory, deadlocked, burdened, handicapped, saddled with, in debt, hairy (Sl).

bloody blood-stained, bloodshot, gory, sanguineous, incarnadine (Arch), bleeding, haemic, haemal, haemogenic.

blue sky blue, pale blue, powder blue, Cambridge blue, Wedgwood blue, grey-blue, saxe blue, slate blue, green-blue, duck-egg blue, eggshell blue, aquamarine, turquoise, peacock blue, kingfisher blue, cobalt blue, cyan, cerulean, sapphire, air-force blue, electric blue, ultramarine, royal blue, Oxford blue, midnight blue, navy blue, navy, French navy, perse, azure, in-

bluish digo, hyacinthine. *See also* bluish, depressed, indecent.

bluish black-and-blue, livid, bruised, cyanotic, caesious, freezing.

blunt blunted, unsharp, unwhetted, dull, worn, smooth, faired, stubby, snub, blunt-nosed, rounded, square, curving, flat, edgeless, unpointed, dull-edged, bated. *See also* outspoken, dull, toothless.

blurred hazy, fuzzy, vague, indistinct, obscure, unclear.

blushing flushed, red, ruddy, reddening, crimsoning, nervous, awkward, shamefaced, sheepish.

boastful proud, arrogant, exhibitionistic, ostentatious, self-opinionated, stuck-up, peacockish, know-it-all, dogmatic, opinionated, puffed up, blatant, swaggering, pompous, pretentious, affected, smart-alecky (Inf), smart-arsed (Sl).

bogus sham, fake, counterfeit, fraudulent, false, spurious.

bohemian offbeat, avant-garde, unconventional, unorthodox, exotic.

boisterous bouncy, lively, noisy, riotous, rumbustious, uproarious, stormy, turbulent, tempestuous, blustery.

bold brave, valiant, courageous, audacious, daring, enterprising; insolent, cheeky, rude, brash, brazen; colourful, eye-catching, loud, conspicuous, flashy, striking.

bombastic boasting, bragging, raving, inflating, self-glorifying,
hyping, magniloquent, grandiloquent, pompous, fustian.

bored tired, fatigued, drowsy, dreary, weary, world-weary, jaded, sated, satiated, dissatisfied, disinterested, sullen, fed-up (Inf).

boring tedious, tiresome, tiring, uninteresting, dull, dreary, dreich (Scot), drab, wearisome, wearing, irksome, slow, inactive, languorous, time-killing, thumb-twiddling, disliked, unenjoyable, repeated, repetitious, plain, flat, tasteless, insipid, cloying, satiating, too much, monotonous, uniform, unvarying, invariable, humdrum, pedestrian, suburban, prosaic, prosy, commonplace, stale, unfunny, humourless, soporific, sleep-inducing, unreadable, arid, dry, dry-as-dust, long-winded, drawn out, prolix, dragging, stodgy, banal, indifferent, world-weary, deadly (Inf), draggy (Sl), heavy (Sl), blah (Sl). *See also* bored.

born newborn, begotten, by, fathered, sired, mothered, dammed, foaled, dropped, spawned, littered, laid, hatched, produced.

borrowed loaned, mortgaged, secured, money-raising, repayable, outstanding, credit-card, instalment, pawned, adopted, appropriated, infringed, plagiarized, copied, pirated, imitated, fake, ersatz, stolen, plastic (Inf). *See also* adoptive.

botanical botanic, phytological, phytographic(al).

broad

bottom base, basic, undermost, lowest, fundamental, last.

bought purchased, charged, emptional, ransomed, redeemed, bribed, bribable. *See also* buying.

bound tied, chained, fettered, shackled, yoked, harnessed, leashed, tethered, lassoed, manacled, handcuffed, secured, locked, bolted, latched, padlocked, battened, clamped, clasped, gripped.

boundless unlimited, unconfined, infinite, vast, immense, endless.

bountiful plentiful, abundant, lavish, profuse, copious; magnanimous, munificent, princely, openhanded, benevolent.

brainy intellectual, clever, bright, intelligent, smart.

branched arborescent, treelike, dendriform, branchlike, ramose, Y-shaped, V-shaped, forked, furcate, bifurcate(d), pronged, trident-like.

brave heroic, macho, dashing, gallant.

breathless out of breath, gasping, winded, panting, wheezing; eager, agog, open-mouthed, excited, astounded, avid.

breathtaking awe-inspiring, impressive, stunning, magnificent, amazing, astonishing.

bred well-bred, fattened-up, grown.

breezy windy, blowy, fresh, gusty.

brief transitory, fleeting, momentary, short-lived, swift; concise, compressed, short, succinct, limited; abrupt, curt, terse, sharp, short, surly.

bright vivid, brilliant, flamboyant, garish, lurid, flashy, effulgent, splendid, resplendent, kaleidoscopic, shining, dazzling, fluorescent, blinding, glaring, flashing, sparking, coruscating, glinting, sparkling, scintillating, twinkling, glittering, fiery, flaming, blazing, flaring.

brilliant lustrous, radiant, dazzling, bright, luminous, shining; exceptional eminent, outstanding, famous; clever, astute, accomplished, gifted, brainy, talented.

brisk lively, energetic, nimble, agile, alert, active; sharp, crisp, bracing, fresh, invigorating.

brittle fragile, frangible, delicate, papery, wafer-thin, flimsy, frail, unsturdy, unsteady, insubstantial, shoddy, gimcrack, jerry-built, dilapidated, tumbledown, weak, vulnerable, breakable, bursting, explosive, crackable, chipping, shatterable, splitting, splintery, scissile, tearable, crushable, crumbly, short, friable, fissile, flaky, powdery, crispy, inelastic, rigid, like parchment, crazy (Arch).

broad wide, wide-set, splayed, patulous, transverse, extensive, expansive, roomy, ample, deep, widespread, wide-ranging, spread-out, beamy, broadcast, open, wide-open, full, wide-cut, flared, bell-bottomed, baggy, wide-angle, wide-screen, broad-gauge, broadloom. *See also* broad-shaped, broad-minded.

broad-minded open-minded, liberal, open, unprejudiced, unbiased, impartial, disinterested, unbigoted, free-thinking, free, direct, frank, candid, explicit.

broad-shaped broad-bottomed, broad-based, wide-bottomed, broad-beamed, wide-hipped, broad-tailed, wide-bodied, broad-brimmed, broad-leaved, broad-billed, wide-billed, broad-toothed, wide-mouthed, wide-eyed, broad-nosed, broad-backed, broad-shouldered, broad-chested, broad-winged.

broken destroyed, smashed, shattered, burst, fractured, severed; weakened, exhausted, run-down, spent, beaten; interrupted, disturbed, discontinuous, fragmentary, intermittent; defeated, oppressed, subdued, tamed, crushed, crippled.

brokenhearted devastated, inconsolable, grief-stricken, wretched, despairing, sorrowful.

brown oatmeal, beige, buff, fawn, biscuit, mushroom, café-au-lait, ecru, snuff-coloured, dun, khaki, hazel, walnut, amber, bronze, tawny, fulvous, sorrel, nutbrown, tan, foxy, bay, roan, chestnut, auburn, mahogany, copper, russet, rust-coloured, rubiginous, ferruginous, liver-coloured, maroon, puce, peat-brown, mocha, chocolate, coffee, fuscous. *See also* browned.

browned bronzed, dark, brunette,

tanned, suntanned, sunburnt, toasted, grilled, charred, singed.

brutal savage, cruel, bloodthirsty, ferocious, inhuman; severe, harsh, callous, heartless; coarse, vulgar, crude, beastly, uncouth, gross.

bubbly foamy, frothy, fizzy, effervescent, aerated, yeasty.

bumpy jolting, agitated, turbulent, choppy, tempestuous.

bungling incompetent, awkward, clumsy, inept, gauche, ham-fisted.

buried interred, inhumed, entombed, coffined, urned, cremated, embalmed, mummified, below ground. *See also* funeral.

burly sturdy, thick-set, beefy, hefty, strapping, strong.

busy active, bustling, hustling, humming, hectic, lively, eventful, pottering, astir, employed, in harness, engaged, occupied, slogging, overworked.

buying purchasing, shopping, marketing, teleshopping, cash-and-carry, cut-price, bidding, bargaining, haggling, investing, speculative, bullish, pre-emptive, redemptive, acquisitive.

C

cajoling wheedling, inveigling, blandishing, coaxing, ingratiating.

calamitous disastrous, devastating, catastrophic, ruinous, dreadful, dire.

calculable computable, reckon-

categorized

able, estimable, countable, numer-able, measurable, mensurable, quantifiable.

calculative computative, numer-ative, enumerative, estimative, cal-culating, computing, numerical, quantifying, statistical, actuarial, psephological. *See also* calculable, mathematical.

callous unfeeling, unnatural, ob-durate, hard, hard-hearted, heartless, cold, cold-hearted, cold-blooded, steely, stony, flinty, harsh, rough, severe, stern, grim, dour, gruff, rugged, tough, austere.

calm composed, Stoic.

cancelled off, played out, called off, scrapped.

candid open, blunt, frank, honest, straightforward, truthful.

cantankerous bad-tempered, peevish, crotchety (inf), grumpy, ir-ritable, quarrelsome.

capable competent, able, adept, proficient, accomplished, clever.

capricious arbitrary, erratic, fit-ful, uncertain, unpredictable, idio-syncratic, unexpected, volatile, mer-curial, inconsistent, inconstant, vari-able, changeable, unstable, unreli-able, fickle, feckless, irresponsible, flighty, flirtatious, coquettish, friv-olous, skittish, giddy, feather-brained, light-minded, whimsical, fanciful, fantastic, eccentric, off-beat, freakish, quirky, humoursome, temperamental, moody, crotchety, irascible, fretful, weird, crazy, mis-chievous, prankish, wanton, mo-

tiveless, wayward, perverse, con-trary, undisciplined, refractory, wil-ful, particular, faddy, captious, un-reasonable.

careful attentive, mindful, diligent, heedful, assiduous, thorough, metic-ulous, circumspect, watchful, wide-awake, alert, vigilant, observant, guarding, watching, on-guard, ready, prepared, prudent, scrupu-lous, precise, painstaking, pedantic, perfectionist, fastidious, pernickety, faddy, particular, exact, orderly, tidy, neat.

careless negligent, neglectful, slack, remiss, sloppy, slapdash, slip-shod, hit-or-miss, dizzy, flighty, rash, precipitous, disregarding, inattentive, lax, heedless, rash, devil-may-care.

carnivorous unguiculate, canine, doggy, foxy, vulpine, lupine, ursine, weaselly, musteline, viverrine, fe-line, leonine, tigrine.

cast-off shed, exuvial, moulting, ecdysial, desquamated.

casual accidental, fortuitous, un-foreseen, unexpected, random, chance; informal, relaxed, blasé, nonchalant, offhand, unconcerned.

catcalling jeering, booing, hoot-ing, disapproving, derisive, scorn-ful.

categorical classificatory, hierar-chical, taxonomic(al).

categorized classified, codified, grouped, pigeonholed, compart-mentalized, placed, graded, ranked, rated, seeded, stratified, sorted, sifted, screened, selected, analysed, processed, tabulated, alphabetized, catalogued, indexed, listed, filed, on record.

causal causative, etiological, explanatory, creative, inventive, original, aboriginal, primary, primal, primordial, primitive, basic, fundamental, intrinsic, foundational, elemental, ultimate, radical, effectual, pivotal, determinant, decisive, crucial, central, significant, productive, genetic, generative, germinal, seminal, embryonic, inceptive, rudimentary, formative, initiatory, suggestive, inspiring, influential, impelling, compelling, responsible, answerable, blameworthy.

caused effected by, reacting to, resulting from, ensuing, following from, coming from, due to, owing to, developing from, deriving from, evolving from, arising from, descending from, inheriting from, hereditary, genetic, dependent, attributed to, consequent upon, contingent upon, subject to, subsequent, sequential, secondary, unoriginal, emergent, eventual, born of, out of, by.

causeless groundless, unmotivated, undesigned, unplanned, unpremeditated, unmeant, unintended, unintentional, inadvertent, unaccountable, inexplicable.

cautious careful, wary, chary, watchful, vigilant, alert, heedful, mindful, prudent, circumspect, sceptic, suspicious, doubtful, tenta-

tive, reluctant, slow, hesitant, nervous, experimental, gingerly, anticipatory, provident, thrifty, economical, frugal, canny, guarded, secretive, conservative, discreet, reticent, politic, judicious, overcautious, unadventurous, cagey (Inf).

ceaseless continuous, endless, eternal, constant, perpetual, nonstop.

celebrative celebratory, festive, merry, gay, convivial, dithrambic. *See also* commemorative, ceremonial, congratulatory, centennial.

celibate unmarried, single, sole (Fml), spouseless, unpartnered, mateless, spinsterly, old-maidish, bachelorly, unwooed, unasked, unconsummated, independent, unattached, free, fancy-free, misogamic, misogynous, misandrous. *See also* virginal, monastic.

cellular multicellular, unicellular, single-celled, acellular, plasmic, protoplasmic, cytoplasmic, ectoplasmic, endoplasmic, reticular, coenocytic, syncytial, mitochondrial, ribosomal.

censored proscriptive, deleted, blue-pencilled, blacked out, unprintable, unmentionable, unsayable, classified, top-secret, restricted, banned.

censured castigated, chastised, reprimanded, rebuked, reproached, upbraided, rebuked, scolded, admonished, lambasted, berated, assailed, attacked, abused.

censuring castigatory, chastising,

reprimanding, rebuking, reproaching, upbraiding, chiding, scolding, admonitory, stern.

centennial bicentennial.

central middle, mid, median, mean; principal, essential, main, key, fundamental, chief.

ceramic enamelled, stanniferous, glazed, underglazed, overglazed, fired, encaustic, hand-painted, gilded, blunged, hand-turned, wedged, thrown, down-drawn, crystallized, devitrified.

ceremonial ritual, solemn, triumphal, crowning.

ceremonious ritual, solemn, pompous, liturgic, stately.

certain known, factual, actual, historical, real, true, veracious, definite, sure, secure, absolute, given, verifiable, demonstrable, well-grounded, proved, documented, certified, ascertained, demonstrated, established, safe, self-evident, unmistakeable, ostensible, obvious, necessary, realistic, accurate, authoritative. *See also* convinced, decided, guaranteed, inevitable, infallible, particular.

cetacean cetaceous, pinnipedian, sirenian.

chance random, unpredictable, unforeseeable, fortuitous, indeterminable, incalculable, uncertain, stochastic, aleatory, haphazard, hit-or-miss, sink-or-swim, catch-as-catch-can (US), casual, aleatory, serendipitous, accidental, adventitious, contingent, unexpected, un-

foreseen, noncausal, epiphenomenal, incidental, coincidental, lucky, fortunate, unlucky, unfortunate, risky, chancy (Inf), fluky (Inf), dicey(Inf), iffy (Inf). *See also* causeless.

changeable mutable, alterable, mobile, versatile, varied, variegated, protean, kaleidoscopic, iridescent, inconsistent, inconstant, variable, irregular, imbalanced, plastic, pliant, soft, supple, flowing, melting, fluid, fluctuating, ever-changing, alternating, tidal, vibrating, oscillating, uncertain, unreliable, unpredictable, unstable, unsteady, floating, loose, unattached, labile, wobbly, rocky, shaky, swaying, tottering, teetering, unsettled, impermanent, transient, rootless, homeless, rambling, precarious, fitful, shifting, ephemeral, spasmodic, flickering, wavering. *See also* changed, transformative, exchangeable, irresolute.

changed varied, altered, modified, qualified, diversified, modernized, renewed, redecorated, rearranged, reorganized, restructured, reordered, restyled, remodeled, reshaped, revised, emended, amended, improved, repaired, restored, revived, deteriorated, degenerated.

changeless permanent, immutable, imperishable, incorruptible, indestructible.

characteristic distinctive, distinguishing, typical, specific, particular, peculiar, defining, discriminating, idiosyncratic.

chargeable rateable, taxable, dutiable, tax-free, deductible.

charged deferred, overdrawn.

charged high-tension, magnetic, polarized, mechanized, electric, electronic, souped-up (Inf). *See also* in credit.

charitable beneficent, hospitable, philanthropic, Christian, generous, bountiful, magnanimous, altruistic, unselfish, big-hearted, openhanded, liberal, giving, alms-giving.

charming appealing, delightful, engaging, bewitching, alluring, fascinating.

chaste pure, virginal, unsullied, immaculate, innocent, simple, undefiled.

cheap inexpensive, unexpensive, uncostly, reasonable, sensible, manageable, affordable, modest, moderate, down-market, bargain-basement, five-and-ten (US), dime-store (US), twopenny-halfpenny, goodvalue, low-price(d), low, underpriced, catchpenny, brummagem, going cheap, sale-price(d), off-season, off-peak, excursion, economyclass, tourist-class, second-class, bucket-shop, concessional, nominal, budget, economy-size, bargain, discount, half-price, cut-price, cutrate (US), markdown, knockdown, reduced, slashed, sacrificial, rockbottom, giveaway, declining, falling, slumping, bearish, deval-

ued, depreciated, superfluous, oversupplied, dirt-cheap (Inf), cheapo (Inf). *See also* shoddy, free of charge.

checked chequered, plaid, tartan, tortoiseshell, inlaid, tessellated, patched, piebald, pinto, skewbald, fasciate.

cheeky brazen, mouthy, brassy, saucy, sassy, crusty, gally, nervy, smart-alecky (Inf), smart-arsed (Sl).

cheerful cheery, happy, glad, joyful, radiant, sunny, smiling, grinning, beaming, laughing, genial, good-natured, good-humoured, optimistic, sociable, light-hearted, exhilarated, merry, jolly, jovial, convivial, genial, gay, funny, buoyant, carefree, vivacious, lively, sparkling, high-spirited, bouncy, chirpy, bonhomous, high (Sl), up (Sl). *See also* cheering.

cheering heartening, reassuring, encouraging, promising, auspicious, propitious, favourable, bright, sunny, golden, rosy, rose-coloured, rose-tinted.

cheerless bleak, dreary, dull, depressing, dismal, miserable.

chemical physiochemical, organic, inorganic, analytic(al), synthetic, crystallographic, catalytic, photochemical, radiochemical, biochemical, astrochemical, metallurgical, zymurgic, alchemical (Arch). *See also* crystalline, elemental, structural, reactive.

chilly cool, breezy, draughty, fresh,

cold, nippy; unfriendly, unwelcoming, hostile, cool.

chiropteran dermopteran, winged, flying.

chivalrous knightly, heroic, gallant, manly, soldierly.

choice exclusive, select, handpicked, prize, rare, valuable.

chosen selected, picked, sorted, assorted, seeded, well-chosen, worth choosing, select, choice, A-1, recherché, hand-picked, elite, elect, designate, elected, returned, adopted, deselected, on approval, preferable, better, desirable, advisable, preferred, special, favourite, fancy, pet, God's own, by appointment.

chronicled recorded, logged, documented, minuted, archival, reported, biographical, autobiographical, factual, actual, authentic, genuine, valid, verifiable, traditional, legendary, mythical.

churlish rude, morose, boorish, sullen, surly, brusque; mean, niggardly, stingy, close-fisted.

circuitous roundabout, deviating, digressive, periphrastic, discursive, excursive, indirect, circumlocutory, long-winded, devious, diffuse, oblique, meandering, backhanded, ambagious (Arch).

circular annular, discoid, spherical, orbital, orbicular, spheric, spherelike, spheroidal, rounded, round, ring-shaped, semicircular, cyclic, elliptic, ovate, oval, ovoid, egg-shaped, rotund, circulatory, circumferential, cyclical, gyratory, coiled, looped.

circumlocutory circuitous, periphrastic, ambagious (Arch), roundabout, deviating, digressive, discursive, excur..ive, rambling, wandering, oblique, indirect, irrelevant, pointless, aimless, sidetracked.

circumstantial relative, given, contingent, conditional, indirect, inferential, hearsay, conjectural, presumed, implied, provisional, adventitious, situational, surrounding, environmental, background, situated, placed, contextual, changeful, variable, transient, incidental, eventual, eventful.

civilized enlightened, cultured, refined, sophisticated, educated, human.

classed classified, categorized, grouped, ranked, graded, rated, sorted, ordered, placed, pigeonholed.

classic best, first-rate, excellent, outstanding; ideal, standard, model, archetypal, traditional; lasting, abiding, ageless, enduring.

classical refined, polished, elegant, well-proportioned; Greek, Grecian, Hellenic, Roman, Latin, Augustan, Attic.

classificatory categorical, hierarchical, taxonomic(al), indexical, tabular. *See also* typical, classed.

clean unsoiled, unsullied, undefiled, virginal, untainted, unmuddied, untarnished, unstained, immaculate, spotless, stainless, blank, perfect, dainty, nice, fastidious, fresh, dewy, pure, unmixed, unadulterated, unpolluted, uncontaminated, hygienic, sanitary, sterile, aseptic, antiseptic, salubrious, spruce, dapper, well-groomed, neat, tidy, spick-and-span, orderly, bright, shining, white, snowy, kosher, ritually clean, untouched, natty (Inf). *See also* cleaned, cleansing.

cleaned freshened, disinfected, trimmed, shaven, washed, scrubbed, scoured, swept, brushed, polished, whitened, bleached, laundered, starched, ironed, cleansed, purified, purged, expurgated, decontaminated, sterilized, pasteurized, refined, distilled, filtered.

cleansing lustral, purificatory, disinfectant, hygienic, sanitary, purgative, purgatory, cleaning, detergent, abstergent, ablutionary, balneal.

clear lucid, pellucid, perspicuous, limpid, transparent, pure, coherent, intelligible, comprehensible, apodictic, plain, unadorned, simple, austere, stark, straightforward, direct, unambiguous, explicit, clear-cut, definite, distinct, obvious, exact, accurate, uninvolved; plain, bright, signposted, distinct, defined, sharp, high-definition, open, exposed, uncovered, showy, vivid, brilliant, spectacular, eye-catching, remarkable, outstanding, striking, prominent, stark, lucid, visual, highlighted, spotlighted, illuminated, high-profile.

clever able, gifted, intelligent, knowledgeable, talented, smart.

closed unopened, shut, locked, bolted, barred, latched, padlocked, burglar-proof, fastened, secured, buttoned up, zipped up, sealed, hermetically sealed, vacuum-packed, airtight, watertight, waterproof, lightproof, nonporous, impermeable, impervious. *See also* stopped, closed down, enclosed.

closed down shut down, wound up, finished, resolved, completed, ended.

cloudy overcast, overclouded, dull, dreich (Scot), gloomy, grey, cirrose, cirriform, cumuliform, cumulous, stratous, stratiform, cumulonimbiform, nephological.

clumsy cumbersome, unwieldy, awkward, ungainly, hulking, ponderous, bulky, lumbering.

coarse rough-grained, cross-grained, grainy, granulated, gravelly, stony, rocky, craggy, scraggly, snaggy, nodose, lumpy, slubbed, hispid, villous, spiny, nubby, studded, knobby, knobbly, knotted, gnarled, knurled, bouclé, shattered, broken, jagged, sharp, serrated, ridged, rough-edged, deckle-edged, corrugated, grated, tweed, potholed, furrowed, rutty, pitted, pockmarked, pimply, scabby, encrusted, scaly, warty, blistered, cracked, chapped; tasteless, inelegant, insensitive, undiscriminating, racy, tacky, tawdry, gauche, gaudy, vulgar,

commanding

crude, crass, indecent, obscene, sick (Inf), gross (Inf).

coated plated, veneered, faced, lined, overlaid, overlaying, overlapped, sheathed, laminated.

cocky perky, pert, bumptious, pompous, aggressive, self-confident, swanky, pretentious, affected, obtrusive.

coelenterate hydroid, polypoid, medusoid, hydrozoan, scyphozoan, anthrozoan, coralline, ctenophoran.

cold fresh, bracing, nippy, sharp, inclement, parky, breezy, invigorating, raw, chill, cool, shivery, pinched, biting, bitter, bleak, wintry, severe, snowy, sleety, frosty, icy, snow-bound, iced up, perishing, ice-cold, algid, glacial, frigid, freezing, frozen, gelid, polar, Arctic, Siberian, frost-bitten, frozen solid, frosted, hoar, frappé, iced, glazed, on ice, cold enough to freeze the balls off a brass monkey (Inf). See also heat-resistant.

collected amassed, accumulated, hoarded, stockpiled, heaped, piled, stacked, put together.

colossal huge, immense, massive, gigantic, titanic, vast, enormous.

colourful brilliant, vivid, intense, rich, bright, multicoloured; distinctive, lively, interesting, stimulating, interesting, characterful.

colourless washed out, bleached, achromatic, wan, ashen, pale; dull, insipid, lack lustre, boring, dreary, characterless.

columned columnated, columnar,

supported, pilastered, buttressed, fluted, Doric, Tuscan, Corinthian, Composite.

combative aggressive, hostile, adversarial, opposing, inimical, agonistic, antagonistic, bellicose, belligerent, pugnacious, militant, militaristic, warlike, expansionistic, imperialistic, jingoistic, chauvinistic, hardline, crusading, buccaneering, piratical, bloodthirsty, rowdy, rough, tough, thuggish, trigger-happy (Inf), gung-ho (Inf). See also argumentative, martial.

combined integrated, fused, composed, blended, mingled, mixed, syncretic, harmonized, interwoven, intertwined, networked, connected, joined, conjugate, yoked, linked, united, unified, centralized, incorporated, embodied, inbred, ingrained, impregnated, absorbed, digested, coalescent, symphystic. See also cooperative, assembled.

comfortable easy, secure, well, prosperous, lucky, opportune, suitable, auspicious, favourable; soothing, relaxing, restful, dulcet, mellow, emollient, easy, cosy, snug, comfy (Inf).

comforting reassuring, consoling, cheering, soothing, succouring, easing.

comic amusing, humorous, droll, funny, witty, joking.

commanding ordering, imperative, directive, compelling, ruling, regulatory, enacted, legislative, prescriptive, encyclical, papal, pontifical, authoritative, governmental, mandatory, obligatory, compulsory, dictatorial, prohibitive, proscriptive, injunctive, countermanded, interdicted, vetoed, banned, embargoed. *See also* self-assured.

commemorative ceremonial, solemn, memorial, honourable.

commercial economic, monetary, financial, fiscal.

commissioned delegating, devolutionary, decentralized, representational, deputized, empowered, inaugural, responsible, assigned, appointed, accredited, nominated, authorized, vicarious, warranted, mandated, plenipotentiary, bureaucratic, ambassadorial, legationary, gubernatorial, offical, agential. *See also* engaged.

committed pledged, responsible, obligated, liable, charged, promised.

common regular, standard, normal, usual, ordinary, average, unexceptional, run-of-the-mill, customary, habitual, routine, everyday, equotidian, familiar, accustomed, middlebrow, middle-of-the-road, conventional, pedestrian, vernacular, vulgar, downmarket, plebeian, provincial, titleless, low-down, second-class, low-born, low-caste, proletarian, plebby (Sl).

commonplace trite, platitudinous, hackneyed, uninspired, unimaginative, jaded, overused, stereotyped.

common-sense wise, practical, prudent, level-headed, astute, shrewd.

communal shared, collective, joint, common, public, general.

communicational transmissional, oral, verbal, epistolary, postal, telecommunicational, telephonic, telegraphic, transmitted, relayed, propagated, amplified, modulated, demodulated, broadcast, announced, advertised, radioed, televised, repeated, received, read, seen, heard, transcribed, recorded, taped, videoed.

compact compressed, dense, condensed, packed, solid, thick; short, brief, succinct, terse, pithy, laconic.

compassionate humane, kind, sympathetic, soft-hearted, understanding, benign.

compatible conforming, corresponding, coinciding, congruent, congruous, consistent, matching, equal, uniform, synchronized, parallel, similar.

compelling compulsive, coercive, irresistible, hypnotic, mesmeric, cogent, convincing, inspiring, influential, persuasive, involuntary, unavoidable, inevitable, necessary, commanding, imperative, urgent, overriding, pressing, driving, high-pressure, oppressive, dictatorial, enforcing, binding, restraining, constraining, steamroller, forceful, violent, bludgeoning, strong-arm (Inf), bulldozing (Inf). *See also* compulsory.

compensable amendable, rectifiable, recoupable, reclaimable, repleviable, redeemable, remittable, requitable, restorable, recoverable, satisfiable, propitiable, atonable.

compensated recompensed, indemnified, reimbursed, refunded, repaid, paid off, rewarded, remunerated, remitted, requited, satisfied, propitiated, overcompensated, avenged, revenged, replaced, restored, restituted, recouped, recovered, rectified, redressed, remedied, expiated, redeemed, atoned. *See also* compensable, compensatory, counterbalancing.

compensatory reparatory, restitutory, restorative, indemnificatory, amendatory, retributive, redemptory, remedial, expiatory, propitiative, piacular, penitential.

competent capable, able, skilful, proficient, masterful, adept.

competitive keen, cutthroat, dog-eat-dog, keenly contested, ding-dong, close-run, cliffhanging, well-fought.

complete entire, integral, intact, unbroken, unimpaired, undivided, self-contained, self-sufficient, united, whole, plenary, quorate, sufficient, adequate, all there, unexpurgated, unabridged, uncut, unabbreviated, all-in, comprehensive, absolute, utter, total, exhaustive, full-scale, detailed, thorough, wholesale, unqualified, pure, out-and-out, consummate, full-blown, full-grown, full-fledged, mature, perfect, faultless, finished, accom-

plished, achieved, compleat (Arch), finalized, concluded, closed, terminated, over, done. *See also* full.

completed whole, entire, total, exhaustive, thorough, utter, perfect, well done, consummate, fulfilled, fully realized, thoroughgoing, comprehensive, unabridged, intact, unbroken, full-blown, blooming, ripe, full-grown, matured, polished, secured, accomplished, achieved, compassed, attained, effected, implemented, executed, realized, discharged, disposed of, cleaned up, wrapped up, tied up. *See also* concluded.

complex involved, elaborate, intricate, tangled, tortuous, knotty.

compliant willing, obedient, acquiescent, submissive, yielding, sheep-like, lemming-like, tractable, complaisant, accommodating, agreeable, passive.

complicated elaborate, complex, intricate, tangled, knotty, convoluted.

component constituent, integral, ingredient, elemental, formative, fractional, segmental, departmental, categorical. *See also* modular, belonging, composing.

composed orchestrated, improvized.

composing constituting, comprising, including, inclusive of, containing, embodying, incorporating.

compressible squeezable, padded, foam-filled, pneumatic, pillowed, podgy, pudgy, spongy,

compromising mashy, soggy, squashy, squishy, squelchy, juicy, overripe, pulpy, pithy, medullary, muddy, boggy, marshy, mossy, grassy.

compromising accommodating, adjusted, negotiable, adaptable, averaging out, agreeing, arranged, conceding, give-and-take, settled, halfway, balancing. *See also* half-measure, irresolute.

compulsory mandatory, necessary, unavoidable, ineluctable, obligatory, required, requisite, prerequisite.

concave hollow, incurvate, depressed, sunken, cavernous, indented, cup-shaped, bowl-shaped, dented, dimpled, pockmarked, pitted, porous, spongy.

concealed hidden, covert, unseen, unmanifested, unexposed, invisible, screened, backroom, underground, skulking, lurking, stealthy, hiding, private, secluded, sequestered, unspied, undetected, undisclosed, undercover, veiled, muffled, masked, disguised, coded, cryptographic, secret, classified, restricted, off-the-record, obscure, murky, dark, arcane, unintelligible, impenetrable, undiscoverable, closed. *See also* disguised, silent, noncommittal.

conceited vain, arrogant, pompous, insolent, brazen, unblushing, unabashed, condescending, haughty, self-admiring, affected, uppity, self-praising, snobbish, vainglorious, purse-proud, strutting, conceited, nose-in-the-air, snooty, smug, toffee-nosed (Inf).

concentrating contemplative, pensive, reflective, absorbed.

concerned interested, involved, active, implicated; anxious, uneasy, distressed, bothered, worried, solicitous.

concise brief, short, succinct, pithy, crisp, compact, terse, curt, brusque, taciturn, monosyllabic, laconic, brisk, exact, incisive, trenchant, pointed, brachylogous, tight-knit, portmanteau, compressed, telegraphic, elliptic, syncopal, clipped, abbreviated, contracted, truncated, shortened, compendious, epitomical, aphoristic, epigrammatic, sententious, outlined, summarized, condensed, abridged, cut.

concluded finished, terminated, ended, finalized, wound up, done, crowned, last, final, ultimate, terminal.

conclusive definite, final, positive, decisive, clinching, indisputable.

concurrent concurring, coincident, coinciding, simultaneous, contemporary, contemporaneous, parallel, correlative, coexistent, coexisting, symbiotic, cohabiting.

condensed consolidated, concentrated, solidified, binding, congealed, coagulated, constipated, costive, curdled, clotted, jelled, set, frozen, indissoluble, infusible, crystalline, caked, matted, knotted, ropy, tangled.

condescending snooty, snobbish, lofty, toffee-nosed, supercilious, pompous.

conditional qualificatory, reserved, stipulatory, parametric, obligatory, requisitional, provisional, provisory, specified, defined, mandatory, determined, limiting, restricted, circumscribed, contingent, bound, confined, controlled, checked, curbed, demarcated, delimited, prescribed, proscribed.

confident positive, certain, sure, satisfied, assured, convinced; self-assured, self-reliant, self-possessed, bold, courageous, fearless.

confidential private, secret, restricted, classified, off the record, intimate.

conformable adaptable, adjustable, flexible, pliant, malleable, soft, plastic. *See also* conforming, compliant, conformist, everyday.

conforming equal, correspondent, standard, normalized, uniform, mechanical, identical, regimented, mass-produced, ready-to-wear, off-the-peg, undifferentiated, monolithic, plain, faceless, characterless, featureless, blank, bland, normal, automatic, orderly, aligned, computerized, stereotyped, typecast.

conformist orthodox, kosher, conservative, law-abiding, conventional, traditional, bourgeois, provincial, correct, proper, pedantic, formal, old-fashioned, staid, strait-laced, prim, prudish, square (Inf), stuffy (Inf), stodgy (Inf), grey (Inf), uptight (Inf).

confused bewildered, disconcerted, worried, perplexed, nonplussed, confounded, baffled, puzzled, discomposed, embarrassed, shy, timid, difficult, enigmatic, problematic, cryptic.

congested crowded, jammed, clogged, packed, stuffed, crammed.

congratulatory welcoming, complimentary, auspicious.

conjunctive adjunctive, connective, copulative, coagulating, solidifying, condensing, possessive, copulatory, venereal, sexual, fucked (Tab), hitched (Sl), hooked (Sl), laid (Sl), screwed (Sl).

connected tied, linked, joined, united, merged, coupled, interfaced, fastened, attached, interconnected, interwoven, entangled, laced, braided, plaited, knotted, lashed, bound, stitched, sewn, tacked, zipped (up), buttoned (up), buckled, hooked, wired (up), pinned, nailed, stapled, pegged, riveted, screwed, hinged, stuck, bonded, glued, bracketed, hyphenated, bridged.

connective conjunctive, cohesive, adhesive, sticky, interconnective, communicative, liaising, associated, related, joint, coherent. *See also* connected, bound.

conscientious painstaking, thorough, meticulous, careful, faithful, particular; principled, high-minded, honest, upright, moral, honourable.

conscious awake, sleepless, insomniac.

consecutive successive, following, serial, seriate, sequential, in order, running, ongoing, progressive, chronological, catenary, ordinal, linear. *See also* repercussive, continuous, cyclical.

consenting consentient, assentient, affirming, confirming, approving, recognized, agreed, ratified, authorized, accredited, backed, endorsed.

consequent resulting, ensuing, caused.

conservative traditional, right-wing, true-blue, reactionary, obstinate, stubborn, old-fashioned, unprogressive, die-hard, dyed-in-the-wool, dry (Inf), stick-in-the-mud (Inf).

considerate kind, thoughtful, charitable, solicitous, benevolent, obliging.

consistent regular, constant, steady, dependable, unchanging, persistent; harmonious, corresponding, agreeing, congruous, compatible.

conspicuous distinct, well defined, unblurred, clear-cut, obvious, eye-catching.

constant permanent, regular, habitual, even, fixed, steadfast; perpetual, nonstop, ceaseless, endless, continous; loyal, true, faithful, dependable, staunch, devoted.

constructive practical, positive, useful, helpful, valuable.

contagious infectious, catching, communicable, infective, morbific, pathogenic, germ-carrying, zymotic, pestiferous, plague-stricken, malarious, aguish, epidemic, pandemic, endemic, epizootic, enzootic, sporadic, unsterilized, nonsterile, infected, septic, contaminated, dirty.

containing holding, enclosing, covering, enveloping, wrapping, sheathed, surrounded, cocooning, stabling. *See also* loaded, itemized.

contemporary contemporaneous, coexistent, synchronous; modern, current, up-to-date, fashionable, recent, present.

contemptuous scornful, disdainful, pejorative, supercilious, lofty, haughty, arrogant, snobbish, snooty, contumelious, snotty (Inf).

contending battling, fighting, grappling, struggling, competing, contesting, challenging, racing, rival, vying, outdoing, surpassing, agonistic, athletic, sporting, starting, running. *See also* contentious, competitive.

content satisfied, at ease, glad, willing, comfortable fulfilled.

contentious argumentative, quarrelsome, irritable, irascible, aggressive, combative, fight-hungry, pugilistic, gladiatorial, pugnacious, bellicose, warmongering, warlike, hawkish, at loggerheads, at odds, at war, belligerent, warring, head-to-head, close.

continental Australasian, Asian,

European, African, American, subcontinental, insular, islander, isleted, archipelagic, estuarial, coastal, littoral, ashore, sandy, pebbled, shingled, swampy, boggy, marshy, paludal, deltaic, flat, plain, rocky, peninsular, isthmian, promontory, campestral, volcanic, thermal.

continual continuous, in progress, ongoing, constant, steady, incessant, progressive, sequent, additional, repetitive, recurrent, unbroken, uninterrupted, interconnected, interrelated, cohesive, sustained. *See also* protracted.

continuing forever ceaseless, unceasing, continuous, constant, unending, nonstop, interminable, incessant.

continuous constant, incessant, perpetual, nonstop, endless, unending, never-ending, ceaseless, unremitting, interminable, unrelieved, unbroken, solid, smooth, serried, seamless, uninterrupted, uniform, undifferentiated, featureless, monotonous.

contracting shrinking, constringent, astringent, styptic, compressive, tightening, crushing, pinching, cramping, constricting, limiting, restricting, circumscriptive, strangling, deflationary, implosive, collapsing, shortening, stunting, narrowing, gathering, puckering, pursing, shrivelling, searing, wasting, tabescent, emaciating, thinning,

slimming, decreasing, reducing, lessening, waning.

contractual contracting, contracted, obligatory, promised, pledged, ratified, endorsed, authentic, signed, sealed, and delivered.

contradictory jarring, grating, paradoxical, absurd, oxymoronic, antinomic, contrary, opposite, mismatched, misallied, ill-chosen, maladjusted, unnatural, abnormal, mutant, distorted, anomalous, odd, uncharacteristic.

contrary opposite, reverse, inconsistent, incompatible, contradictory, repugnant, antithetical, diametric(al), adversative, irreconcilable, polarized, con (Inf).

contrite sorry, repentant, remorseful, humble, conscience-stricken, sorrowful.

contrived unnatural, artificial, laboured, overdone.

controversial disputed, open to question, debatable, dialectic.

convenient handy, helpful, practical, pragmatic, practicable, usable, workable, effective, adapted to, applicable, suitable, commodious, appropriate, fit, seemly, proper, expedient, advantageous, beneficial, useful, commendable, desirable, worthwhile, acceptable, timely, well-timed, auspicious, opportune, seasonable. *See also* nearby.

convergent confluent, uniting, concurrent, meeting, focal, focusing, confocal, centrolineal, centripetal, asymptotic(al), radial, ra diating, tangential, centring, pointed, tapering, narrowing, conical, pyramidal, knock-kneed. *See also* advancing.

conversational colloquial, informal, chatty, gossipy, newsy, informative, forthcoming.

conversing talking, chatting, interlocutory, confabulatory, talkative, loquacious, communicative, unreserved. *See also* discussing, conversational.

converted changed, transformed, transposed, transfigured, metamorphosed, transmuted, mutated, translated, bewitched, enchanted, brainwashed, proselytized, assimilated, naturalized, improved, regenerated, degenerated. *See also* converting, influenced, naturalized.

converting changing, becoming, growing, developing, maturing, altering, transforming, mutating, processing, fermenting, leavening, crystallizing, melting, transmuting, transfiguring, evolving, progressing, regenerating, improving, deteriorating.

convex bulbous, bulging, swelling, gibbous, billowing, protruding, distended, humped, prominent, excrescent, tumescent, swollen, meniscoid, arcuated, bowed out, arched, vaulted, lenticular.

convinced certain, sure, positive, believing, accepting, trusting, unquestioning, undoubting, unswerving, unhesitating, undeviating, as-

sured, satisfied, persuaded, confident, self-assured, self-confident, opinionated, cocksure, assertive, overconfident, doctrinaire, dogmatic, orthodox, narrow-minded, obstinate, stubborn, bigoted, biased, partisan, fanatical.

convolutional winding, twisted, involutional, circumlocutory, sinuous, undulatory, intricate, braided, wavy, twirled, entwined, corrugated, tortuous, meandering, labyrinthine, serpentine, vermiform, wriggling, squirming, squiggly, coiled, spiral, helical, cochleate, whorled, turbinate. *See also* ambiguous.

convulsive jerky, jolting, jarring, jolty, twitchy, twitchety, jumping, jumpy, palsied, fitful, spasmodic, paroxysmic, eclamptic, spastic, vellicative, orgasmic, saltatory, choreic, choreal, epileptic, cataleptic.

cool chilly, nippy, frosty, icy, snowy, slushy, sleety, arctic, parky (Inf), perishing (Inf).

cooperative symbiotic, in agreement, in harmony, associated, orchestrated, leagued, in league, conspiratorial, cabbalistic, allied, federated, confederate, coagent, concurrent, synchronized, coincident, conjunctive. *See also* joint, associating.

copious abundant, profuse, extensive, plentiful, lavish, ample.

core nuclear, focal, pivotal, inner, inside, interior.

corporate limited, public, nationalized, private, privatized, merged.

correct factual, authentic, genuine, truthful, literal, true-to-the-letter, word-perfect, true-to-life, unerring, verbatim, faithful, lifelike, realistic.

correlated correspondent, balanced, aligned, equal, uniform, harmonious.

correlative correspondent, comparable, analogous, allegorical, parallel, symmetric(al), proportional, patterned, matching, equivalent, similar, identical.

correspondent corresponding, correlative, reciprocal.

corrosive erosive, wearing, corroding, acid, acrid, caustic; cutting, biting, sarcastic, incisive, trenchant, caustic.

corrupt fraudulent, dishonest, bent (Inf), rotten, shady, unprincipled, unscrupulous; immoral, degenerate, wicked, profligate; decayed, putrid, rotten, defiled.

cosmetic superficial, beautifying.

cosmopolitan worldly, universal, catholic.

costly high-priced, expensive, dear, overpriced, exorbitant, inflationary, sky-high, unaffordable, prohibitive.

cosy homely, comfortable, snug, warm, secure.

counteracting opposing, contravening, polarized, contrary, conflicting, clashing, antipathetic, antagonistic, inimical, hostile, resistant, recalcitrant, intractable, reactionary, retroactive, reactive, frictional, restraining, frustrating, interfering, repressive, suppressive, intolerant, obstructive, preventive, antidotal, contraceptive, remedial, corrective, balancing, offsetting, moderating, neutralizing, invalidating, nullifying, compensatory.

counterbalancing balancing, compensating, counterpoised, equipoised, in equilibrium, equiponderant, equalized, countervailing, levelled, evened up, offsetting, corrected, attuned, adjusted, return, counter, counterposed, counteracted, retroactive, neutralized, cancelled out, written off, nullified, deactivated, antidotal, retaliating, avenging.

countered repudiated, retracted, disclaimed, disowned, abjured, abnegated, abrogated, revoked, renounced, denied, disavowed, reneged, retorted, refuted, confuted, negated, invalidated, annulled.

counterfeit faked, fraudulent, bogus, imitation, sham.

countering answering, defensive, apologetic, retaliatory, confutative, refutative, contrary, counteractive, rebutting, denying, contradictory, oppositional, apostatic, hypocritical, equivocal. See also countered.

courageous brave, heroic, gallant, valiant, mettlesome, plucky, daring, audacious, bold, hardy, fearless, dauntless, undaunted, spirited, stout-hearted, lion-hearted, unflinching, unshrinking, unshake-

able, unbowed, undismayed, indomitable, doughty, tough, spunky (Sl), gutsy (Sl), ballsy (Sl). *See also* chivalrous, militant, self-reliant, adventurous, encouraging.

courteous polite, civil, urbane, agreeable, affable, genial, amiable, gracious, humble, fair, considerate, thoughtful, solicitous, decent, tactful, discreet, generous, benevolent, charitable, accommodating, lenient, even-humoured, gentle, mild, good-humoured, obliging, amenable, sociable, friendly, kind, sweet, nice, welcoming, gallant, chivalrous, courtly, graceful, old-fashioned, old-world. *See also* good-mannered, deferential.

covered topped, capped, corked, glazed, varnished, stained, painted, whitewashed, copperplated, roofed, tiled, thatched, faced, bricked, panelled, papered, wallpapered, roofed in. *See also* protected, covering, inclusive, substitutive.

covering overlaying, overlying, spanning, superimposed, epidermal, cuticular, integumental.

cowardly dastardly, craven, recreant (Arch), pusillanimous, timid, shy, spineless, soft, namby-pamby, chicken-hearted, lily-livered, faint-hearted, weak-kneed, timorous, wet, fearful, afraid, scared, frightened, rattled, daunted, cowed, panicky, unheroic, defeatist, cowering, chicken (Sl), gutless (Inf), sissy (Inf), windy (Sl), yellow (Inf), yellow-bellied (Sl).

coy demure, bashful, shy, modest, coquettish.

cracked cleft, cloven, fissured, cut, slit, split, riven, ruptured, rent, torn, broken, fractured, open, gaping, gappy, grooved, furrowed, rimose, dehiscent.

crackling crepitant, sizzling, spitting, clicking, rattling, popping, staccato.

crafty sly, cunning, deceitful, devious, scheming, artful.

cramped confined, crowded, hemmed in, packed, overcrowded, congested.

crapulous hung over, dizzy, giddy, sick.

crass stupid, insensitive, boorish, oafish, obtuse, thick.

crazy mad, mental (Sl), lunatic, dafts, nuts (Inf), potty (Inf); silly, inane, foolish, asinine, half-baked (Inf); peculiar, odd, bizarre, outrageous, fantastic; infatuated, ardent, passionate, obsessive.

created materialized, made, actualized, evolved.

creative imaginative, clever, talented, artistic, original, ingenious.

credible believable, likely, plausible, conceivable; honest, trustworthy, dependable, reliable.

crestfallen downcast, down-hearted, dispirited, dejected, despondent, disappointed.

criminal law-breaking, felonious, fraudulent, underhanded, thieving, light-fingered, embezzling, swindling, bribing, shady (Inf), crooked (Inf), fishy (Inf), bent (Sl).

crisp crispy, crunchy, crumbly, firm, brittle; fresh, bracing, invigorating, refreshing; brusque, short, brief, terse, abrupt.

critical censorious, disparaging, denigrating, maligning, decrying, denunciatory, defamatory, slanderous, libellous, vituperative, abusive; crucial, decisive, momentous, pivotal, key.

criticized dispraised, uncommended, run down, panned (Inf), slated (Inf).

crooked curved, bowed, deformed, distorted, misshapen, twisted; lopsided, askew, slanted; deceitful, fraudulent, shifty, underhand, bent (Inf), corrupt.

cross angry, ill-tempered, in a bad mood, peevish, fractious, vexed; crosswise, transverse, oblique, crisscrossing, contrary, adverse.

crossing intersecting, interchanging, interconnecting, intersectional.

crowded packed, crammed, congested, dense, close, serried, seething, teeming, swarming, bristling, milling, crawling, jam-packed (Inf), chock-a-block (Inf); thronged, mobbed, congested, massed, packed, jam-packed, crushed, cluttered, overpopulated, overrun.

crucial essential, pivotal, central, critical, imperative, urgent.

crude coarse, obscene, lewd, vulgar, rude, smutty; natural, unre-

fined, unpolished, unproce... clumsy, rudimentary, makesh... sketchy, primitive.

cruel inhumane, subhuman, dehumanized, atrocious, outrageous, barbaric, brutal, savage, bestial, vicious, ferocious, violent, sadistic, monstrous, terrorful, heinous, bloodthirsty, cannibalistic, murderous, fiendish, devilish, satanic, demoniac, diabolical, hellish, infernal.

crumbly friable, crisp, flaky, scaly, scurfy.

crumpled creased, rumpled, wrinkled, ruffled, puckered, crushed.

crusty crispy, brittle, well-done, friable; irritable, peevish, testy, cantankerous, gruff, surly.

crying sobbing, sighing, groaning, moaning, whimpering, weeping, wailing, howling, ululant, blubbering, blubbing (Inf).

crystalline microcrystalline, crystallized, crystalloid, noncrystalline, amorphous, supernatant.

culinary gastronomic, epicurean, mensal, prandial, pre-prandial, postprandial, dressed, oven-ready, prepared, ready-to-cook, made-up, ready-to-serve, cooked, done, well-done, overcooked, burnt, al dente, underdone, undercooked, red, rare, raw, roasted, browned, toasted, grilled, barbecued, devilled, curried, fried, deep-fried, sautéed, stir-fried, scrambled, coddled, boiled, steamed, poached, stewed, braised, beaten, stuffed, chopped, ground, minced, au gratin, au naturel, table d'hôte.

cultivated ploughed, worked, tilled, farmed, planted, harvested; cultured, polished, refined, educated, well-bred, civilized; encouraged, supported, patronized, nurtured.

cultural artistic, educational, enriching, edifying, civilizing.

cultured accomplished, polished, genteel, well-bred, erudite, scholarly.

cumbersome awkward, clumsy, burdensome, heavy, unwieldy, bulky.

cumulate glomerate, conglomerate, agglomerate, aggregate, convergent, confluent, collective, combined.

cunning sly, wily, foxy, artful, crafty, clever, skilful, knowledgeable, resourceful, inventive, ingenious, guileful, imaginative, disingenuous, subtle, serpentine, vulpine, feline, tricky, tricksy, devious, secret, stealthy, clandestine, underhand, scheming, contriving, practising, plotting, planning, intriguing, conspiring, calculating, Machiavellian, arch, knowing, intelligent, smart, sharp, astute, shrewd, wise, acute, sophisticated, urbane, canny, pawky (Dial), experienced, reticent, reserved, cautious, wary, tactical, strategical, well-laid, insidious, perfidious, shifty, slippery, timeserving, temporizing, equivocal, sophistical, flattering, beguiling, hyp-

ocritical, insincere, deceitful, rascally, crooked, dishonest, knavish (Arch), slick (Inf), fly (Sl), cagey (Inf).

cured healed, healthy, better, convalescent.

curious inquisitive, inquiring, inquisitorial, questioning, interested, keen, adventurous, sightseeing. *See also* prying.

curricular intramural, extramural, extracurricular, doctoral, collegiate, varsity, canonical, doctrinal, technical.

cursed damned, blighted, doomed, jinxed, hexed, ill-fated; detestable, hateful, loathsome, damnable, abominable, infamous.

cursing swearing, profane, obscene, vulgar, scurrilous, naughty, offensive, indelicate, blue, four-letter, Anglo-Saxon, invective, dirty, filthy, vile, indecent, ribald, bawdy, Rabelaisian, risque, foul, foulmouthed, scatological(al), dysphemistic, blasphemous, sacrilegious. *See also* vituperative, maledictive.

curt brusque, abrupt, rude, short, terse, offhand.

curved cambered, curviform, curvilinear, bent, concave, convex, turning, sloping, stooped, bowed, vaulted, arciform, arched, spiraled, curled, coiled, looped, round, oval, semicircular, circular, crescentic, lunar, meniscal, parabolic, hyperbolic, domical, sinusoidal. *See also* well-rounded.

dated

customary habitual, accustomed, wonted, conventional, traditional, regulation, standard, routine, usual, normal, typical, copybook, regulated, methodical, systematic, orderly.

cyclic circular, orbital, revolving, rotational, routine, hourly, daily, diurnal, quotidian, nightly, tertian, weekly, hebdomadary, fortnightly, monthly, seasonal, biannual, annual, perennial, bissextile, biennial, Metonic cycle, biorhythmic, menstrual, oestrous.

cyclical periodic, rhythmic, recurrent, repetitive.

cynical sardonic, derisive, scornful, sceptical, mocking, contemptuous.

D

dainty delicate, fine, pretty, graceful, neat, petite.

damnable blasted, confounded, bothersome, execrable, accursed, diabolic, dratted (Inf), blankety-blank (Inf), infernal (Inf), devilish (Inf), hellish (Inf).

damned cursed, doomed, condemned, lost; hateful, detestable, loathsome, revolting, atrocious.

damp wet, clammy, moist, humid, soggy, drizzly.

dangerous perilous, treacherous, hazardous, risky, unknown, uncertain, unlit, venturous, difficult, chancy, tricky, critical, serious, nasty, ugly, menacing, threatening, ominous, foreboding, alarming, frightening, at stake, in question, inflammable, explosive, radioactive, toxic, deadly, life-threatening, harmful, unhealthy, infectious, sticky (Inf), dicey (Inf), dodgy (Inf), iffy (Inf), hairy (Sl). *See also* unsafe, vulnerable, endangered.

daring daredevil, bold, fearless, reckless, adventurous, brave.

dark unlit, unilluminated, dim, ill-lit, underexposed, lightproof, lightless, sunless, moonless, starless, pitch-dark, shady, umbrageous, overcast, thundery, louring, dusky, gloomy, dingy, murky, tenebrous, black, Stygian, Cimmerian, nocturnal; deep, achromatic, dim, dingy, murky, smudgy, smoky, dusky, swarthy, swart (Arch), pigmented, melanistic, dark-complexioned, Black, Negro, Negroid. *See also* darkening, dark-coloured, benighted.

dark-coloured dark, brunette, swarthy, dusky, darkling, black, pitch-black, jet-black, inky, ebony, melanic, sable, livid, leaden, grimy, dirty, stained, drab, funereal.

darkening extinguishing, shading, shadowing, screening, obscuring, dimming, dipping, dyeing.

dashing dynamic, bold, debonair, gallant, swashbuckling, valiant; showy, elegant, flamboyant, dazzling, dapper, jaunty.

dated old hat, out of date, old-fashioned, obsolete, archaic, unfashionable.

dazed confused, bemused, baffled, bewildered, perplexed, stunned.

dazzled blinded, astonished, stunned, amazed, impressed; blinded, bedazzled, dazed, blurred, confused.

dead deceased, defunct, demised, lifeless, breathless, still, inanimate, exanimate, no more, passed away, released, departed, gone, stillborn, extinct, finished, in Paradise, late, lamented, regretted, killed, murdered, kaput (Inf), cold (Sl), stiff (Sl).

deadly lethal, killing, mortal, fatal, deathly, fell (Arch), life-threatening, capital, death-bringing, malignant, poisonous, toxic, asphyxiant, suffocating, stifling, unhealthy, miasmic, insalubrious, inoperable, incurable, terminal. *See also* murderous.

deaf unhearing, hearing-impaired, stone deaf, deaf-mute, tone deaf, unmusical, deafened. *See also* unhearing, deafening, unheard.

deafening ear-splitting, piercing, ear-shattering.

dear expensive, costly, high-priced, extravagant, fancy, luxury, up-market, exorbitant, excessive, overcharging, unreasonable, prohibitive, extortionate, inflationary, rising, climbing, soaring, spiralling, mounting, rocketing, high-cost, sky-high, bullish, usurious, profiteering, pricey (Inf), ritzy (Sl), stiff (Inf),

steep (Inf), skyrocketing (Inf). *See also* valuable.

deathly cadaverous, ghastly, livid, pale, pallid, wan, ashen, ghostly, haggard, skeletal.

debatable questionable, arguable, controversial, moot, doubtful, uncertain.

decadent dissolute, corrupt, immoral, depraved, degenerate, decaying.

deceased dead, lifeless, departed, expired, defunct, gone.

deceitful duplicitous, fraudulent, fake, artificial, false-hearted, cunning, sneaky, artful, guileful, wily, crafty, manipulative, malingering, lying, fibbing, fabricating, prevaricating, slandering, libelling, perjuring, forswearing, perfidious, collusive, treasonous, treacherous, flimflam (Inf).

deceived duped, tricked, hoaxed, fooled, outsmarted, hookwinked, victimized, outmanoeuvred, bluffed, cheated, outwitted, ensnared, entangled, manipulated, misled, misguided, misdirected, misinformed, mocked, ridiculed, ragged, flimflammed (Inf), spoofed (Inf), diddled (Inf), done (Inf), swizzled (Inf).

deceiving misleading, double-dealing, conniving, contriving, covering up, whitewashing, colluding, dodging, feinting, designing, scheming, cheating, calculating, cunning, sharp, artful, guileful, wily, crafty, tricky, shifty, devious, dishonest, sneaky, furtive, surreptitious, indirect, smooth, slippery, conning (Inf), dodgy (Inf). *See also* deceptive, deceived, hypocritical, treacherous, imitative, disguised, trapped.

decent seemly, proper, presentable, fitting, decorous, modest; kind, polite, courteous, nice, thoughtful, accommodating.

decentralized devolved, shared, deputized, assigned, consigned, deconcentrated, regionalized, localized, federalized.

deceptive false, fallacious, duplicitous, dishonest, conspiratorial, fraudulent, sorcerous, insidious, illicit, underhand, gerrymandered, contrived, gimmicky, misleading, tongue-in-cheek, fixed (Inf).

decided settled, fixed, established, undisputed, unrefuted, irrefutable, undeniable, uncontestable, unchallengeable, incontrovertible, indubitable, unimpeachable, unambiguous, unequivocal.

decisive definite, conclusive, final, categorical, crucial, critical; forceful, resolute, firm, strong-minded, incisive.

declared innocent cleared, acquitted, exonerated, exculpated, absolved.

decorated ornamented, garnished, ornate, embellished, enriched, enhanced, bejewelled, gilt, gilded, embroidered, trimmed, worked, inlaid, enamelled, patterned, ornamental, fancy, pretty-pretty (Inf), non-functional, scenic, picturesque, baroque, rococo; knighted, honoured. *See also* decorated.

decreasing declining, falling, dwindling, waning, fading, evanescent, abating, softening, diminuendo, decrescendo, sinking, subsiding, detumescent, ebbing, decaying, diminished. *See also* decrescent.

decrepit feeble, frail, crippled, infirm, aged, weak; ramshackle, worn-out, rickety, broken-down, antiquated.

decrescent declinate, reductive, depressive, debilitative, deflationary, depreciatory, loss-making, regressive, corrosive, deliquescent, decompressive, decadent, decayable, declinable, deductible.

dedicated committed, wholehearted, devoted, single-minded.

deep bottomless, unfathomable, fathomless, unsounded, unplumbed, abysmal, abyssal, plunging, cavernous, yawning, gaping, ankle-deep, knee-deep, deep-down, deep-set, sunken, engraved, incised; low, sepulchral, sonorous, vibrant, booming, thundering, full, rich, plangent, mellow, melodious, rounded, orotund, full-throated. *See also* deep-seated, wise, under, bathymetric.

deep-seated intense, extreme, sincere, profound, serious, heartfelt, earnest.

defamatory slanderous, libellous, calumnious, scandalous, scurrilous, abusive, insulting, aspersive, insin-

uating, gossiping, whispering, mud-
slinging, smearing, besmirching,
blackening, tarnishing, damaging,
injurious, destructive, venomous,
caustic, bitter, back-biting, snide,
catty (Inf), bitchy (Inf).

defeated beaten, bested, lost, outmanoeuvred, outclassed, out-
matched, outgunned, outplayed,
outshone, outvoted, outwitted,
thrashed, in retreat, routed, overthrown, knocked out, licked (Inf),
pipped (Sl), KO'd (Sl).

defective broken, faulty, poor, disappointing, blemished, shop-soiled,
imperfect, inadequate, perfunctory,
cursory, substandard, inferior,
catalectic, failing.

defensive resistant, hostile, dis-
missive.

deferential obeisant, compliant,
condescending, complaisant, glib,
fulsome, sycophantic, ingratiating,
bowing, nodding, kowtowing,
smug, oily, unctuous, buttery (Inf),
soapy (Inf), slimy (Inf).

defiant outspoken, assertive, emphatic, assured, unabashed, audacious, bold, arrogant, presumptuous, stubborn, obstinate, stiff-
necked, bumptious, offensive, impudent, impertinent, pert, insolent,
insulting, contemptuous, disdainful,
derisive, shameless, brash, brassy,
brazen, courageous, daring, reckless, saucy, cocky, cheeky. *See also*
defying.

definite absolute, categorical, un-

equivocal, unquestionable, undisputed, indisputable, indubitable.

deflated punctured, depreciated,
cut-down, cut-back.

deformed distorted, warped,
twisted, malformed, hunchbacked,
clubfooted, disfigured, imperfect,
ugly, hideous, grotesque, defaced,
scarred, marked, pockmarked,
spotty, pitted, blemished, ill-made,
zitty (Sl); handicapped, disabled,
blind, deaf, dumb, mute, mutilated,
maimed, lame, crippled.

defying challenging, disagreeing,
disobedient, recalcitrant, refractory,
obstinate, antagonistic, belligerent,
provocative, aggressive, rebellious,
militant, warlike.

degraded debased, downgraded,
demoted, humiliated, downcast, depressed, kowtowing, kneeling,
grovelling, courteous, deferential.

deified divinized, immortalized,
canonized, beatified, sanctified, an-
gelized, haloed, glorified, saved, redeemed, martyred, consecrated, enshrined, elevated, dedicated, dignified, ennobled, magnified, exalted,
adulated, idolized.

dejected crestfallen, downcast,
dispirited, depressed, sad, despondent.

delayed detained, checked, arrested, obstructed, impeded, retarded, restrained, slack, backward,
behind, late, hysteretic, dilatory, lingering, dawdling, loitering, dilly-
dallying (Inf), shillyshallying (Inf).

delaying slowing, procrastinating,

obstructive, hindering, retarding, blocking, restraining, detaining, lagging, late-running, following.

delegated elected, nominated, appointed, representative, Parliamentary, ministerial, diplomatic, ambassadorial, legatine, legationary, consular, intermediary, deputy. *See also* decentralized.

deliberate intentional, willed, premeditated, prepense, planned, preplanned, considered, measured, weighed, calculated, designed, prearranged, preset, pre-established, fixed, set, controlled, studied, advised, devised, contrived, packed, primed, stacked, loaded, put-up (Inf), set-up (Inf), framed (Inf).

delicate dainty, filmy, gossamery, finespun, thin-spun, subtle, finedrawn, wire-drawn.

delicious tasty, appetizing, mouthwatering, palatable, delectable, scrumptious; exquisite, delightful, enchanting, charming.

delighted thrilled, enchanted, captivated, joyous, pleased, jubilant.

delightful lovely, wonderful, marvellous, heavenly, enchanting, gorgeous, entrancing, charming, enthralling, captivating, Elysian (Fml).

deliverable saveable, salvable, rescuable, extricable, redeemable, salvageable, saved, rescued, liberated, free, saving.

demanding claiming, requisitionary, injunctive, forcible, threatening, blackmailing, extortive; imperative, urgent, exigent, exacting, pressing, squeezing, pinching.

democratic popular, egalitarian, self-governing, republican, representative.

demonstrable provable, confirmable, attestable, verifiable, evident, self-evident, obvious, undeniable, apparent, perspicuous, distinct, indisputable, unquestionable, positive, certain, conclusive, clear-cut.

demonstrated obvious, manifest, plain, clear, express, explicit, displayed, exhibited, disclosed, exposed, revealed, published, publicized, expository, exhibitional, revelatory, apodeictic. *See also* demonstrative, explanatory, demonstrable, proven, demonstrating.

demonstrating protesting, objecting, opposing, dissenting, agitating, rallying, marching, parading, striking, picketing, boycotting.

demonstrative open, unrestrained, frank, candid, warm, affectionate, effusive, expansive, ostentatious, showy, flashy, flamboyant, dramatic, stagy, theatrical, exhibitionist, emotional, exhibitionistic, histrionic.

dense thick, compact, cohesive, close-packed, firm, incompressible, full, assembled, serried, massed, heavy, weighty, monolithic, solid, concrete, rigid, constrictive, strong, unbreakable, infrangible, indivisible, inseparable, consistent, impenetrable, thickset, impermeable, impervious; full-bodied, semiliquid,

viscous, condensed, congealed, coagulated, clotted, thickened, intensified, boiled-down, reduced,
crowded, abundant, packed, swarming, teeming, jammed, chock-a-
block, impenetrable; stupid, thick.
See also condensed.

dental oral, orthodontic, exodontic,
endodontic, prosthodontic, peri-
odontic, periodontal.

departed gone, gone away, gone
off, left.

departing leaving, farewell, valedictory, parting, leave-taking, last,
final. *See also* departed, outgoing.

dependent weak, defenceless,
helpless, reliant, vulnerable; de-
pending, liable to, contingent, conditional, subject to.

deplorable wretched, disastrous,
lamentable, calamitous, distressing;
disgraceful, shameful, scandalous,
reprehensible.

depraved corrupt, degenerate,
profligate, abandoned, lewd, perverted.

depressed melancholic, downcast, low, droopy, dreary, joyless,
dejected, dispirited, despondent,
atrabilious, lugubrious, grey, lack-
lustre, listless, gloomy, morose,
glum, dismal, long-faced, moody,
moping, suicidal, blue (Inf), sunk
(Inf).

depressing bleak, dismal, miserable, gloomy, black, dreary, sad.

deprived disadvantaged, bereft,
needy, poor, wanting, lacking.

deputizing representing, acting,

standing in, substituting, diplomatic,
ambassadorial, plenipotentiary, consular, proconsular, ministerial,
deputy, intermediary, temporary,
temporary, imitative, ersatz, second-
best.

deranged disordered, unhinged,
unbalanced, maladjusted, disturbed,
demented, neurotic, psychotic, unstable, mad, insane, hung-up (Sl),
gaga (Sl).

derelict deserted, ruined, dilapidated, forsaken, neglected, discarded; remiss, neglectful, negligent.

derisive ridiculing, satirical, sarcastic, sardonic, quizzical.

descending down, downward,
decurrent, declivitous, deciduous,
downflowing, downrushing, pouring, downturning, sinking, declining, bearish, decreasing, lowering,
subsiding, slumping, drowning,
foundering, tottering, tumbling,
crashing, collapsing. *See also*
drooping, falling.

descriptive representational,
graphic, vivid, detailed, full, informative, illustrative, explicatory, explanatory, elucidating, illuminating,
expository, interpretive, amplifying,
well-drawn, true-to-life, realistic,
naturalistic, photographic, eidetic,
convincing, picturesque, expressive,
impressionistic, evocative, moving,
poignant, thrilling, exciting, striking, highly coloured, forceful. *See
also* narrative, representing.

desensitized numb, frozen, paralysed, anaesthetized, dopey, groggy, torpid, sluggish, drugged, stupefied, comatose, unfeeling, unconscious, quiescent, inert, dead.

desert arid, Saharan, dusty, powdery, sandy, barren, bare, brown, grassless.

deserted abandoned, desolate, derelict, neglected, uninhabited, empty.

deserved earned, merited, just, well-earned, suitable, fair.

desirable acceptable, welcome, pleasurable, pleasant, attractive, likeable, appealing, inviting, tempting, appetizing, mouth-watering, admirable, creditable, laudable, praiseworthy, meritorious, deserving, worthwhile, good, beneficial, advantageous, profitable, expedient, convenient, suitable, fitting, apt, proper.

desired wished for, wanted, needed, necessary, required, requested, longed for, yearned for, coveted, envied, in demand, popular, sought-after. *See also* desirable, desirous, hungry, lustful.

desirous wishful, wanting, needing, demanding, longing for, coveting, craving, itching for, dying for, ardent, passionate, avid, eager, keen, partial to, fond, covetous, envious, gluttonous, voracious, greedy, acquisitive, possessive, insatiable, hoping, aspiring, yearning, pining, wistful, nostalgic, homesick.

desisting denying, refraining, abstaining, abstemious, forbearing.

desolate wild, uninhabited, barren, bleak, bare, desert; abandoned, bereft, friendless, forsaken, sad, miserable.

despairing anxious, despondent, hopeless, dejected, downcast, grief-stricken.

desperate foolhardy, impetuous, headstrong, rash, dangerous, risky; critical, urgent, grave, dire, acute; wretched, forlorn, despairing, hopeless, inconsolable.

despondent depressed, dejected, disheartened, glum, hopeless, miserable.

despotic oppressive, tyrannical, autocratic, dictatorial, authoritarian.

destined headed, directed, bound; intended, fated, doomed, predestined, certain, sure.

destitute poor, poverty-stricken, penniless, needy, down and out, hard up (Inf); bereft, deficient, wanting, lacking, deprived, deficient.

destroyed wiped out, ruined, devastated, crushed, ground, pulverized, pulped, shredded, broken up, disintegrated, shattered, wrecked, torpedoed, sunk, done for, dished, in tatters, in ruins, crumbling, falling apart, doomed, bankrupt, bust, in liquidation, in receivership, buggered (Sl), kaput (Inf).

destructive devastating, ruinous, internecine, cut-throat, annihilating, consuming, raging, rampaging, suicidal, deadly, lethal, fatal, disastrous, catastrophic, apocalyptic, cataclysmic, overwhelming, subversive, revolutionary, anarchistic, incendiary, insidious, pernicious, noxious, harmful, injurious, baneful. *See also* destroyed.

detached unemotional, imperturbable, unruffled, unconcerned, dispassionate, cool, calm, collected, composed, level-headed, equanimous, tolerant, self-controlled, stoical, patient, serene, placid.

detailed meticulous, elaborate, minute, incidental, particular, full, precise, exact, specific, special, fussy, finicky, pernickety, nit-picking (Inf).

detained quarantined, shut-in, housebound, snowbound, fogbound, besieged, custodial, arrested, sentenced, incarcerated, imprisoned, in custody, on remand, confined, captive, kidnapped, enslaved, gagged, muzzled, in irons.

deteriorated worse, exacerbated, aggravated, worsening, failing, going downhill, decreasing, in decline, falling off, in recession, impoverished, falling, slipping, sliding, tottering, senile, spoilt, gone bad, off, rotten, corked, stale, flat, bland, tasteless, impaired, damaged, effete, worn out, exhausted, drained, run-down, useless, weakened, undermined, sapped, faded, decaying, withered, sere (Arch), wasting away, ebbing, retrogressive, regressive, retrograde, outdated, recidivist, tergiversating, degenerate, depraved, corrupt. *See also* dilapidated.

determined resolute, resolved, certain, sure, iron-willed, inflexible, unwavering, tough, hard, steely, obstinate, stubborn, obdurate, imperturbable, cool (Sl).

detrimental damaging, destructive, deleterious, harmful, injurious, hurtful, distressing, troublous, baleful, baneful, pernicious, noxious, toxic, corruptive, corrosive, malignant, catastrophic, dire, mortal, deadly.

devastating overwhelming, overpowering, deadly, caustic, withering, savage.

developed matured, ripened, mellow, seasoned, weathered, hardened, veteran, adult, full-grown, fledged, blooming, fruiting, well-done, elaborate, wrought, laboured, completed, perfected.

developing maturing, cooking, stewing, brewing, marinating, brooding, hatching, incubating, in progress, afoot, forthcoming, impending, under consideration, mooted, planned, probationary.

developmental ontogenic, germinal, embryonic, ectodermal, endodermal, mesodermal, fetal, amniotic, chorionic, allantoic, juvenile, larval, pupal, neotenous, paedogenetic.

deviant misdirected, nonconformist, aberrant, eccentric, off-centre, exorbitant. *See also* indirect, undirected, oblique, diverging, wandering, diffractive.

devilish devil-like, evil, satanic, diabolic, diabolical, demonic, demoniac, demon-like, Mephistophelean, fiendish, fiendlike, fallen, damned, hell-born, hellish, infernal, sulphurous, chthonian, chthonic, subterranean, pandemonic, Plutonian, Avernal, Tartarean, abysmal, purgatorial.

devious circumlocutory, periphrastic, circuitous, roundabout, indirect, sidelong, furtive, backhand, evasive, equivocal, hedging, deceptive, distorted, euphemistic, dissembling, fraudulent, spurious, shady (Inf), fishy (Inf).

devoted dedicated, supportive, loyal, true, tried-and-true, tested, faithful, steadfast, constant, committed, firm, fast, staunch, trustful.

diagnostic symptomatological, symptomatic, prognostic, indicative.

diagonal crosswise, oblique, slanting, angled.

diagrammatic graphic, tabular, schematic, analytic.

different dissimilar, deviating, divergent, variant, odd, alien, unsuitable, discordant, discrepant, incompatible, incongruous, unequal, ambiguous, ambivalent, inconsistent, misfit, mismatched, misaligned, mistimed.

difficult hard, arduous, strenuous, laborious, toilsome, demanding, exacting, challenging, tough, heavy,

onerous, burdensome, effortful, physically demanding, wearisome, backbreaking, gruelling, punishing, exhausting, fatiguing, uphill, oppressive, formidable, superhuman, herculean, steep (Inf), stiff (Inf); awkward, critical, crucial, pivotal, decisive, troublesome, exigent; confusing, puzzling, baffling, perplexing, complex, complicated, recondite, abstruse, elusive, amorphous, obscure, enigmatic, inscrutable, mysterious, nebulous, vague, unclear, ambiguous, equivocal, paradoxical. *See also* rough, problematic, inconvenient, troublesome, clumsy, troubled.

difficult to see partly visible, half-seen, inconspicuous, infinitesimal, microscopic, subliminal, distant, remote, darkened, faint, pale, indefinite, unclear, indistinct, unfocused, undefined, blurred, bleared, hazy, misty, foggy, filmy, shadowy, obscured, dim, low-definition, ill-defined, fuzzy.

diffident hesitant, shy, backward, reluctant, doubtful, modest.

diffractive refractive, refrangible, scattered, reflected, diffuse, dispersed.

diffuse profuse, prolific, copious, abundant, detailed, minute, amplified, expanded, extended, protracted, drawn out, padded, long, loose-knit, lengthy, never-ending, nonstop, epic, repetitive, reiterative, tautologous, pleonastic, superfluous, excessive, talkative, verbose, loquacious, fluent, gushing, effuse, inspired, exuberant, rich, fertile, flowing, polysyllabic, sesquipedalian, wordy, waffling, prosy, prolix, long-winded, fustian, flatulent, pretentious, empty, incoherent, ornate, rhetorical, magniloquent, bombastic, turgid, voluminous, tedious, boring. *See also* circumlocutory.

dignified distinguished, majestic, grand, stately, honourable, imposing.

digressive parenthetic, nonserial, nonlinear, nonsequential.

dilapidated in disrepair, falling apart, in ruins, in shreds, beyond repair, cracked, broken, leaking, battered, weather-beaten, decrepit, rickety, tottery, shaky, unsteady, ramshackle, derelict, tumbledown, run-down, exhausted, weakened, ruined, slummy, worn, shopsoiled, frayed, shabby, tatty, unkempt, dingy, holey, in tatters, in rags, seedy, down-at-heel, down-and-out, rusty, mouldering, moth-eaten, worm-eaten, dog-eared, kaput (Inf), wonky (Inf), flea-bitten (Inf).

diligent studious, painstaking, meticulous, fastidious, sedulous, assiduous, undistracted, singleminded, rapt, engrossed, obsessed, fixated, pedantic, preoccupied, purist, hung-up (Inf).

dilute watered down, liquefied, evaporated, boiled away, vaporized, dissipated.

diluted saturated, watered-down, wishy-washy (Inf).

dim half-lit, semidark, twilit, crepuscular, waning, ill-lit, dark, darkish, sombre, livid, leaden, dusky, grey, dull, overcast, cloudy, louring, stormy, sunless, shady, shadowy, tenebrous. *See also* murky, dimmed, stupid.

dimmed clouded, dull, faded, drab, dingy, gloomy, lack-lustre, matt, unpolished, tarnished, rusty, dusty, dirty.

dingy dull, dark, murky, gloomy, drab, shabby.

diplomatic discreet, tactful, prudent, politic, sensitive, subtle.

dire dreadful, frightful, awful, horrible, shocking, disastrous; gloomy, ominous, portentous, dismal.

direct unsophisticated, simplistic, homespun, unqualified, unmitigated, wholehearted, single-minded, downright, sincere, unpretentious, honest, honourable, unaffected, undisguised, naked, bare.

directional advancing, progressive, backward, regressive, retrogressive, backtracking, refluent, downward, sinking, plunging, descending, subsiding, upward, ascending, rising, soaring, mounting, climbing, rapid, speedy, slow, toddling, pottering, regular, recurring, rhythmic, periodic, uniform, continuous, circuitous, rotary, centripetal, centrifugal, axial, radial, oscillating, fluctuating, vibrating, agitating, irregular, sideward, oblique, angular, random, Brownian, gyratory, kinetic, dynamic.

dirty unclean, soiled, defiled, mucky, grubby, grimy, filthy, dusty, sooty, smoky, polluted, unwashed, unswept, littered, foul, squalid, sleazy, slummy, untidy, unkempt, bedraggled, frowzy, slatternly, slovenly, sluttish, black, dingy, unpolished, unburnished, tarnished, stained, spotted, smudged, besmirched, messy, greasy, oily, muddy, slimy, clotted, caked, matted, encrusted, murky, furred up, clogged, scummy, musty, mouldy, fusty, cobwebby. *See also* unclean, obscene.

disabled handicapped, incapacitated, crippled, lame, mutilated, weak.

disagreeable unharmonious, dissenting, hostile, adverse, opposite, antipathetic, inimical.

disagreeing differing, argumentative, polemic(al), contentious, dissenting, dissident, discordant, disharmonious, noncooperative, hating, unpleasant, controversial, confrontational, disputing, quarrelsome, criticizing, bickering, wrangling, divisive, polarizing, schismatic, incompatible, irreconcilable, irascible, provocative, cantankerous, prickly, hostile, inimical, aggressive, antagonistic, belligerent, fighting, squabbling, brawling, warring, at cross-purposes; conflicting, at variance, contrary, unresolved. *See also* different.

disappeared vanished, absent, gone, missing, lost, dead, extinct, obsolete, past, nonexistent, invisible, eclipsed, occulted, hidden, concealed, buried, disguised, camouflaged, dispersed, dissipated, worn away, eroded.

disappearing vanishing, evanescent, fugitive, going, departing, escaping, transient, fleeting, passing, fading, waning, dying, dissolving, evaporating, hiding, obsolescent. *See also* disappeared.

disappointed disenchanted, disillusioned, expecting more, let down, frustrated, thwarted, balked, bilked, foiled, baffled, confounded, confused, hindered, hampered, denied, refused, stonewalled, rejected, jilted, defeated, disconcerted, crestfallen, dejected, depressed, disheartened, discouraged, mortified, chagrined, humiliated, humbled, disgruntled, soured, dissatisfied, discontented, sad, upset, hopeless, heartbroken, crushed, devastated. *See also* deceived, disappointing, deceptive.

disappointing frustrating, unfulfilling, unsatisfying, insufficient, inadequate, falling short, second-best, second-rate, poor, inferior, abortive, unsuccessful.

disapproved rejected, refused, opposed, excluded, ostracized, blacklisted, banned, barred, boycotted, vetoed.

disapproving disapprobatory, dissatisfied, discontented, unhappy,

disarranged

disappointed, displeased, disgruntled, indignant, disrespectful. *See also* disagreeing, critical, fault-finding, blaming, censuring, disapproved, unsatisfactory, criticized, censured, blameworthy.

disarranged deranged, disordered, disorganized, muddled, confused, roiled.

disastrous catastrophic, devastating, dire, dreadful, tragic, ruinous.

disbanded dissolved, dismissed, demobilized, deactivated.

disbelieved discredited, exploded, unbelievable, incredible, impossible, improbable, implausible, untenable, far-fetched, unreliable, suspect, suspicious, so-called, self-styled, questionable, disputable.

disbelieving incredulous, sceptical, scornful, doubtful, dubious, uncertain, hesitant, distrustful, mistrustful, suspicious, dissenting, heretical, atheistic, agnostic, pagan, heathen, faithless, unfaithful. *See also* disbelieved.

disciplined controlled, restrained, law-abiding, peaceable, docile, obedient, well-behaved, decorous, mannerly.

disclosed revealed, shown, visible, clear, obvious, transparent, open, exposed, leaked, confessed, admitted, avowed, acknowledged, uncovered, unearthed, unmasked. *See also* disclosing, revelatory.

disclosing revealing, divulging, maieutic, open, candid, frank, downright, unreserved, outspoken, forthcoming, informative, communicative, talkative, garrulous, loquacious, indiscreet, imprudent, chatty, leaky.

discomposed discomfited, disconcerted, unsettled, disturbed, perturbed, upset, deranged, convulsed.

disconcerting disturbing, upsetting, bewildering, alarming, baffling, perplexing.

disconnected disjointed, disarticulated, dislocated, unhinged, disengaged, dismembered, detached, separated.

disconsolate desolate, unhappy, miserable, forlorn, wretched, melancholy.

discontinued nonrecurrent, unrepeated, ended, ceased, stopped, halted, terminated, finished.

discontinuous unsuccessive, disconnected, disjointed, disunited, discrete, fragmented, broken, unjoined, unconnected, irregular, intermittent, fitful, spasmodic, sporadic, erratic, random, desultory, episodic, periodic, alternate, stop-go, on-off, nonuniform, uneven, rough, choppy, scrappy, snatchy, jerky, bumpy, jolty, scrappy, bitty, patchy, spotty, dotted. *See also* discontinued, interrupted, digressive.

discordant disagreeing, contentious, dissentient, dissident, different, conflicting, clashing, adversarial, confronting, head-on, challenging, defiant, rival, competitive, competing, contending, at odds, at issue, anti (*Inf*).

discounted marked down, cut-price, cut-rate, bargain, cheap, rebated, shop soiled.

discouraged deterred, put off, disheartened, dissuaded, inhibited, hindered.

discouraging depressing, unfavourable, daunting, disappointing.

discourteous impolite, uncivil, disagreeable, inurbane, ungracious, ungallant, uncourtly, ungentlemanly, unladylike, unpleasant, surly, sullen, crusty, nasty, unkind, thoughtless, offhanded, inconsiderate, unsolicitous, tactless, insensitive, inattentive, cavalier, abusive, vituperative, unsmiling, grim, unsociable, unfriendly, uncomplimentary, unflattering, disrespectful, familiar, gruff, blunt, harsh, severe, rough, rugged, brutal, brusque, curt, short, abrupt, impatient, discontented, peevish, testy, acerbic, sharp, tart, snappy, biting, growling, bearish, acrimonious, aggressive, beastly (Inf). *See also* bad-mannered.

discoverable findable, recognizable, identifiable, perceptible, detectable, heuristic.

discovered found, located, seen, spotted, unearthed, uncovered, exposed, unmasked, revealed.

discovering finding, warm, revelatory, inventive, pioneering, exploratory, experimental. *See also* discovered, discoverable.

discreet diplomatic, tactful, considerate, careful, thoughtful, prudent.

discriminating judicious, selective, tasteful, sensitive, differential, separating, discerning, divisional, critical, diagnostic, interpretational, appreciative, epicurean, perceptive, insightful, refined, delicate, fastidious, meticulous, perfectionist, pedantic, quibbling, hair-splitting (Inf), choosy (Inf), picky (Inf). *See also* discriminatory, judged.

discriminatory prejudicial, one-sided, partisan, jaundiced, inequitable, unfair, partial, preferential, nepotistic, prejudiced, biased, bigoted, narrow-minded, blinkered, small-minded, petty, intolerant, dogmatic, insular, parochial, elitist, classist, ageist, sexist, misogynous, misandrous, homophobic, racist, anti-semitic, xenophobic, jingoistic, ethnocentric, fascist, Nazi, chauvinist(ic), fundamentalist, fanatical.

discussing conferring, in conference, in committee, consultatory, advisory.

disdainful contemptuous, scornful, proud, haughty, sneering, arrogant.

diseased infected, contaminated, tainted, stricken, distempered, pathological, pathogenic, morbid, morbific, peccant, insalubrious, unhygienic, iatrogenic, psychosomatic, gangrenous, infectious, contagious, poisonous, toxic, purulent, degenerative, consumptive, phthtic, tuberculous, diabetic, hydrocephalic, anaemic, leukaemic, haemophilic, arthritic, rheumaticky, rickety, palsied, paralytic, spastic, epileptic, leprous, carninomatous, cancerous, oncogenic, carcinogenic, syphilitic, venereal, oedematous, gouty, bronchial, croupy, sniffly, snuffly, asthmatic, allergic, pyretic, febrile, feverish, delirious, shivering, aguish, sore, tender, painful, ulcerous, inflamed, rashy, spotty, erysipelatous, spavined, mangy.

disentitled disfranchised, dispossessed, deprived, disqualified, disestablished, unfrocked, deposed, dethroned, denaturalized, deported, expelled, criminalized, banned, forbidden, prohibited, vetoed, censored.

disgraceful shocking, shameful, disreputable, scandalous, degrading, outrageous.

disgruntled irritated, peevish, sulky, grumpy, annoyed, displeased.

disguised concealed, hidden, camouflaged, incognito, masquerading, masked, veiled, cloaked, varnished, painted, whitewashed, glossed; false, seeming, sham, fake, imitation, simulated, dissembled, glossed, varnished, gilded, embellished, embroidered, overdone, dressed-up, touched-up, falsely coloured.

disgusted outraged, scandalized, repelled, appalled, nauseated, revolted.

disgusting foul, hateful, loathsome, nauseating, sickening, repugnant, obnoxious.

dishonest false, duplicitous, deceitful, treacherous, mendacious, insincere, disingenuous, Machiavellian, cunning, sly, wily, cheating, defrauding, swindling, impersonating, pretending, shamming, humbug, fraudulent, fake.

dishonourable dishonest, disreputable, shameful, worthless, good-for-nothing, evil, wicked, bad, villainous, nefarious, corrupt, unprincipled, unethical, bribable, depraved, venal, disrespectful, disgraceful, ignoble, contemptible, debased, base, indecent, immoral, rotten, unscrupulous, ungentlemanly, unsportsmanlike, devious, opportunistic, scheming, unfair, biased, prejudiced, unjust, insincere, hypocritical, disingenuous, uncandid, untruthful, lying, tricky, foxy, vulpine, slippery, wrangling (Inf), shady (Inf), crooked (Inf), low-down (Inf). *See also* faithless, criminal.

disillusioned disappointed, brought down to earth, disabused.

disintegrated smashed, shattered, destroyed, demolished, broken down, dissolved, melted, liquefied, separated, decomposed, deconstructed, rotted, putrid, corrupted, decayed, rusty, corroded, dilapidated, ruined. *See also* disintegrating.

disintegrating crumbling, falling apart, tumbledown.

disinterested indifferent, detached, impersonal, impartial, unbiased, unprejudiced, objective, equitable, non-partisan, fair, fair-minded, open, just, neutral, non-aligned, uninvolved, self-controlled, dispassionate, stoical, cool (Sl). *See also* unselfish.

disliked unlikeable, unpopular, unappreciated, disapproved, disfavoured, unwanted, avoided, undesired, unprepossessing, unloved, rejected, jilted, spurned, thrown over, unchosen, unwelcome, unrelished, distasteful, disagreeable, insufferable, intolerable, despised, loathsome, fearsome, abhorrent, disgusting, repulsive, repugnant, rebarbative, abominable, revolting, unsavoury, nauseating, yucky (Sl).

disliking displeased, discontented, dissatisfied, disenchanted, disillusioned, loveless, undesirous, disinclined, loath, unwilling, reluctant, averse, disaffected, squeamish, queasy, dissenting, averse, resentful, fearful, hostile, antipathetic, antagonistic, bitter, inimical, repelled, disapproving, disgusted, despising, abhorring, loathing, detesting, hating, sickened, sated, nauseous, allergic (Inf). *See also* disliked.

dislodged displaced, uprooted, deracinated, extricated, disengaged, liberated, eliminated, extracted.

disloyal false, unfaithful, treacherous, subversive, disaffected, recreant.

dismal bleak, gloomy, dreary, melancholy, depressing, dark, drab.

dismissed discharged, fired, sacked, laid off.

disobedient noncompliant, non-cooperative, nonobservant, undutiful, unwilling, opposing, recalcitrant, obstinate, stubborn, intractable, obstructive, insubordinate, obstreperous, undisciplined, transgressing, restless, wild, unmanageable, misbehaving, mischief-making, naughty, delinquent, disorderly, riotous, tumultuous, unruly, dissenting, defiant, recusant, disloyal, perfidious, tergiversatory, criminal, immoral, wicked, sinning, bloody-minded (Inf). *See also* subversive.

disordered in disarray, disarranged, deranged, disrupted, disorganized, muddled, jumbled, shuffled, displaced, misplaced, disjointed, dislocated. *See also* unordered, irregular, untidy, confused, discomposed, muddled, disorderly.

disorderly chaotic, lawless, unruly, undisciplined, uncontrolled, unmanageable, boisterous, disruptive, stroppy (Inf), laddish (Inf), rowdy, hell-raising, harum-scarum, wild, turbulent, rampageous, riotous, rebellious, insubordinate, contumacious, mutinous, obstreperous, disobedient, anarchic, nihilistic.

disparaging deprecatory, depreciatory, decrying, detractory, derogatory, pejorative, denigratory, belittling, slighting, minimizing, critical. *See also* defamatory, scornful.

disparate dissimilar, different,

contrasting, unrelated, unlikely, unusual, strange, foreign, alien, exotic, diverse, variant, discrepant, nonuniform, inconsonant, incongruent, immiscible, incommensurate, heterogeneous, disproportionate, asymmetric(al), irregular, odd, inconsistent, ambiguous, ambivalent, equivocal, unequal. *See also* contradictory, nonconforming, disagreeing, unfit.

dispassionate objective, detached, neutral, impartial, fair, just; cool, calm, collected, unruffled, serene, unmoved, poised.

dispersed scattered, diffuse, widespread, sparse, infrequent, sporadic, dotted about. *See also* separated, disbanded, distributed, divergent, sprawled, decentralized, dilute, dispersive; displaced, dislodged, dislocated, disorientated, derailed.

dispersive scattering, spreading, diffractive, diffusive, distributive, disseminative, dissipative.

dispirited down, downcast, crestfallen, gloomy, morose, disheartened.

displaced dislocated, dislodged, disturbed, disarranged, deranged, derailed, shifted, shunted, moved, relocated, transferred, switched, swerved, veered, deflected. *See also* removed, replaced, relegated, disconnected, misplaced.

displayed exhibited, presented, shown, on view, made public, manifested, apodictic, featured, visible,

apparent, produced, cited, quoted, confronted, worn, sported, paraded, flaunted, brandished, flourished, advertised, publicized, promoted, published. *See also* manifest, open.

disposed (**of**) dispensed with, relinquished, released, discarded, freed, liberated, abandoned, divorced, disowned, disinherited, forgone, forsworn. *See also* dismissed, for sale, unclaimed.

disqualified barred, precluded, excluded, eliminated, ruled out, prohibited.

disregardful neglectful, dishonourable, disreputable, contemptible, despicable, worthless, shameful, base, low.

disreputable ignominious, degrading, notorious, infamous, nefarious, shady, questionable, scandalous, dishonourable, shameless, immoral, underhand, fraudulent, devious, suspicious, iffy (Sl), dodgy (Inf).

disrespectful irreverent, blasphemous, scurrilous, rude, discourteous, impolite, unmannered, uncivil, impertinent, cheeky, saucy, pert, impudent, insolent, insubordinate, brazen, bold, audacious, forward, familiar, fresh (Inf). *See also* insulting, disregardful, contemptuous, ridiculing, taunting, humiliating, unrespected, undervalued.

disrupted interrupted, interfered with, molested, sabotaged, hindered, obstructed, inconvenienced, distracted.

dissatisfied displeased, disgruntled, discontented, malcontented, sulking, brooding, disaffected, complaining, whingeing, disappointed, disillusioned, disapproving, unimpressed, critical of, perjorative, disgusted, contemptuous, scornful, derisive. *See also* unsatisfactory.

dissenting differing, at odds, opposing, conflicting, heterodox, unorthodox, heretical, sceptical, unconvinced, dissatisfied, protesting, unwilling, resistant, intolerant, dissident, seditious, divisive, separatist, schismatic, party-minded, partisan, clannish, sectarian, nonconformist, protestant, schismatical, secessionist, breakaway, rebel, recusant, rebellious, quarrelling, arguing, cantankerous, irascible, bellicose, warlike, contentious, disputatious.

dissimilar different, disparate, divergent, diverse, various, multiform, unequal, asymmetrical, nonuniform, unresembling, unlike, incongruous, incompatible, contrasting, poles apart, unrealistic, scarcely like, discrepant, distinctive, peculiar, original, singular, unrelated, new, unique, peerless, matchless, nonpareil, untypical, unprecedented, incomparable, incommensurate, something else.

dissipated dissolute, riotous, fast-living, high-living, free-living, licentious, debauched, profligate.

dissolute debauched, abandoned, depraved, corrupt, licentious, degenerate.

dissonant discordant, inharmonious, jangling, jarring, clashing, grating, scraping, rasping, harsh, raucous, cacophonous, strident, shrill. *See also* disagreeing, unmelodious.

dissuaded discouraged, disenchanted, disillusioned, disheartened, dampened, reluctant, unwilling.

dissuasive discouraging, contrary, contradictory, cautionary, warning, monitory, expostulatory, chilling, damping, disheartening, deterrent. *See also* dissuaded.

distant far, far off, far away, far-flung, remote, yonder, yon (Dial), ulterior, farther, further, outlying, offshore, inaccessible, out-of-the-way, godforsaken, exotic, antipodean, hyperborean, overseas, transcontinental, transpolar, distal, peripheral, long-distance, long-range, farthermost, furthermost, ultimate, unget-at-able (Inf); remote, innaccessible, unapproachable, unavailable. *See also* reserved.

distasteful offensive, repugnant, repulsive, obnoxious, unpalatable, unsavoury.

distinct well-defined, plain, clear, lucid, apparent, evident; separate, different, detached, individual, unlike.

distorted asymmetric, unsymmetrical, unbalanced, misshapen, irregular, lopsided, crooked, askew, disproportionate, unequal, off-target, off-centre, skewwhiff (Inf), cockeyed (Inf). *See also* deformed, exaggerated.

distracted flustered, harrassed, bewildered, puzzled, agitated, perplexed; frantic, mad, deranged, frenzied, crazy, raving.

distressed worried, anxious, disturbed, desolate, distraught, troubled.

distressing depressing, dispiriting, sorry, lamentable, heartbreaking, harrowing, painful, tragic, grievous.

distributed disseminated, diffused, broadcast, spread, deployed, strewn, sown, propagated, circulated, published, issued, dispensed.

distrustful mistrustful, suspicious, doubtful, watchful, vigilant, Argus-eyed, solicitous, anxious, apprehensive.

disturbed perturbed, agitated, convulsed, upset, distressed, unsettled, disconcerted, disquieted, discomfited, discomposed, uncomfortable, uneasy, confused, flustered, ruffled, shaken, rattled, alarmed, concerned, worried, anxious, troubled, bothered, annoyed, irritated, vexed, bugged (Sl). *See also* disarranged, dispersed, disrupted, deranged, disturbing.

disturbing upsetting, distressing, unsettling, disconcerting, alarming, worrying, bothersome, annoying, vexatious, muddling, disruptive, distracting, off-putting (Inf).

disused derelict, abandoned, discarded, cast-off, jettisoned, scrapped, laid up, mothballed, decommissioned, frozen, rusting, in limbo, neglected, done with, used up, run down, worn out, retired, supplanted, superseded, superannuated, discontinued, discredited, obsolete, junked (Inf).

divergent forking, radiating, branching, ramiform, dendriform, centrifugal; divaricate, separated, aberrant, different, contradictory, deviating. *See also* radiating, fanlike, branched.

diverging divaricating, branching, once removed.

diverse varied, nonuniform, heterogeneous, dissimilar, contrasting, deviant, diverging, different, manifold, incongruous, variegated, chequered, abnormal, freakish, unique, inconsistent, changeable, unstable, spasmodic, sporadic, erratic, haphazard, fitful, inconstant. *See also* assorted, dissenting.

dividing line radius, diameter, co-ordinate, equator, bisector, longitudinal line, latitudinal line.

divinatory prophetic, clairvoyant, clairaudient, clairsentient, premonitory, precognitive, augural, haruspical, sibylline, oracular, astrological.

divine godly, godlike, deistic, theistic, Yahwistic, Elohistic, Christlike, Christly, messianic, incarnate, theomorphic, epiphanic, numinous, holy, hallowed, sacred, sacrosanct, transcendent, transcendental, enlightened, blessed, sublime, perfect, supreme, sovereign, majestic, theocratic, providential, omnipresent, ubiquitous, all-seeing, all-knowing, prescient, omniscient, all-powerful, omnipotent, almighty, absolute, immortal, eternal, infinite, immeasurable, ineffable, mystical, oracular, supernatural, supramundane, extramundane, unearthly. *See also* heavenly, deified, devilish.

divorced dissolved, separated, legally separated, split, estranged, living apart, deserted, abandoned. *See also* widowed.

dizzy light-headed, giddy, bemused, shaky, bewildered, unsteady; scatterbrained, flighty, capricious, silly, feather-brained, fickle.

docile amenable, submissive, manageable, compliant, biddable, obedient.

dogmatic opinionated, overbearing, assertive, obdurate, insistent, intolerant.

dominant dictatorial, magisterial, authoritative, ruling, overriding, governing, ordering, imperial, sovereign, royal; wide-ranging, international, multinational, monopolistic, prevailing, ubiquitous, all-pervading.

dominating overpowering, overcoming, controlling, conquering, suppressive, oppressive, repressive, intimidating, colonial, tyrannical.

doomed ill-fated, cursed, fated, dammed, ill-omened.

dormant asleep, inert, hibernating, sleeping, resting, inactive.

double twin, duplicate, geminate, repeat, second, duplicated, geminated, copied, repeated, cloned.

double-edged double-barrelled, ambiguous, ironic, ambivalent, duplicitous, two-faced, hypocritical, double-crossing, Janus-like, two-timing (Inf).

doubtful unsure, hesitating, wavering, uncertain, tentative, undecided; questionable, ambiguous, unclear, vague, dubious, obscure.

dowdy old-fashioned, shabby, drab, frumpy, frowzy.

downcast depressed, dejected, disheartened, discouraged, dismayed, sad.

downplayed toned-down, moderated, de-emphasized, watered-down, reduced, diminished, curtailed, restrained, constrained, disregarded, shrugged-off.

downward descending, declining, slipping.

dramatic dramaturgic, melodramatic, spectacular, theatrical, mimetic, musical, operatic, choral, balletic, choreographic, Terpsichorean, histrionic, Thespian, stagy, protagonistic, antagonistic; histrionic, theatrical, sensational, daring, stagey, cosmetic. *See also* tragic.

drastic extreme, powerful, violent, forceful, radical, strong.

dreadful horrible, frightful, terrible, dire, appalling, awful, ghastly,

dreary

dreary dully, boring, grim, bleak, melancholy, sombre.

dressed clothed, clad, attired, garbed, apparelled, bedecked, arrayed, vested, invested, habited, habilimented, wrapped, draped, robed, frocked, mantled, cloaked, gowned, hatted, capped, bonneted, hooded, bewigged, gloved, shod, shoed, booted, decked out, turned out, rigged, kitted out, costumed, uniformed, liveried. See also dressed up, styled.

dressed up smart, clothes-conscious, fashionable, stylish, modish, chic, dapper, spruced up, spruce, well-dressed, groomed, tricked out, natty (Inf).

dried-out drained, evaporated, squeezed dry, mangled.

dried-up dried, dehydrated, desiccated, exsiccated, withered, shrivelled, sere (Arch), faded, wizened, parchment-like, mummified, corky, bone-dry.

drinkable potable, milky, lactic, white, diluted, watery, undiluted, black, nonalcoholic, soft, fizzy, alcoholic, fermented, distilled, spiritous, hard, vinous, sparkling, still, sweet, dry, light, full-bodied, vintage.

drinking nursed, suckled, breast-fed, imbibing, swilling, tippling, bibulous, vinous, drunken, dipsomaniacal, boozing (Inf). See also drinkable.

droll funny, comical, amusing, entertaining, quaint, whimsical.

drooping sagging, depressed, downcast, demoted.

drugged doped, incapacitated, insensible, high (Sl), stoned (Sl), zonkers (Sl), zonko (Sl), floating (Sl). See also addicted, addictive.

drumming rolling, thrumming, reverberant, resonant, throbbing, pounding, beating, loud, insistent, persistent, incessant, repeated. See also humming, rattling, pealing.

drunk inebriated, intoxicated, ebriate, tight (Sl), merry (Inf), happy (Inf), high (Inf), pissed (Sl), well-oiled (Sl), well-lubricated (Sl), pickled (Sl), pixilated (Sl), rat-arsed (Sl). See also drunken, intoxicating.

drunken inebriate, intemperate, alcoholic, dipsomaniac(al), sottish, sodden, gin-sodden, beery, vinous, bibulous, tippling, swilling, swigging, guzzling, hard-drinking, carousing, wassailing, red-nosed, bloodshot, gouty, liverish, boozy (Sl), pub-crawling (Inf).

dry arid, waterless, moistureless, unirrigated, unmoistened, undamped, anhydrous, droughty. See also thirsty, dried-up, dried-out, rainless, desert, adapted to drought, baked, drying, waterproof.

drying desiccative, dehydrating, exsiccative, siccative.

due deserved, merited, earned.

dull obtuse, insensitive, unperceptive, hebetudinous, dense, slow, numb, unfeeling.

duplicate triplicate, copied, faxed, photographic, reprinted, offprinted, reproduced, holographic, replicated, moulded, stamped.

duplicitous deceiving, dissembling, two-faced, Janus-faced, double-dealing, false, equivocal, ambidextrous backhanded, tongue-in-cheek, ambidextrous, false.

durable long-lasting, endurable, hard-wearing, abiding, persistent, stable.

dutiful duteous, conscientious, scrupulous, punctilious, ethical, moral, principled, virtuous, honourable, decent, upright. *See also* loyal, liable, duty-bound, obligatory, on duty.

duty-bound bound, obliged, obligated, beholden, tied, committed, engaged, pledged, sworn, saddled.

dwarf small, baby, pocket, miniature, tiny.

dying expiring, deathly, deathlike, cadaverous, skeletal, terminally ill, hopeless, fey (Scot), moribund, half-dead, slipping away, sinking fast, fading, going. *See also* dead, deadly, deathly, post-mortem.

dynamic forceful, energetic, powerful, vigorous, vital, active.

E

eager enthusiastic, keen, prompt, alacritous, zealous, overenthusiastic, fanatical.

early first, earliest, prompt, punctual, immediate, expeditious, ready, advanced, alacritous, quick, hurried,

---

eccentric

hasty, summary. *See also* imminent, primeval, precursory, premature.

earnest sincere, genuine, resolute, determined, purposeful, intent, dedicated, committed, eager, enthusiastic.

earthy rocky, stony, gravelly, pebbly, sandy, loamy, silty.

easily seen through open, guileless, ingenuous, direct, forthright, straightforward, frank, candid, open-hearted, undisguised, evident, obvious, patent, manifest, plain, unambiguous, lucid.

easy facile, undemanding, effortless, painless, unburdensome, smooth, uncomplicated, simple, uninvolved, straightforward, plain, clear, intelligible, elementary, glib, superficial, dead simple, cushy (Inf), easy-peasy (Sl). *See also* feasible, made easy, wieldy, easygoing, relaxed.

easygoing undemanding, lenient, tolerant, permissive, indulgent, tractable, docile, relaxed, calm, serene, acquiescent, compliant, submissive, biddable.

eating feeding, dining, grazing, carnivorous, creophagous, cannibalistic, omophagic, insectivorous, herbivorous, graminivorous, frugivorous, vegetarian, vegan, omnivorous, greedy, gluttonous, hungry, ravenous, voracious, well-fed, full. *See also* edible.

eccentric offbeat, idiosyncratic, quirky, individual, singular, original, rare, unusual, exotic, unique,

exceptional, far-out, way-out, odd, queer, curious, peculiar, strange, bizarre, outlandish, weird, freakish, grotesque, monstrous, oddball (Inf), freaky (Inf), kooky (Inf), funny (Inf), rum (Sl), dolally (Inf).

echinodermal echinodermatous, crinoidal, asteroid, ophiuroid, echinoid, holothurian.

economic fiscal, monetary, pecuniary, financial, budgetary, inflationary, deflationary, mercantile, commercial, marketable, profitable, taxable, nationalized, privatized.

ecstatic blissful, overjoyed, euphoric, elated, delirious, rapturous.

edging bordered, marginal, extreme, seaside, waterfront, coastal, littoral, beach, riverside, waterside, roadside, wayside, sideline, peripheral. *See also* skirting, advantaged.

edible consumable, esculent, comestible, digestible, nutritious, alimental, alimentary, palatable, palate-tickling, mouth-watering, tasty, calorific, fattening, succulent, delicious, scrumptious, moreish (Inf).

educatable teachable, trainable, bright, autodidactic, self-taught, apt, willing, motivated, ready, receptive, curious, inquisitive, susceptible, impressionable, docile.

educated scholarly, intellectual, erudite, learned, cultured, literary.

educational instructive, informative, illuminating, enlightening, edifying, remedial, progressive, communicative, helpful, authoritative, academic, scholastic, pedagogical, preachy, schoolmarmish. *See also* educatable, curricular.

eerie unearthly, ghostly, weird, uncanny, frightening, spooky (Inf).

effective forceful, powerful, productive, useful, functional, operational, procedural, professional, managerial, executive.

efficient capable, skilled, proficient, able, adept, skilful.

effusive gushing, expansive, candid, frank, communicative, sociable, chatty, conversational, gossipy, tattling, prattling, prating, blabbing, yakking (Inf), big-mouthed (Inf), mouthy (Inf), lippy (Inf), flip (Sl).

egoistic conceited, vain, narcissistic, self-loving, self-absorbed, self-centred, egocentric.

eighth eightfold, octuple, octonary, octennial, octadic, octagonal, octangular, octahedral, octatonic.

elastic rubbery, stretchable, supple, plastic, extensible, distensible, flexible, pliant, tensile, ductile, tonic, springy, well-sprung, coiling, resilient, giving, yielding, snapping, recoiling, rebounding, bouncy. *See also* adaptive.

elated euphoric, exhilerated, ecstatic, exultant, jubilant, animated.

elected selected, chosen, delegated, appointed, authorized, granted.

elective electoral, voting, enfranchised, vote-catching, electioneering, canvassing, psephological.

electric dynamic, exciting, charged, thrilling, rousing, stirring.

electronic electric, electrical, photoelectric, thermoelectric, piezoelectric, hydroelectric, electrodynamic, electrolytic, electromagnetic, electromechanical, electromotive, electrostatic, negative, positive, neutral, live, resistive, capacitive, inductive, rechargeable.

elegant stylish, smart, graceful, delicate, harmonious, euphonious, tasteful, fine, beautiful, majestic, stately, exquisite, polite, courtly, refined, sophisticated, suave, cultivated, perspicacious, plain, simple, restrained, dignified, distinguished, distinctive, natural, idiomatic, correct, expressive, classic, well-proportioned, symmetrical, gracile, rhythmic, fluid, smooth, flawless, mellifluous, fluent, apt, fitting, felicitous, polished, manicured, soigné, well-groomed, finished, well-turned, artistic, elaborate, ornamented, classical, Attic, Augustan, Ciceronian.

elemental metallic, metalloid, inert, transuranic, superheavy.

elementary basic, rudimentary, fundamental; clear, simple, straightforward, easy.

eleventh undecennial, hendecagonal, twelfth, duodenary, duodecimal, fifteenth, quindecagonal, quindecennial, sixteenth, hexadecimal, umpteenth.

eligible fit, appropriate, qualified, suitable, acceptable.

elongated oblong, rectangular, elliptical.

eloquent silver-tongued, smooth-talking, rhetorical, grandiloquent, magniloquent, tub-thumping, ranting, declamatory, bombastic.

elusive intangible, transient, fleeting; shifty, slippery, evasive, deceptive.

emaciated malnourished, undernourished, underfed, starved, anorexic, wizened, shrivelled, withered, wasted, peaked, tabescent, marasmic, gaunt, haggard, hollow-cheeked, sunken-eyed, drawn, pinched, cadaverous, corpselike, skeletal, frail, wraithlike.

embarrassing humiliating, distressing, shameful, touchy, awkward, mortifying.

embryonic budding, nascent, germinal, inchoate, developing, fetal, pregnant, gestatory, parturient, dawning, emergent, new, fresh, raw, newborn, baby, infant, unfledged, young.

eminent prominent, distinctive, important, salient, reputable, esteemed, glorious, impressive, exalted, primary.

emotional passionate, demonstrative, fervent, heated, ardent; warm, tender, sensitive, sentimental, feeling; touching, poignant, moving, emotive.

emotive affecting, touching, moving, heartfelt, overwhelming.

emphasized stressed, accentuated, highlighted, enhanced, under-

emphatic

lined, in italics, pointed out, pointed up, marked, pronounced, *accusé* (Fr).

emphatic vehement, earnest, insistent, urgent, firm, uncompromising, dogmatic, iterative, reiterative, repetitive, enthusiastic, fervent, passionate, impassioned, ardent, fiery, spirited, inspired, vigorous, zestful, bold, vivacious, positive, affirmative, categorical, unequivocal, definite, sure, certain, incisive, penetrating, keen, trenchant, pointed, sententious, pithy, meaty, thought-provoking, pungent, sharp, mordant, piquant, poignant, vivid, graphic, strong, eloquent, compelling, convincing, effective, cogent, forceful, powerful, strenuous, energetic, brisk, peppy (Inf), punchy (Inf), zingy (Sl). *See also* emphasized, serious.

employed busy, working, active, occupied.

empty hollow, vacant, void, bare, blank, uninhabited; useless, aimless, futile, worthless, vain, inane, silly; absent, expressionless, vacant, vacuous.

enamoured attracted, charmed, fervent, doting, devoted, gallant, enslaved, ensnared, enraptured, infatuated, enchanted, captivated, fascinated, bewitched, besotted, mad, insane, crazed, lovesick, lovelorn, languishing, smitten.

enchanting captivating, fascinating, bewitching, alluring, delightful, beguiling.

enclosed fenced-in, walled-in, shut-in, hemmed-in, built-in, penned, pent-up, indoor, cloistered, monastic, conventual, intramural, closed in, shut up, jailed, imprisoned, confined, claustrophobic.

encouraging heartening, assuring, reassuring.

endangered in peril, at risk, in jeopardy, slipping, drifting, surrounded, trapped, at bay, cornered, under siege, under sentence, condemned.

endearing affectionate, demonstrative, sentimental, fond, loving, amorous, courting, wooing, pursuing, dating, familiar, flirtatious, coy, coquettish, toying, clinging, caressing, fondling, philandering, attached, engaged, sloppy (Inf), lovey-dovey (Inf).

ended finished, complete, finalized, terminated, concluded, decided, settled, done, through, over.

ending last, final, ultimate, terminal, concluding, conclusive, completing, closing, finishing, definitive, culminating, consummative, crowning, capping, apocalyptic, catastrophic, eschatological. *See also* ended, cancelled, annihilated, limiting, hindmost.

endurable tolerable, bearable, sustainable.

engaged employed, functional, paid, mercenary.

enjoyable agreeable, pleasant, delightful, entertaining, satisfying.

enlargeable extendable, extensile,

stretchable, elastic, spreadable, dispersive, expandable, expansile, expansionary, dilatable, distensible, inflatable, augmentative, multipliable, magnifiable, amplifiable.

enlarged magnified, amplified, dilated, maximized, inflated, expanded, aggrandized, heightened, blown-up, puffed-up.

enlightened elucidated, clarified, (crystal) clear, lucid, illuminated, bright, brilliant, intelligent, sparky (Inf).

enlisted conscripted, drafted, commissioned, noncommissioned, regular, irregular, reserve, combatant, noncombatant.

enormous huge, immense, gigantic, colossal, vast, tremendous.

entering ingressive, inward, incoming, ingoing, inbound, immigrant, imported, allowed in, homing. *See also* invasive.

enterprising resourceful, innovative, pioneering, adventurous, speculative, daring, courageous, go-ahead, progressive, opportunist, ambitious, responsible, managerial.

enthusiastic keen, ardent, avid, excited, fervent, passionate.

entitled warranted, justified, qualified, worthy, just, rightful, legitimate, lawful, legal, licit, inviolable, inalienable, admitted, permitted, allowed, sanctioned. *See also* meritorious, due, entitled to, owed, fit.

entitled to due.

entomological apiarian, sericultural, arachnological, acarological.

envious jealous, covetous, green-eyed, jaundiced, desirous, longing, resentful, grudging, spiteful, malicious.

environmental territorial; local; conservationist, green, environment-friendly, green, environment-friendly, ozone-friendly.

equal same, similar, parallel, convertible, identical, equivalent, corresponding, egalitarian, democratic, equitable, just, fair, impartial, sharing, homologous, congruent, coextensive, equilateral, equidistant, coordinate, coincident, equable, stable, static, homeostatic, self-regulating, steady, fixed, rounded, squared, flush, even-sided, regular, well-ordered, commensurate, tantamount, equipollent, correspondent, proportionate, uniform, Dutch (Inf); coequal, symmetrical, balanced, equiponderant, equidistant, level, impartial, par, tied, drawn, love-all, stalemated, deadlocked, neck-and-neck, half-and-half, fifty-fifty (Inf), level-pegging (Inf), quits (Inf).

equine equestrian, horse-riding, horseracing, hunting, show-jumping, mounted, thoroughbred, purebred.

equivalent corresponding, concordant, accordant, harmonious, agreeing, congruent, equipollent, interchangeable, reciprocal, representative, parallel, similar, homoiousian, coincidental, synchronous, synonymous, homogeneous, homographic, homonymic, homophonic,

equivocal analogous, metaphoric(al), reflective, shadowing.

equivocal ambiguous, ambivalent, epicene, double-tongued, two-edged, prevaricating, vague, evasive, misleading, roundabout, circumlocutory, oracular, amphibolous, homonymous, anagrammatic. *See also* equivocating.

equivocating tergiversating, shuffling, slippery, perfidious, double-dealing, hypocritical, two-faced, false, unfaithful, disloyal, traitorous, treacherous, apostate, recanting, renegade, recidivist, back-pedalling, vacillating, irresolute, fickle, whimsical, capricious, timeserving, flattering.

errant erring, fallible, culpable, guilty, sinful, aberrant, deviant, perverse, perverted, heretical, unorthodox.

erratic inconsistent, changeable, irregular, unstable, capricious, fitful.

erroneous wrong, untrue, incorrect, false, fallacious, illogical, faulty, flawed, falsified, inaccurate, inexact, loose, inconsistent, self-contradictory, distorted. *See also* errant, mistaken.

eructative flatulent, belching.

erudite learned, scholarly, cultivated, literate, cultured, refined.

escaping evasive, elusive, fugitive, runaway, truant, escaped, loose, free, scot-free, reprieved, acquitted, immune, exempt, relieved, emancipated, liberated, untied, unbound, unchained.

essential crucial, vital, necessary, paramount, indispensable, requisite, obligatory, mandatory, compulsory, imperative, inalienable, uninfringeable, unquestionable. *See also* intrinsic, integral, quintessential, characteristic.

established official, de rigueur, done, practised, approved, accepted, received, admitted, acknowledged, recognized, understood, accredited, instituted, institutionalized, hallowed in, fashionable, modish.

esteemed admired, cherished, revered, treasured, venerated, honoured.

estranged alienated, separated, irreconcilable, distant, disloyal, unfaithful, disaffected, at variance, divided, disunited.

eternal everlasting, neverending, unending, infinite, perpetual, timeless, sempiternal, permanent, enduring, durable, incorruptible, imperishable, immortal, undying, deathless, unchanging, immutable, evergreen. *See also* agelong, continuing forever.

ethical high-principled, faithful, charitable, loving, prudent, just, honest, dutiful, obedient, temperate, sober, self-controlled, chaste, pure, virginal.

evasive equivocal, ambivalent, double-talking, shifty, shuffling, dodging, fencing.

even even-sided, regular, consistent, uniform, eurhythmic, beautiful, shapely.

evening afternoon, postmeridian, vesperine, twilight, dusky, crepuscular, nocturnal, dark, nightly, night-time, benighted (Arch).

eventful notable, busy, active, momentous, significant, important.

everlasting eternal, abiding, endless, ceaseless, infinite, perpetual, eternal.

everyday quotidian, ordinary, unexceptional, common, commonplace, familiar, household, typical, stock, standard, general, usual, identikit, stereotyped, average, median, middling, normal, straight.

evident apparent, manifest, obvious, self-evident, visible, prominent, ostensible.

evidential prima facie, significant, factual, relevant, informed, witnessed, attested, circumstantial, direct, documented, recorded, reported, documentary, corroborative, probative, constructive, indicative, pointing, demonstrative, tell-tale, authentic, empirical, verified, confirmed, proved, certain. *See also* evident.

evil bad, wicked, mean, wrong, sinful, sinister, nefarious, malevolent, maleficent, malignant, malicious, vicious, diabolic(al), demonic(al), ungodly, hateful, unkind, untruthful, prejudicial, vindictive, revengeful, mischievous, obnoxious, offensive, odious, iniquitous, immoral, corrupt, defiled, blighted, depraved, foul, vile, nasty, wretched, deplorable, rotten, worthless, terrible, dreadful, horrible, awful, atrocious, despicable, detestable, contemptible, reprehensible, deadly, beastly (Inf), lousy (Sl). *See also* afflicted, detrimental, inauspicious.

exact accurate, faultless, concise, correct, definite, literal, precise; methodical, careful, orderly, meticulous, scrupulous, painstaking, punctillious.

exaggerated overemphasized, overstated, sensationalized, overdone, inflated, hyped, puffed, overrated, overpraised, oversold, flattered, embellished, embroidered, varnished, highly coloured, far-fetched, excessive, intensified, overstressed, overenthusiastic, overemphatic, hyperbolic, exacerbated, exorbitant, extreme, inordinate, aggravated, superlative, prodigious, stretched, strained, laboured, overestimated, overvalued, overcompensated, enhanced, overacted, histrionic, melodramatic, teratologic, ballyhooed (Inf). *See also* enlarged, extravagant, bombastic.

exalted eminent, prominent, promoted, upgraded, lofty, sublime, high-flown, elevated, enshrined, deified, canonized, lionized, beatified, apotheosized.

excellent expert, specialist, professional, scholarly, intellectual, masterly, skilful, adept, proficient, first-rate, supreme, consummate, competent, good at, experienced, qualified, ace (Inf), highbrow (Inf), bossy (Inf).

exceptional rare, unusual, odd, peculiar, strange, extraordinary; remarkable, special, extraordinary, outstanding, phenomenal.

excessive redundant, overflowing, brimming over, overfull, flooding, streaming, flowing, overwhelming, saturated, supersaturated, drenched, soaked, abundant, exuberant, luxuriant, riotous, profuse, plentiful, plethoric, overpopulated, bristling, teeming, swarming, crawling, outnumbered, too much, exorbitant, extreme, inordinate, disproportionate, cloying, satiating, nauseating, replete, overfed, gorged, crammed, stuffed, bloated, congested, bursting, overstretched, overburdened, overcharged, exaggerated, overdone, overacted, effusive, gushing, overpolite, overexcited. *See also* superfluous.

exchangeable interchangeable, tradeable, substitutable, commutable, permutable, transpositional, replaceable.

exchanged interchanged, substituted, transposed, traded, bartered, converted, switched, swapped, pawned, reciprocated, requited, compensated, ransomed.

excitable nervous, edgy, testy, touchy, volatile, quick-tempered.

exciting sensational, titillating, thrilling, stimulating, keen, breathtaking, impressive, stirring, emotive, poignant, striking, electric, hair-raising, itchy, prickly, tingly, tickly.

excluded absent, missing, left out, omitted, excepted, excused, exempt, barred, banned, embargoed, forbidden, taboo, rejected, deleted, dismissed, evicted, expelled, shut out, shunned, blackballed, blacklisted, disbarred, struck off, outcast, exiled, unsaid, inadmissible, peripheral, extra, foreign, not considered, disregarded, outclassed, forestalled, prevented.

excluding closed, close-knit, clannish, cliquish, narrow, restrictive, xenophobic, racist, sexist, restricted, limited, private, elite, select, choice, unique, sole, exemptive, interdictory, prohibitive, preventive, preemptive, preclusive, silent about. *See also* excluded.

exclusive unique, limited, sole, single, restricted; aristocratic, closed, private, select, snobbish, posh, elegant.

excretory egestive, eliminative, ejective, exudative, transudative, secretory. *See also* faecal, urinary, purulent, sweaty, salivating, bleeding, menstrual, cast-off.

exempt immune, nonliable, not responsible, unaccountable, unanswerable, privileged, excepted, excluded, shielded, protected, unpunishable. *See also* acquitted, independent, tax-free.

exhaustive comprehensive, thorough, extensive, far-reaching, indepth, full.

existing being, living, subsistent, coexistent, occurring, present, prevalent, current, extant, manifest, necessary, obvious, in force, in effect. *See also* intrinsic, lasting, real, self-existent, created, vegetating.

expectant anticipating, confident, assured; pregnant, gravid, with child.

expected predicted, foreseen, unsurprising, designated, chosen, promised, due, anticipated, probable, likely, apparent, predictable, foreseeable, sure, certain, long-awaited, prospective, contemplated, impending, imminent, hoped for, desired, feared, dreaded.

expecting hopeful, confident, sanguine, optimistic, desiring, wanting, sure, certain, anticipating, prepared, ready, waiting, on stand-by, forewarned, forearmed, unsurprised, vigilant, watchful, on tenterhooks, in suspense, excited, eager, prognostic, apprehensive, dreading, pessimistic, anxious. *See also* expectant, expected.

expedient advantageous, suitable, judicious, seemly, proper, practical.

expended spent, disbursed, paid, paid out, invested, contributed, blown (Sl).

expending spending, sumptuary, out-of-pocket, generous, liberal. *See also* spendthrift, expended, used.

expensive dear, costly, high-priced, extravagant, exhorbitant, lavish, valuable.

experimental empirical, pragmatic, scientific, analytic, instrumental, probational, exploratory, investigative, experimenting, inquiring, trying, testing, researching, verifying, determining, speculative, conjectural, tentative, provisional, mock, rough, trial, test, dummy, practice, model, simulated. *See also* original, tested.

expert masterly, skilled, accomplished, experienced, tried, seasoned, veteran, versed in, instructed, trained, practised, well-prepared, qualified, specialized, proficient, competent, efficient, professional, businesslike.

explanatory explicatory, illustrative, indicative, descriptive, representative, exemplificatory, illuminating, exegetic, explained, clarified, cleared up, elucidated, illustrated, described, depicted, delineated, illuminated, exemplified, expounded.

exposed divested, unveiled, denuded, bare, topless, discalced, pornographic, X-rated, stripped.

expository discursive, disquisitional, critical, interpretive, interpretative, exegetical, illuminating, editorial, glossarial, annotative.

expulsive expellent, ejective, ejaculative, eliminant, explosive, eruptive, radiating, emitting, secretory, sweaty, sudatory, salivary, sickening, emetic, purgative, laxative, cathartic, sialagogue, emmenagogic. *See also* vomiting, eructative.

extensive regional, widespread, far-reaching, wide-ranging, far-flung, global, worldwide, interstellar, intergalactic, universal, boundless, infinite, unconfined, uncircumscribed, unrestricted.

exterior external, surface, outer, front, facing, faceted, crusty, covered, enveloped, integumental, epidermal, cuticular, exoskeletal. *See also* outside, apparent, externalized, extraneous.

external extrinsic, exterior, extraterrestrial, distant, outward, outer, outside, ulterior, peripheral, superficial, foreign-made, imported, incoming, invading, infringing, interloping, intrusive, trespassing, gatecrashing, externalizing, projecting, supernatural, paranormal.

externalized exteriorized, projected, open, outward, extroverted.

extinct dead, obsolete, ended, extinguished, lost, gone.

extra new, fresh, surplus, spare, superfluous, decorative, ornamental, dressed up.

extractive eductive, eradicative, removable, uprooting, elicitory, evocative, arousing, stimulating. *See also* dislodged.

extraneous irrelevant, irrelative, immaterial, inessential, superfluous, extra, superficial, redundant, pleonastic, pointless, inapplicable, unrelated, unconnected, incidental, adventitious, secondary, insignificant, trivial; foreign, alien, exotic,

strange, otherworldly. *See also* foreign, separate, external.

extraordinary weird, strange, peculiar, unusual, bizarre, rare.

extravagant excessive, flamboyant, ostentatious, outrageous, profuse, lavish, grandiose, overindulgent, overspending, pound-foolish, intemperate, inordinate, exorbitant, overdone, overshot, overstepped, meretricious, piled-on (Inf); wasteful, lavish, uneconomic, spendthrift, prodigal, profligate, thriftless, unthrifty, improvident. *See also* unrestrained, costly.

extreme severe, acute, maximum, intense, fanatical, radical, drastic; farthest, ultimate, utmost.

F

fabulous legendary, fantastic, fictitious, unbelievable, astounding, mythical.

facetious joking, comical, flippant, frivolous, humorous, witty, droll.

facile easy, effortless, skilful, smooth, fluent, adept.

factual genuine, accurate, true, correct, exact, faithful.

faded bleached, washed out, discoloured, pale, dim, dull.

faecal feculent, excremental, scatologic, stercoral, shitty, dungy, cathartic, purgative, laxative, aperient.

failed unsuccessful, ineffective, insufficient, unproductive, hopeless, insolvent, bankrupt, negligent, neglectful, unlucky, unfortunate, bungling, blundering, stillborn, abortive, weak, ailing, fruitless, bootless, profitless, useless, futile, dud (Inf), ploughed (Sl), kaput (Sl). *See also* defeated.

faint soft, quiet, low, gentle, distant, indistinct, inaudible, soundproof, just caught, half-heard, weak, feeble, dying away, unemphatic, unstressed, unaccented, piano, hushed, muted, muffled, damped, nonresonant, dead, dull, soft-pedalled, subdued, suppressed, stifled, bated, voiceless, whispered, hoarse, husky, wheezy, rasping, gravelly, murmuring, sighing, purring, gurgling, rustling, hissing, pattering, stealthy.

faint-sounding subdued, hushed, muted, low, quiet, soft, gentle, piano, pianissimo, indistinct, unclear, distant, weak, whispered, murmured, muttered, mumbled, inaudible, imperceptible. *See also* nonresonant.

fair just, impartial, honest, honourable; blond(e), light, pale, flaxen; attractive, pretty, handsome, good-lookng; middling, average, mediocre, so-so; sunny, fine, cloudless.

faithful loyal, true, true-blue.

faithless unfaithful, perfidious, deceitful, false, two-faced, untrustworthy, unreliable, undependable, questionable, shaky, disloyal, disobedient, double-crossing, duplicitous, deserting, betraying, treacherous, treasonous, seditious, rebellious.

fake sham, mock, artificial, imitative, counterfeit, bogus, tinselled, rubbishy, junky, phoney (Inf).

fallen sunk, soused, submerged, downcast, downthrown, defenestrated.

fallible imperfect, human, mortal, frail, erring.

falling tumbling, stumbling, titubant, tripping, sprawling, flopping, spilling, lurching, plunging, plummeting, diving, dipping, nosediving, dropping, falling, swooping, stooping, ducking, sliding, slipping, slithering, skidding, gliding, coasting.

false fallacious, erroneous, mendaceous, inveracious, untrue, ungenuine, spurious, dissembling, dishonest, deceptive, delusive, Machiavellian. *See also* duplicitous, hypocritical, spurious, deceitful, pretending, fraudulent, falsified, fake, evasive, disguised.

falsified faked, misrepresented, exaggerated, distorted, twisted, stretched, half-true, counterfeit, fabricated, confabulated, invented, slanderous, libellous, perjurious, manipulated, concocted, fictional, imaginative, mythologized, fabled, legendary, made-up, cock-and-bull, trumped-up, contrary-to-fact.

familiar known, everyday, household, ordinary, commonplace, unexceptional, unoriginal, stock, trite,

famous banal, hackneyed, clichéd, well-worn, trodden, beaten, current, prevalent, widespread, obtaining, universal; natural, simple, plain, homely, folksy, common, unaffected.

famous celebrated, well-known, eminent, distinguished, great, legendary.

fancy elaborate, ornate, intricate, elegant, showy; fanciful, whimsical, capricious.

fanlike deltoid(al), palmate(d), splayed, spread-eagled.

fantastic fanciful, bizarre, eccentric, exotic, odd, strange; wonderful, excellent, first-rate, splendid.

fantastical unreal, bizarre, grotesque, extravagant, whimsical, fanciful, airy-fairy (Inf), preposterous, absurd, outlandish, impractical, Heath Robinson, visionary, otherworldly, starry-eyed, quixotic, Laputan.

farmable arable, cultivable, ploughable, tillable, fertile, productive, fruitful, farmed, cropped, ploughed, broken down, tilled, grazed, fallow, undersown.

far-reaching far-ranging, wide-ranging, far-flung.

fascinating bewitching, alluring, captivating, spellbinding, charming, enchanting.

fashionable smart, stylish, snazzy, clothes' conscious, well-dressed, dressy, tasteful, classy, posh, glamorous, well-groomed, chic, cool (Sl), with-it (Sl), crucial (Sl), hip (Sl), groovy (Sl).

fast fixed, sound, steadfast, stable, steady, immovable, irremovable.

fasting abstinent, abstemious, anorexic, unfed, empty, Lenten, Quadragesimal, Spartan, slimming, reducing, austere, ascetic, underfed, thin, half-starved, starving, famished, ravenous, hungry, wasting away, anorexic.

fat obese, overweight, endomorphic, gross, fleshy, flabby, bloated, puffy, swollen, distended, full, plump, podgy, tubby, chubby, bonny, adipose, stout, corpulent, portly, rotund, round, roly-poly, well-fed, overfed, squab, dumpy, full-faced, chubby-cheeked, double-chinned, pot-bellied, paunchy, buxom, busty, bosomy, full-bosomed, well-endowed, top-heavy, steatopygic, hippy (Inf), well-upholstered (Inf), fat-arsed (Sl).

fatal deadly, harmful, calamitous, ruinous, catastrophic, lethal; final, killing, deadly, lethal, malignant; decisive, critical, fated, crucial.

fated destined, predestined, preordained, sure, certain.

fateful crucial, critical, significant, momentous, portentous, important.

fatigued tired, weary, sleepy, drowsy, nodding, yawning, dozy, half-asleep, exhausted, tired out, worn out, spent, weak, drained, dull, stale, strained, overworked, over-tired, overfatigued, overstrained, overwrought, burned out, weakened, enervated, fainting, swooning, stiff, footsore, footweary, travel-weary, jet-lagged, hollow-eyed, haggard, worn, drooping, flagging, languid, listless, lethargic, dopey (Inf), dog-tired (Inf), dog-weary (Inf), beat (Sl), half-dead (Inf), bushed (Inf), whacked (Inf), knackered (Sl). *See also* bored, panting, fatiguing.

fatiguing tiring, exhausting, laborious, tiresome, wearying, wearing, gruelling, punishing, exacting, tough, demanding, irksome, vexatious, annoying, trying, tedious, boring, monotonous.

fatuous foolish, mindless, silly, idiotic, inane, senseless.

fault-finding captious, carping, cavilling, pettifogging, hairsplitting, nagging, niggling, quibbling, fastidious, censorious, crabbing (Inf), nit-picking (Inf).

faultless blameless, immaculate, spotless, flawless, innocent, pure; impeccable, accurate, classic, correct, perfect, model.

faulty damaged, defective, imperfect, inaccurate, broken, out of order.

favourable beneficial, helpful, promising, auspicious, propitious, advantageous, useful, profitable.

fearful nervous, timorous, apprehensive, anxious, uneasy, alarmed, disquieted, agitated, jittery, jumpy, timid, tremulous, trembling, shaky, quaking, twitchy, tense, strained, highly strung, nervy, panicky, distressed, on edge, on tenterhooks, uptight (Inf).

fearless bold, courageous, daring, intrepid, plucky, valiant.

feasible practicable, workable, possible, useful, labour-saving.

feckless hopeless, incompetent, shiftless, useless, weak, worthless.

feeble weak, frail, languid, debilitated, infirm, sickly; powerless, incompetent, unconvincing, flimsy.

feeling sensing, sentient, sensible, perceptive, aware, conscious, knowing, realizing, understanding, responsive, sensitive, impressionable, susceptible. *See also* intuitive, sensitive, passionate, emotive.

feeling pain suffering, hurting, distressed, sore, aching, in agony, wincing, writhing, tormented, tortured, afflicted, martyred, raw, black-and-blue, bleeding, blistered, traumatized.

female feminine, womanly, womanish, ladylike, girlish, maidenly, matronly, child-bearing, feminist, Amazonian, lesbian.

feminine girlish, ladylike, soft, tender, delicate; effeminate, womanish, sissy, effete.

ferocious fierce, savage, violent, brutal, bloodthirsty, relentless.

fertile fecund, fruitful, fructiferous, productive, profitable, paying, lucrative, remunerative, high-yielding, generative, prolific, philoprogenitive (Rare), multiparous, teeming, streaming, pouring, copious, abundant, plentiful, profuse, boun-

fervent

tiful, fat, lush, verdant, luxuriant, rich, rife, exuberant, thriving, flourishing, prosperous, booming, pregnant, parturient, procreant, propagatory, regenerative, creative, inventive, resourceful.

fervent fervid, passionate, intense, earnest, animated, enthusiastic.

festive carnival-like, entertaining, fun, joyous, Christmassy.

few some, not many, hardly any, little, not much, precious little. *See also* sparse, fewer.

fewer less, reduced, diminished, least, minimum, minimal, too few, inquorate.

fickle changeable, flighty, capricious, eratic, unpredictable, vacillating.

fierce brutal, savage, ferocious, vicious, menacing, wild.

fifth fivefold, quintuple, quintuplicate, quinary, quinquennial, quintic, quinquepartite, pentadic, pentagonal, pentangular, pentahedral, pentatonic. *See also* sixth, seventh, eighth, ninth, tenth, eleventh, twentieth, hundredth, thousandth, millionth.

filled full, chock-a-block, flush, replete, sated, stuffed, glutted, bloated, satisfied, contented, well-provided, well-provisioned, well-stocked, well-furnished, teeming, crawling, overflowing, multitudinous.

filthy mucky, dirty, grimy, polluted, unclean, squalid; coarse, vulgar, smutty, obscene, lewd, pornographic.

final last, closing, concluding, ultimate; absolute, definitive, definite, decisive.

financial monetary, economic, budgeting, pecuniary.

fine fair, bright, sunny, dry, calm, clear, cloudless, mild, settled, fresh, bracing, brisk, crisp, invigorating; finespun, threadlike, hairlike, filamentous, filiform, spindle-shaped, bacilliform, spidery, wispy, scanty, tenuous, exiguous, delicate, fragile; light, insubstantial, flimsy, sheer, diaphanous, gossamer, gauzy, lacy, papery, wafer-thin.

finished ended, stopped, over, complete, closed, in recess, adjourned, interrupted, pending, on hold, on ice, redundant, fired (Inf), sacked (Inf).

firm compact, dense, rigid, inflexible; secure, stable, fixed, anchored, rooted; staunch, steadfast, determined, tenacious.

first chief, head, principal, top, leading; earliest, initial, original, primeval; basic, fundamental, key, primary.

fishlike fishy, piscine, pisciform, piscatorial, ichthyic, ichthyoid(al), ichthyomorphic, sharklike, sharkish, selachian, clupeoid, gadoid, percoid, cyprinoid, anguilliform. *See also* ichthyological.

fit right, proper, appropriate, condign.

fitful irregular, erratic, fluctuating, intermittent, sporadic, variable.

fitting befitting, belonging, pertaining, pertinent, apposite, expedient, suitable.

fixed staunch, true-blue, dyed-in-the-wool, ingrained, implanted, deep-rooted, deep-seated, imbued, permeated, soaked, dyed.

flabbergasted astounded, amazed, astonished, dumbfounded, overwhelmed, stunned.

flagrant bold, brazen, barefaced, blatant, immodest, notorious.

flamboyant showy, ornate, elaborate, rococo, flashy, gaudy.

flashy gaudy, loud, extravagant, flamboyant, exhibitionist, bombastic, garish, frilly, glittering, tinselly, tawdry, meretricious, colourful, dazzling, painted, foppish, rakish, jaunty, snazzy (Inf), snappy (Inf).

flat even, level, horizontal, smooth, unbroken; dull, insipid, bland, uninteresting, tedious, monotonous; reclining, outstretched, prostrate, recumbent; direct, absolute, positive, downright, out-and-out; punctured, deflated, collapsed, burst.

flattened levelled, smoothed, pressed, ironed, rolled, consolidated, beaten flat, squashed flat, well-trodden, trampled down, spread.

flattering adulatory, complimentary, laudatory, praising, insincere, hypocritical, tongue-in-cheek. *See also* honeyed, cajoling, unctuous, sycophantic.

flatulent windy, gassy.

flawed broken, blemished, imperfect, defective, damaged, cracked.

fleeting brief, ephemeral, transitory, short-lived, temporary.

flexible plastic, elastic, supple, stretchy; adaptable, variable, compliant, adjustable; amenable, docile, biddable, manageable.

flickering flickery, sputtering, spluttering, guttering, sputtery, wavery.

flimsy frail, delicate, fragile, slight, unsubstantial; feeble, implausible, inadequate, poor, unconvincing, weak.

flippant rude, offhand, pert, cheeky, impertinent, saucy.

flooded deluged, inundated, swamped, awash.

floral flowered, flowery, bloomy, floristic, flower-like, fragrant, florid, ornate, floreate, floriate(d). *See also* flowering.

florid ruddy, flushed, high-coloured, rosy; flowery, flamboyant, fussy, ornate, elaborate, showy.

flourishing blooming, prospering, thriving, successful.

flowering in flower, in bloom, blossoming, blooming, flourishing, florescent, inflorescent, efflorescent.

flowery ornate, elaborate, high-flown, rhetorical, grandiloquent, embellished.

flowing fluent, fluxive, watery, runny, juicy, sappy, moist, succulent, squashy.

fluffy downy, fuzzy, velvety, velutinous.

fluid liquid, fluidic, liquiform, uncongealed, unclotted. *See also* flowing, rheumy, milky, bloody, liquefied, liquefying, liquefiable.

fluvial fluviomarine, fluent, effluent, profluent, affluent, confluent, convergent, streaming, running, coursing, meandering, serpentine, ripply, racing, torrential, vortical, inundant, falling, ebbing, refluent. *See also* flooded, hydrologic(al).

focused subjective, angled, pointed, founded, based, supposed, proposed, programmed, thematic, central, basic.

foggy fogbound, smoggy, misty, hazy, nebulous.

folded bent, pleated, plicate, flexuous, doubled over, turned over, dog-eared, rolled, creased, rucked up, flexed, corrugated. *See also* closed.

fond affectionate, loving, caring, warm, devoted, doting.

foolhardy reckless, hotheaded, rash, impetuous, irresponsible, madcap, daredevil.

foolish stupid, inept, inane, mad, ill-advised, ill-considered, unwise, imprudent, injudicious, uncircumspect, incautious, rash, reckless, foolhardy, harebrained, heedless, inattentive, hotheaded, hellbent, headstrong, prodigal, devil-may-care, frivolous, flippant, silly, asinine, idiotic, imbecilic, moronic, lunatic, insane, senseless, brainless, ignorant, unintelligent, dim-witted, feeble-minded, empty-headed, simple, slow, doltish, dull, gormless, fatuous, pointless, absurd, ludicrous, ridiculous, nonsensical, preposterous, childish, puerile, senile, eccentric, bird-brained (Inf), nutty (Inf), daft (Inf), crazy (Inf), barmy (Sl), spaced-out (Sl), potty (Inf), gaga (Inf).

forbidden prohibited, denied, disallowed, blocked, barred, banned, stopped, cancelled, ruled out.

forced compulsory, mandatory, obligatory, compelled, unwilling; affected, contrived, unnatural, wooden, stiff, laboured.

forceful compelling, powerful, dynamic, weighty, potent, convincing.

foreign alien, unrelated, other, continental, overseas, transatlantic, tramontane, strange, different, deviating, outlandish, unknown, exotic, barbaric, wandering, travelling, rambling, roaming, nomadic, gypsy, migrant, homeless, stateless.

foremost first, leading, head, primary, main, supreme.

foreseeable predictable, probable, forecast.

foreseeing predictive, prophetic, prognostic, precognitive, prospective, clairvoyant, intuitive, telepathic, second-sighted, prescient, farsighted, longsighted, weatherwise, expectant, anticipant, anticipatory, prudent, provident, cautious, careful, circumspect, wise, sagacious. *See also* foreseeable.

foreseen foretold, predicted, expected, anticipated, awaited, looked for, hoped for, promised.

forgivable pardonable, venial, excusable, easily excused.

forgiven pardoned, excused, granted amnesty, reprieved, spared, absolved, shriven, indulged, remitted, acquitted, cancelled, discharged, released, delivered, freed, let off, exonerated, condoned, exculpated, vindicated, justified, reconciled, redeemed, pacified, rehabilitated, atoned, restored, reinstated, taken back.

forgiving pardoning, excusing, reprieving, sparing, absolving, shriving, exonerating, condoning, vindicating, justifying, reconciling, conciliatory, redeeming, pacifying, rehabilitating. *See also* merciful, forgiven, forgivable, overlooked.

forgotten unmemorable, past, lost, beyond recall.

forlorn miserable, wretched, comfortless, unhappy, woebegone, destitute.

formal formulary, formalistic, legalistic, pedantic, stately, dignified, ceremonious, stiff, refined, starchy, sedate, staid, stilted, rigid, solemn, royal, correct, smart, precise, conventional, ritual, procedural, official, stylized, prim, punctilious, precise, scrupulous, fastidious, precious, puristic, exact, meticulous, orderly, methodical, elegant, decorous, proud, grave, pompous, weighty. *See also* dressed up, ceremonious.

formed orderly, systematic, conformable, configurational, creative, made, constructed, produced, shaped, sculptured, carved, moulded, modelled, tailored, thrown (pot), blown (glass), turned, rounded, squared, fashioned, set-up, composed, styled, stylish, expressive, morphologic, morphogenic, isomorphic, Platonic, concrete, solid, plastic, fictile. *See also* prototypical, formal, on form.

former previous, prior, erstwhile, one-time, sometime, quondam, retired, emeritus, ex (Inf).

formidable terrifying, shocking, alarming, threatening, menacing, awful; powerful, mighty, colossal, great, impressive, indomitable.

forsaken abandoned, deserted, disowned, ignored, outcast, marooned.

for sale available, transferable, inheritable.

fortunate favoured, happy, lucky, successful, blessed, prosperous, well-off.

forward progressive, advanced, up-to-date, forward-looking, go-ahead, enterprising, reformist, gogetting (Inf). *See also* ongoing.

fossilized petrified, mineralized, fossiliferous.

foul dirty, disgusting, contaminated, tainted, polluted, offensive; wicked, evil, vile, obscene, gross, profane; unfair, dishonest, unsportsmanlike, underhand; rainy, murky, stormy, wet, gloomy.

found discovered, pinpointed, detected, unearthed, tracked down, pinned down.

four quaternary, quadratic, quadruple, quadruplex, fourfold, fourth. *See also* quadrilateral, tetramerous, quartered.

four humours phlegmatic, sanguine, choleric, melancholic.

fractional half, quarter, partial, fragmentary, incomplete, proportional, sectional, segmental, divisional, subdivisional, aliquot. *See also* small.

fragile brittle, flimsy, frail, delicate, feeble, weak.

fragrant sweet-smelling, scented, perfumed, aromatic, flowery, floral, spicy, musky, fruity, pungent, heady, camphorated, balmy, ambrosial, aromatherapeutic.

frail brittle, flimsy, delicate, weak, fragile, vulnerable.

frantic frenetic, beserk, distraught, frenzied, hysterical, furious.

fraudulent swindling, dishonest, cheating, tricky, false, fake, imposturous, illicit, underhanded, counterfeit, forged, copied, put-up, whitewashed, crooked (Inf), rip-off (Sl), fiddling (Sl).

free emancipated, liberated, franchised, authorized, constitutional, inalienable, national, unilateral, autonomous, self-governing, autarkic, self-determining, unconfined, unrestrained, unregulated, unhindered, unimpeded, unshackled, unfettered, unbridled, uncurbed, unbound, unchecked, ungoverned, acquitted, at large, discharged, released, privileged, exempt, nonliable, excepted, immune, noninvolved, secluded, nonaligned, nonpartisan, neutral, isolationist, noninterventional, free-trade, self-regulating, open, capitalistic, broad-minded, unbiased, unprejudiced, uninfluenceable, cross-bench, undecided, floating, moderate, just, tolerant, liberal. *See also* independent, ranging, unconditional, informal.

free of charge free, scot-free, for free, for nothing, without charge, gratis, given free, giveaway, complimentary, courtesy, gratuitous, honorary, grace-and-favour, voluntary, unsalaried, unpaid, charity, eleemosynary, tax-free, zero-rated, rent-free, post-paid, buckshee (Sl).

freezing biting, icy, bitter, raw, arctic, polar.

frequent common, customary, familiar, everyday; repeated, recurrent, persistent, continual.

fresh new, young, youthful, evergreen, sappy, springlike, vernal, vigorous, flourishing, blooming.

frictional abrasive, anatriptic, irritant, rubbing, attritive, erosive, ablative, gnawing. *See also* rough.

friendly cordial, courteous, amicable, amiable, kindly, peaceable, unhostile, sociable, affectionate, gracious, harmonious, pleasant, congenial, compatible, cooperative, agreeable, favourable, hospitable, demonstrative, effusive, back-slapping, ardent, warm, genial, well-meaning, well-disposed, comradely, simpatico (Inf), matey (Inf), chummy (Inf), pally (Inf), palsy-walsy (Sl), buddy-buddy (Sl). *See also* friends with, familiar, devoted, favourable.

friends with acquainted.

frightened afraid, scared, fearing, fear-stricken, terrified, terror-struck, horrified, horror-struck, aghast, petrified, panic-stricken, terrorized, intimidated, cowed, demoralized, affright (Arch), ashen-faced, frit (Inf). *See also* fearful, worried, frightening.

frightening fearsome, awesome, daunting, dismaying, formidable, menacing, intimidating, alarming, unnerving, startling, scaring, enervating, shocking, horrifying, terrifying, petrifying, terrible, frightful, fearful, dreadful, dire, grim, horrible, horrific, horrendous, ghastly, hideous, awful, appalling, hair-raising, scary (Inf), spooky (Inf).

frightful awful, dire, dreadful, grisly, gruesome, fearful.

frigid chill, cold, icy, frosty, frozen, arctic; formal, aloof, rigid, stiff, prim, forbidding.

front fore, foreground, frontal, entrance, obverse, anterior, preceding, forward, physiognomic, full-faced, head-and-shoulders, full-frontal (Inf); frontal, leading, foremost, head. *See also* outward, assured, arrogant.

frontal cyclonic, anticyclonic.

frosty icy, frozen, chilly, wintry, cold; frigid, off-putting, cool, indifferent, aloof, unfriendly.

fruit-eating frugivorous, vegetarian.

fruitful productive, fertile, fecund, plentiful, teeming, abundant; profitable, successful, worthwhile, rewarding.

fruiting fructiferous, pomiferous, leguminous, fructuous, fruitful, productive, fertile. *See also* fruitlike, fruit-eating, of a fruit.

fruitless useless, futile, unproductive, unprofitable, in vain.

fruitlike fruity, citrus, citrous, citric, citrine.

frustrated disappointed, foiled, thwarted, hindered, defeated, circumvented.

fulfilled satisfied.

full replenished, replete, satisfied, well-stocked, level with, flush, saturated, stuffed, gorged, sated, chock-a-block, crowded, crammed, jam-packed, loaded, overrun.

full of energy dynamic, vigorous, lively, vivacious, animated, spirited, attractive, drawing, pulling, impelling, propulsive, moving, locomotive, kinetic, driven, automated, on line, pro-active, on stream, live.

fundamental

fundamental basic, key, essential, crucial, central, necessary.

funeral burial, funerary, funebrial, funereal, sombre, black, dark, sad, mournful, lamenting, dirgelike, mortuary, cinerary, crematory, sepulchral, memorial, obsequial, eulogistic, elegiac, obituary, necrological, lapidary, epitaphic.

funny amusing, diverting, entertaining, laughable, risible, hilarious, uproarious, side-splitting, hysterical (Inf). *See also* humorous, humouring, four humours.

furious livid.

furrowed scratched, grooved, wheel-tracked, slotted, chinky, rutty, rimose, fluted, scored, corrugated, etched, engraved, ploughed. *See also* wrinkly.

furthest extreme, far, verging, boundary, border, longitudinal, latitudinal.

furtive clandestine, secret, stealthy, sneaking, sly, covert.

fussy finicky, faddy, fastidious, particular, choosy (Inf), discriminating; restless, fretful, fidgety; elaborate, ornate, embellished, overdone.

futile useless, worthless, vain, impossible, purposeless, pointless, Sisyphean, hopeless, idle, unavailing, abortive, unsuccessful, profitless, loss-making, uneconomic, unproductive, fruitless, barren, wasted, squandered, time-wasting, unrewarding, thankless.

future forthcoming, coming, to come, to be, eventual, later, ahead, approaching, oncoming, due, fated, destined, imminent, threatening, overhanging, impending, pending, nigh (Arch). *See also* predictable, foreseen.

G

gainful beneficial, acquiring, obtainable, attainable, available, procurable, inheriting, beneficiary, compensatory, fund-raising, moneymaking, capitalistic, profitable, gross, net, gratuitous, windfall, useful, paid, lucrative, remunerative, rewarding, money-spinning (Inf). *See also* greedy, well-off, acquisitional, yielding.

gaseous gassy, vaporous.

gassy fizzy, effervescent, bubbly, sparkling, carbonated, aerated.

gay jolly, merry, cheerful, joyful, lively, vivacious; bright, colourful, gaudy, flashy.

gelatinous jelly-like, syrupy, treacly, jammy, tremelloid.

general universal, comprehensive, inclusive, whole, all-embracing, all-encompassing, all-covering, all-comprehending, all-pervading, overall, synoptic, heterogenous, diversified, miscellaneous, eclectic, liberal, catholic, ecumenical, cosmopolitan, broad-based, encyclopedic, blanket, extensive, wide, broad, sweeping, across-the-board, panoramic, bird's-eye. *See also* universal, widespread, far-reaching, prevailing, generalized, common, commonplace.

generalized nonspecific, generic, approximate, inexact, imprecise, indefinite, indeterminate, undetermined, unspecified, ill-defined, broad, loose, vague, sweeping, abstract, nebulous.

generous liberal, open-handed, hospitable, giving, unstinting, ungrudging, beneficent, munificent, bountiful, lavish, princely, handsome. See also magnanimous, abundant, big.

genetic genotypic(al), genomic, factorial, hereditary, Mendelian, dominant, recessive, mutant, chromosomal, mitotic, meiotic, haploid, diploid, polyploid.

gentle kind, considerate, compassionate, mild, meek, tender; calm, quiet, placid, tranquil, slow, moderate.

genuine real, true, actual, authentic, natural, pure.

geological mineralogical, petrological, hydrological, geochemical, glaciological, geomorphological, pedological, geodetic, stratigraphical, palaeontological, geochronological, geopolitical. See also geophysical, terrestrial, volcanic, petrographic, earthy.

gestural gesticulative, dactylographic, signing, thumbing, looking, glancing, smiling, winking, grimacing, laughing, sighing, moaning, whistling, clapping, patting, pushing, slapping, stamping.

gifted talented, endowed, born for.

given bestowable, impartable, available, saleable, subventionary, bequeathed, willed, transferable, granted, accorded, bestowed, bonus, gratis, for nothing, voluntary, complimentary, courtesy, sacrificial, votive, oblatory, gratuitous, God-given, donative, contributory, tributary, testate (Fml), endowed, subsidized, dowered, stipendiary, pensionary, insurable, taxable. See also giving.

giving bestowing, imparting, granting, transferring, alms-giving, charitable, benevolent, philanthropic, generous, open-handed, bountiful, liberal.

glad happy, cheerful, pleased, delighted, contented, gay.

gloomy dark, dreary, murky, cloudy, dull, dismal.

glum downcast, down, gloomy, crestfallen, despondent, sullen.

gluttonous greedy, insatiable, intemperate, hedonistic, overeating, self-indulgent, overindulgent, voracious, ravenous, rapacious, well-nourished, edacious, polyphagous, epicurean, gastronomic, omnivorous, devouring, stuffing, cramming, bolting, gobbling, gulping, glutting, gorging, guzzling, wolfing, esurient, piggish (Inf), hoggish (Inf), bingeing (Inf).

good excellent, first-rate, superior, better, superb, splendid, great, famous, fine, exquisite, high-class, wonderful, magnificent, terrific, impressive, meritorious, praiseworthy, admirable, worthy, valuable, profitable, sound, healthy, salubrious, salutary, favourable, propitious, auspicious, heaven-sent, lucky, suitable, apt, right, fabulous (Inf), super (Inf), crackerjack (Inf), topnotch (Inf), dandy (Inf), smashing (Inf), wizard (Inf), brill (Inf), fab (Inf), radical (Sl), rad (Inf), swell (Sl), spiffy (Sl), corking (Sl), crack (Sl), bad (Sl), wicked (Sl), deadly (Sl). *See also* best, kind, well-behaved, proficient, beneficial.

good-mannered well-behaved, well-bred, well-spoken, refined, cultured, cultivated, genteel, gentlemanly, ladylike, correct, urbane, polished, elegant, conventional, suave, bland, smooth, flattering, sweet-talking, formal, de rigueur, ceremonious, diplomatic, respectful.

governing ruling, controlling, dictating, in charge, in power, regnant, regnal, royal, regal, majestic, monarchical, imperial, magisterial.

governmental political, presidential, parliamentary, democratic, republican, independent, constitutional, federal, civic, administrative, executive, ministerial, senatorial, official, bureaucratic, centralized, technocratic, matriarchal, patriarchal, theocratic, monarchical, feudal, aristocratic, meritocratic, oligarchic, plutocratic, dictatorial, to-

talitarian, classless, self-governing, self-ruling, autonomous, autarchic, anarchic, socialistic, communistic. *See also* governing.

graceful elegant, becoming, comely, agile, supple, flowing.

graceless inelegant, clumsy, awkward, ungainly, cumbersome, ill-proportioned, dumpy, clownish, gauche, gawky, undignified, ham-fisted, heavy-handed, cack-handed (Sl). *See also* indecorous, inelegant, ugly.

gradational graded, measured, rated, scaled, calibrated, classified, valued, sized, sorted, differentiated, differential, relative, comparative, proportional, portioned, standard, encompassing, limited, majority, minority, level, regular, frequent, extensive, progressive, gradual, slow-ranging, slow-changing, growing, increasing, waxing, waning, tapering, fading, diminishing. *See also* ranked.

gradual even, steady, graduated, progressive, unhurried, moderate.

grainy gritty, granular, sandy, sabulous, arenaceous, gravelly, shingly, pebbly, brecciated, detrital.

grammatical pronominal, adjectival, verbal, copular, reflexive, transitive, intransitive, participial, adverbial, prepositional, conjunctive, coordinate, interjectional, objective, subjective, direct, indirect, modifying, definite, indefinite, inflectional, inflected, formative, morphemeic, diminutive, intensive, attributive, augmentative, comparative, superlative, masculine, feminine, neuter, singular, plural.

grand awe-inspiring, imposing, splendid, spectacular, scenic, magnificent, gorgeous, resplendent, brilliant, glorious, sumptuous, lavish, luxurious, elegant, elaborate, luxuriant, expensive, impressive, plush (Inf), swanky (Inf), ritzy (Inf), glitzy (Inf), posh (Inf).

grass-eating graminivorous, herbivorous, grazing, browsing.

grasslike gramineous, graminaceous, poaceous, graminiferous, farinaceous, wheaten, oaten.

grassy verdant, verdured, meadowy, swardy, turfy, reedy, rushy, sedgy.

grateful thankful, appreciative, pleased, gratified, indebted, beholden, obliged. *See also* thanking.

greedy avaricious, acquisitive, grasping, plundering, money-grubbing (Inf), gold-digging (Inf).

green emerald, jade, vert, greenish, virescent, chartreuse, eau-de-nil, avocado, celadon, reseda, mignonette, glaucous, aquamarine. *See also* verdant, raw, fresh, environmental.

grim severe, forbidding, stern, harsh, dreadful, ghastly.

grotesque distorted, deformed, bizarre, freakish, strange, outlandish.

grouped clumped, clustered, bunched, bundled, packaged, parcelled, baled, trussed, wrapped, fascicled, congressional, congrega-

tional, factional, cabalistic; categorized, classified, codified, specified, pigeonholed, indexed, catalogued, listed.

growing developing, extending, lengthening, stretching, spreading, sprawling, splaying, patulous, branching, fanning, flabellate, deltoid, expanding, widening, broadening, flaring, dilating, opening, unfolding, swelling, tumescent, turgescent, bulging, bulbous, increasing, waxing, mushrooming, snowballing, rising, developing, germinating, budding, shooting, sprouting, burgeoning, blossoming, blooming, flowering, flourishing, thriving, multiplying, pullulating.

guaranteed warranted, certified, authenticated, assured, certain, reliant, unshaken, gilt-edged, covered, insured, mortgaged, covenanted, pledged, promised; warranted, promised.

guaranteeing authenticating, certified, assured, attested, certain, warranted, underwritten, signed, securing, pledging, committed, bound, obligated, promissory, contracted.

guilty responsible, reprehensible, censurable, inexcusable, injustifiable, unpardonable, unforgivable, reproachable, reprovable, at fault, culpable, impeachable, chargeable, accusable, blameworthy, implicated, censured, peccant, condemned, convicted. *See also* appearing guilty, sinful.

gullible

gullible credulous, innocent, naive, green.

H

habit-forming addictive, obsessive, haunting, besetting, clinging.

habitual customary, accustomed, wonted, predictable, invariable, usual, regular, routine, everyday, quotidian. *See also* familiar, normal, established, fixed, habituated, habit-forming.

habituated used, accustomed, familiar, conversant, practised, trained, tamed, broken in, acclimatized, naturalized, conditioned, inured, seasoned, hardened, confirmed, chronic, inveterate, addicted, given, dedicated, devoted, wedded, frequent, recurrent, constant, perpetual.

hairless bald, thin, tonsured, clean-shaven, smooth, glabrous, depilatory.

half halved, bisected, dichotomous, bifurcated, cloven, cleft, halfway.

half-measure stopgap, temporary, second-best.

handed right-handed, dextral, left-handed, sinistral, ambidextrous, light-handed, neat, delicate, heavy-handed, clumsy, manual, hand-operated, touch-operated, hands-on, able, artistic, skilful.

handsome attractive, elegant, good-looking, personable, becoming, comely; generous, plentiful, ample.

haphazard chance, accidental, random, undirected; disorderly, shipshod, careless, indiscriminate.

happy contented, euphoric, pleased, glad, cheerful, joyful, felicitous, gay, blithe, merry, delighted, exuberant, ebullient, blissful, starry-eyed, elated, overjoyed, thrilled, transported, ecstatic, celebratory, jubilant, captivated, enchanted, enraptured, delirious, intoxicated. *See also* delightful.

hard rigid, stiff, tough, nonelastic, unsprung, firm, difficult, complicated. *See also* tough, hardened.

hardened toughened, fortified, strengthened, stiffened, reinforced, backed, braced, buttressed, proofed, tempered, heat-treated, annealed, indurate, hard-boiled, steeled, armoured, calloused, ossified, hornified, calcified, crusted, crystallized, granulated, vitrified, petrified, fossilized, sun-baked, solidified, set, frozen, icy.

harmful hurtful, injurious, damaging, deleterious, detrimental, prejudicial, disadvantageous, destructive, wasting, pernicious, deadly, virulent, disastrous, calamitous, adverse, degenerative, noxious, malignant, infectious, poisonous, polluting, dangerous, sinister, ominous, dreadful, accursed, spiteful, vindictive, malicious, malevolent, mischief-making, cruel, bloodthirsty,

healthy

violent, harsh, intolerant, outrageous.

harmless innocuous, inoffensive, innocent, mild, gentle.

harmonic tuneful, in tune, tonal, symphonious, synchronous, homophonic, harmonious, melodious, mellifluous, dulcet, singable, catchy.

harmonious coordinated, synchronized, synchronous, coincident, coinciding, conjoint, concomitant, symmetrical, balanced, in equilibrium, regulated, attuned, symphonious, symphonic, unisonous, blended, merged, modulated, in concert, choral, melodic, harmonic, echoing, resounding, resonant, rhyming.

harsh rough, coarse, grating, rasping, strident, discordant; severe, stern, austere, cruel, hard.

hasty rushed, speedy, prompt, brisk, quick, presto, allegro, swift, rapid, fast, fleet, expeditious, impetuous, impulsive, precipitant, headlong, reckless, heedless, rash, hot-headed, feverish, impatient, thoughtless, unthinking, ill-considered, ardent, fervent, rushing, scampering, pushing, shoving, elbowing, uncontrolled, boisterous, furious, violent, breathless, breakneck, urgent, immediate, hotfoot, running, racing, speeding, hard-pressed, driven, hurried, haphazard, slapdash, careless, negligent, cursory, perfunctory, superficial, fleeting, last-minute, rough-and-tumble, unprepared,

forced, stampeded, pushed through, railroaded (Inf).

hated loathed, disliked, abominated, detested, detestable, disgusting, abhorrent, odious, obnoxious, despicable, contemptible, execrable, accursed, unlovable, invidious, unpopular, discredited, disliked, unwelcome, unwanted, baneful, nasty, horrid, repugnant, revolting, repelling, abominable, disgusting, vile, repulsive, nauseous, alien, strange, foreign, unloved, scorned, jilted, unvalued, unmissed, unlamented, unmourned, unchosen, spurned, condemned, beastly (Inf).

hateful loathsome, disgusting, detestable, repulsive, obnoxious, repellent.

hating loathing, detesting, abhorring, antipathetic, antagonistic, hostile, execrative, averse, spiteful, spleenful, vindictive, vicious, contemptuous, malicious, malevolent, maledictive, malignant, rancorous, acrimonious, poisonous, bitter, ill-natured, resentful, grudging, sour, sullen, jealous, envious, green-eyed, venomous, virulent. *See also* hated, angry.

having no effect unsuccessful, failed, addled, abortive.

hazardous perilous, dangerous, risky, chancy, dicey, precarious.

healthful wholesome, nutritious, nourishing, tonic, bracing, invigorating, hygienic, sanitary, salubrious, salutary, beneficial.

healthy fit, well, fine, sound, fight-

ing fit, eupeptic, fresh, thriving, flourishing, blooming, glowing, ruddy, rosy, rosy-cheeked, bouncing, bonny, lusty, energetic, vigorous, strapping, robust, hardy, sturdy, stalwart, great, convalescent, cured, healed. *See also* healthful.

hearable audible, reachable, within earshot, loud, soft, resonant, sonorous, echoing, carrying, listenable, harsh, ear-splitting.

heard hearable, audible, distinct.

heartbroken desolate, heavy-hearted, downcast, dispirited, wretched, miserable.

heartless cruel, callous, cold, pitiless, unfeeling, unkind.

heated insulated, lined, padded, double-glazed, lagged, centrally heated, warmed up, defrosted, heated up, preheated, baked, roasted, boiled, toasted, burnt, singed, scorched, molten.

heat-resistant heat-proof, insulated, air-conditioned, air-cooled, water-cooled, cooling, chilling, refrigerant, frigorific, freezable, freezing, refrigerated, unmelted, quick-frozen, freeze-dried, cryogenic.

heavenly celestial, empyrean, empyreal, on high, Elysian, paradisiac, paradisical, paradisial, Olympian, supernal, ethereal, angelic, angelical, archangelic, seraphic, cherubic, saintly.

heavy weighty, weighing, weighed, heavyweight, middleweight, lightweight, featherweight, leaden, solid, dense, mas-

sive, considerable, great, stout, large, lumpish, bulky, fat, overweight, obese, corpulent, hefty (Inf), beefy (Inf). *See also* loaded, ponderous.

hectic frantic, fevered, frenetic, animated, riotous, boisterous.

heedless thoughtless, careless, unthinking, negligent, reckless, rash.

held up postponed, deferred, adjourned, prorogued, prolonged, extended, protracted, stonewalled, hindered, obstructed, suspended, held-up, blocked, tabled, stalled, restrained, detained, remanded, halted, jammed, log-jammed (US), mothballed.

helpful assistant (Arch), useful, utilitarian, serviceable, convenient, handy, informative, practical, constructive, positive, furthering, promoting, contributory, conducive.

helping aiding, assisting, adjunct, serving, supporting, supplementing, facilitative, instrumental, promoting, favouring; cooperative, collaborative, cordial, gracious, benevolent, philanthropic. *See also* supplementary, supportive, helpful, beneficial, benevolent.

helpless powerless, defenceless, vulnerable, weak, feeble.

heraldic emblematic, blazoned, emblazoned.

herbicidal pesticidal, fungicidal, insecticidal.

heroic brave, valiant, bold, fearless, daring, courageous.

hesitant tentative, softly-softly, cautious, reluctant, lagging, dawdling, drawling, procrastinating, foot-dragging (Inf).

hidden dark, obscure, indistinct, camouflaged, invisible, unseen.

hideous grotesque, repulsive, ugly, frightful, ghastly, gruesome.

hierarchical serial, sequential, gradational, taxonomic(al), progressive, alphabetical, numerical, graded, ranked.

high tall, altitudinal, high-up, sky-high, lofty, elevated, uplifted, up-reared, upraised, high-rise, multi-storey, towering, skyscraping, ascending, rising, uprising, mounting, aspiring, soaring, flying, hovering, topping, overlooking, dominating, overshadowing, overhanging, beetling, cloud-topped, aerial, supernal, ethereal, airy, vertiginous, dizzy, giddy. *See also* higher, exalted, tall, mountainous, altimetric.

higher taller, highest, tallest, superior, upper, upmost, uppermost, topmost.

hindering hindered, impeding, held back, unhelpful, uncooperative, unwilling, contrary, encumbering, obstructive, restrictive, cramping, circumscriptive, limited, interfering, intrusive, interventional, meddling, deterrent, dissuasive, discouraging, off-putting, preventive, defensive, prophylactic, counteractive, repressive, preclusive, prohibitive, thwarting. *See also* blocked, inhibitive.

hindmost rear, back, tail.

hissed booed, taunted, jeered, sneered at, derided, ridiculed.

hissing sibilant, rustling, whispering, sneezing, wheezy, asthmatic, fizzy, effervescent, sizzling. *See also* catcalling.

historic ancient, old, ancestral, prehistoric, protohistoric, diachronic, antediluvian, primordial, primal, aboriginal, antiquated, dated, archaic, former, prior. *See also* historical, chronicled.

historical historiographical, prehistorical, protohistorical, archaeological, Assyriological, Egyptological, Sumerological, palaeological, palaeographical, epigraphical.

hoarse husky, rough, gruff, low, guttural, throaty, gravelly, rasping, cawing, croaky, croaking, grunting, snorting, snoring, stertorous, cracked, nonresonant, dry, rusty, scraping, scratchy, droning, clanking, clinking.

holed perforated, porous, permeated, sievelike, cribriform, honeycombed, spongy, leaky, injected, penetrated, probed, pierced, pricked, punctured, lanced, bayoneted, stabbed, slashed, gashed, shot, bored, hollowed, drilled, burrowed, tunnelled, sunk, excavated, cavernous, spacial, volcanic.

holy religious, devout, godly, pious, sacred, hallowed.

honest honourable, trustworthy, decent, law-abiding, truthful; forthright, frank, candid, fair, just, principled.

honeyed sugary, saccharine, blarneying, honey-tongued, smooth-tongued, smooth-spoken, buttery (Inf), sweet-talking (Inf), soft-soaping (Inf).

honourable respectable, decent, good, reputable, incorruptible, high-minded, principled, fastidious, ethical, moral, upright, upstanding, noble, trustworthy, sure, reliable, dependable, responsible, dutiful, honest, true, truthful, candid, frank, open, above board, law-abiding, veracious, plain, straightforward, sincere, undeceitful, scrupulous, careful, meticulous, conscientious, sound, impartial, fair, straight, equitable, bona fide, just, faithful, constant, steadfast, loyal, true-blue, devoted, chivalrous, gentlemanly, sporting, straight-up (Sl). *See also* pure.

hopeful optimistic, sanguine, cheerful, buoyant, positive, starry-eyed, bullish (Inf), upbeat (Inf), up (Inf). *See also* expectant, aspirant, cheering.

hopeless impractical, unfeasible, unworkable, unachievable, untenable, unviable, inoperable, broken, irreparable, irrecoverable, irrevocable, unattainable, insurmountable, insuperable, inaccessible, unapproachable, unreachable, impenetrable, impervious, unobtainable, unavailable, out, over; forlorn, despondent, comfortless, cheerless,

discouraged, defeated, negative, sceptical, pessimistic, cynical, dejected, downcast, despairing, desperate, suicidal, desolate, disconsolate, melancholic, depressed, gloomy, down (Sl). *See also* past hope, inauspicious, futile, bad.

horizontal flat, level, plane, plain, planar, two-dimensional, tabular, homaloidal, even, smooth, unwrinkled, flush. *See also* flattened, lying.

horrible awful, dreadful, horrid, appalling, revolting, terrible, gruesome.

horrid horrible, unpleasant, nasty, mean; terrible, repulsive, ghastly, horrendous.

horticultural floricultural, ornamental, herbaceous, herbal, vegetal, vegetative, leguminous, cereal, arboricultural, arboreal, silvicultural, pomological, viticultural, vinicultural, aquicultural, hydroponic. *See also* herbicidal.

hostile unfriendly, inimical, uncordial, cool, icy, cold, aloof, inhospitable, antisocial, unsympathetic, unamiable, strained, tense, unharmonious, ill-disposed, acrimonious, antipathetic, bitter, rancorous, sour, sore, resentful, envious, jealous, malevolent, malicious, spiteful, virulent, venomous. *See also* intolerant, estranged, aggressive, hated.

hot thermal, warm, mild, tepid, lukewarm chambré, snug, fuggy, stuffy, stifling, sultry, subtropical, tropical, equatorial, warming, calefacient, calorific, suffocating, piping hot, fiery, scalding, searing, scorching, blistering, cauterizing, roasting, boiling, simmering, steaming, sizzling, sweltering, smoking, red-hot, incandescent, candent (Arch), molten, glowing. *See also* on fire, warm, warm-hearted, heated.

huge gigantic, colossal, enormous, massive, vast, immense.

human mortal, creaturely, fleshly, earthborn, tellurian, anthropoid, humanoid, hominoid, humanlike, subhuman, civilized, anthropological, ethnographical, racial, ethnic, anthropocentric, anthropomorphic, personal, individual, humanistic, bionic. *See also* national.

humble meek, unpretentious, unassuming, modest, mouselike, harmless, inoffensive, undistinguished, unimportant, without airs, without side. *See also* lowly, humbled, self-abasing, submissive, humiliating.

humbled humiliated, embarrassed, mortified, deflated, wounded, shamed, scorned, abject, chagrined, crushed, hangdog, put down, squashed, debunked, slapped down, rebuked, disapproved, discomfited, defeated, reduced, diminished, dejected, degraded, deflated, lowered, brought down, laid low, shamefaced, crestfallen, disconcerted, broken-spirited, dashed, abashed, sheepish.

humdrum dull, boring, mundane, monotonous, uninteresting, tedious.

humiliating degrading, embarrassing, mortifying, wounding, chastening, crushing.

humming whirring, buzzing, droning, stridulous, monotonous, repetitive, unvaried.

humorous witty, funny, jocular, jocose, joking, slapstick, waggish, nimblewitted, quick-witted, smart, comic, droll, amusing, whimsical, quirky, zany, merry, pawky, dry, facetious, farcical, sarcastic, ironic, satirical, flippant, teasing, jokey (Inf), corny (Inf).

humouring pleasing, placating, indulging, pampering, cossetting, spoiling, cajoling, flattering, sycophantic, servile, ingratiating, toadying, unctuous, oily, slimy (Inf), smarmy (Inf), bootlicking (Inf).

hundredth centesimal, centennial, centenary, centenarian, hundredfold, centuple, centuplicate.

hungry starving, famished, ravenous, empty, half-starved, peckish, thirsty, dry, parched, dehydrated.

hunting shooting, fishing, piscatorial.

hurried hasty, quick, rushed, slapdash, cursory, swift.

hygienic sanitary, disinfected, chlorinated, pasteurized, sterilized, clean, pure, aseptic, antiseptic, germ-free, sanative, prophylactic, immunizing, protective, remedial, salubrious, healthy, ventilated, refreshing, restorative, salutary, beneficial, wholesome, nutritious, nourishing, body-building, noninjurious, benign, uninfectious, innocuous, immune, vaccinated, inoculated, protected.

hypocritical false, insincere, disingenuous, meretricious, deceptive, delusive, sanctimonious, religiose, falsely pious, empty, Pharisaic, uncandid, unfrank, unctuous, oily, mealy-mouthed, flattering, Pecksniffian, mocking, unserious, tongue-in-cheek, nonsensical, goody-goody (Inf), sweet-talking (Inf), soft-soaping (Inf).

I

ideal model, exemplary, paradigmatic, epitomical, quintessential, prototypical, archetypical, visionary, fantastic, idealistic, optimistic, utopian, romantic, sentimental, dreamy, impractical, ideological.

idealistic Platonic, Neo-Platonic, Hegelian, Kantian.

ideational mental, cerebral, intellectual, imagined, visualized, conceived, conceptualized, inspired, aware, reflective, inventive, creative, original, ingenious, fanciful.

identified recognized, substantiated, corroborated, identifiable, recognizable, known, designated, denoted, labelled, tagged, marked, hallmarked, trademarked, earmarked, characterized, classified, categorized, referenced, signatory, symbolic(al), sigillary, finger-printed, photographed, branded, tattooed. See also heraldic.

idiotic foolish, imbecilic, halfwitted, stupid, daft, absurd.

idle inactive, unemployed, jobless; lazy, shiftless, indolent; foolish, vain, frivolous, futile.

idolatrous iconolatrous, superstitious, cult, heathen, pagan, totemic, fetishistic, phallic, bibliolatrous, ecclesiolatrous, allotheistic, animistic, anthropomorphic, zoolatrous, theriolatrous, ophiolatrous, heliolatrous, Sabaic, pyrolatrous, dendrolatrous, diabolic, Satanic, mammonolatrous, necrolatrous, ancestor-worshipping.

ignominious shameful, disgraceful, scandalous, dishonourable, humiliating.

ignorant unknowing, nescient, incognizant, unwitting, unaware, oblivious, unconscious, blank, uninformed, misled, unskilled, uninitiated, green, naive, simple, innocent, gauche, awkward, unenlightened, backward, illiterate, uneducated, low-brow, Philistine, stupid, dull, dim-witted, slow-witted, thick, empty-headed, clueless (Sl), dumb (Inf), nerdy (Sl). See also semi-skilled, unknown.

ill sickly, faint, pale, pallid, bloodless, anaemic, asthenic, groggy, languid, feeble, weakly, wasted, thin, skinny, emaciated, skin-and-bone, anorexic, frail, decrepit, infirm, crippled, lame, hobbling, shaky, feeble-minded, slow, dim-witted (Inf), poorly (Inf), gammy (Sl).

immature

illegitimate unlawful, illicit, illegal, forbidden, improper, impermissible; bastard, base, fatherless, spurious.

illogical improbable, impractical, immaterial, incommensurable, nonessential, extrinsic, aleatoric, random, arbitrary, incidental, remote, far-fetched, distant, out-of-the-way, strained, laboured, forced.

illusory imaginary, subjective, fantastic, dreamlike, chimerical, phantasmagorical, fanciful, hallucinatory, figmental, visional, delusory.

imaginable conceivable, thinkable, fanciable.

imaginary unreal, abstract, illusory, fanciful, chimerical, ethereal, unsubstantial, subjective, hypothetical, suppositional, conceptual, notional, ideal, dreamy, visionary, shadowy, fictitious, fictional, storybook, make-believe, created, invented, fabricated, contrived, devised, pretend, simulated, imitated, nonexistent, untrue, unhistorical, mythical, legendary, fabulous.

imaginative creative, inventive, innovative, original, ingenious, resourceful, enterprising, skilful, clever, eidetic, visualizing, perceptive, fertile, fecund, productive, inspired, fancy-led, romancing, high-flown, rhapsodic, enthusiastic, exaggerated, lively, vivid, poetic, fictional, Utopian, idealistic, dreamy. *See also* fantastical, imaginary, imaginable.

imitation mock, sham, fake, forged, plagiarized, copied, counterfeit, ersatz, artificial, synthetic, cultured, man-made, pseudo (Inf), phoney (Inf), so-called, copycat (Inf).

imitative artificial, phoney, synthetic, simulated, substituted, cultured, unnatural, unoriginal, copied, plastic, man-made, fake, bogus, sham, mock, quack, counterfeit, forged, shoddy, rubbishy; derivative, unoriginal, parodied, transcribed, mimetic, onomatopoeic, emulating, echoing, aping, parrot-like, following, posing, apish, echoic, fugal. *See also* imitation.

immaterial insignificant, inessential, irrelevant, unimportant, trivial, inconsequential.

immature ungrown, unripe, green, unmellowed, unseasoned, unblown, unfledged, unlicked, callow, nonadult, adolescent, young, juvenile, childish, puerile, undeveloped, backward, retarded, unhatched, unborn, inchoate, embryonic, rudimentary, elementary, unformed, unfashioned, unhewn, unwrought, unworked, uncut, rough-hewn, unpolished, unfinished, raw, crude, imperfect, coarse, boorish, rude, savage, uncivilized, premature, forward, precocious, forced, abortive; inexperienced, budding, aspiring, upstart, parvenu, amateurish, amateur, novice, apprentice, embryonic, inchoate, newborn, youthful, virginal, dewy, callow, green, raw,

immeasurable

naive, ingenuous, innocent, fresh, clean; larval, pupal, chrysalid.

immeasurable vast, immense, enormous, astronomical, incalculable, uncountable, innumerable, myriad, numberless, untold, indeterminable, inestimable, unfathomable, incomprehensible, transcendent, mind-boggling (Inf).

immediate instantaneous, prompt, quick, fast, rapid, swift, speedy, direct, split-second, urgent, on-the-spot. *See also* allowing no delay, prepared for immediate use.

immersed submersed, submerged, baptized, interred, buried.

imminent forthcoming, impending, looming, expected soon, at hand.

immobile motionless, still, immovable, unmoving, fixed, rooted.

immoral amoral, unethical, unprincipled, unscrupulous, bad, wicked, wrong, evil, criminal, illegal, dishonest; vicious, unvirtuous, ruined, scarlet, unchaste, impure, indecent, obscene, gross, shocking, outrageous, lustful, vulgar, carnal, debauched, degenerate, profligate, depraved, degraded, perverse, amoral. *See also* indecent, unchaste, lecherous, unlawful.

immortal enduring, abiding, everlasting, eternal, undying, endless.

immovable immobile, fixed, secure, stationary, rooted, rigid; steadfast, inflexible, staunch, unshakable, unyielding.

immune exempt, protected, resistant, safe, clear.

impartial equanimous, fair, neutral, nonaligned, mugwumpish, nonpartisan, disinterested, unbiased, unprejudiced, nonjudgmental, uncriticizing, tolerant, liberal, broadminded, just, fair.

impassioned fervent, ardent, passionate, heated, intense.

impatient short-tempered, irritable, testy, abrupt, curt, brusque; eager, impetuous, fretful, nervous, jumpy.

impeccable perfect, flawless, immaculate, spotless, faultless.

impelling impellent, impulsive, pulsive, dynamic, motive, moving, thrusting, thrustful, driving, ramming, smashing, thrashing, flogging.

impenitent unrepentant, incorrigible, inveterate, obdurate, obstinate, brazen, shameless, unreformed, unregretting, unsorry, unapologetic, uncontrite, unmoved, unashamed, unblushing, remorseless, unsorrowful, unregretful, regretless, without compunction, conscienceless, heartless, cold-hearted, hard-hearted, hardened, callous, indurative, untouched, hopeless, lost, irreclaimable, irredeemable, unreconciled, unreformed, unregenerated, unchastened, unrecanting, unshriven, dyed-in-the-wool. *See also* unatoned.

imperative essential, urgent, vital, crucial, obligatory, pressing.

imperceptible inconspicuous, unimpressive, faint, shadowy, vague, indistinct, underwhelming (Inf).

imperfect flawed, faulty, defective, fallible, peccable, irregular, uneven, patchy, unsteady, weak, vulnerable, bungled, botched, damaged, broken, cracked, leaky, unsound, soiled, stained, spotted, marked, scratched, chipped, blemished, tainted, corked, stale, over-ripe, bad, off, off-colour, below par, off form, unfit, unhealthy, unsatisfactory, unacceptable, second-best, second-rate, inferior, poor, unimpressive, worthless, dodgy (Inf). *See also* incomplete, deformed, ordinary.

impermanent temporary, one-off, single-use, throwaway, biodegradable, nondurable, brittle, fragile, mortal.

impersonal remote, detached, cold, formal, objective, dispassionate.

imperturbable cool, calm, self-possessed, unruffled, serene, tranquil.

impetuous reckless, hasty, rash, impulsive, heedless, precipitate.

impious irreligious, ungodly, blasphemous, sacrilegious, profane, accursed, damned, reprobate, infernal, devilish, diabolical, satanic, fiendish, Mephistophelian.

important primary, pre-eminent, urgent, imperative, prominent, distinct, eminent, weighty, grave, solemn, serious, pregnant, big, consequential, significant, considerable, world-shattering, earth-shaking, momentous, critical, crucial, fateful, chief, cardinal, capital, staple, major, main, top, paramount, supreme, prime, foremost, leading, overriding, overruling, uppermost, superior, essential, material, relevant, pivotal, central, basic, fundamental, bedrock, radical, worthwhile, valuable, necessary, vital, indispensable, irreplaceable, key, required, helpful, useful, telling, trenchant, meaningful, high-priority, high-level, top-level, summit, top-secret, confidential, high, grand, noble, great, hush-hush (Inf). *See also* notable.

imposing impressive, majestic, dignified, striking, stately.

impossible inconceivable, unthinkable, unimaginable, unquestionable, unreasonable, illogical, ridiculous, preposterous, irrational, paradoxical, self-contradictory, self-defeating. *See also* unbelievable, hopeless, forbidden.

impotent weak, feeble, frail, debilitated, etiolated, tired, fatigued, exhausted, used up, decrepit, senile, paraplegic, paralytic, unconscious, comatose, catatonic, drugged, insensible, incapacitated, disabled, paralysed, crippled, incontinent, prostrate, supine, irresolute, spineless, unnerved, demoralized, shell-shocked, helpless, drifting, rudderless, grounded, fixed (Inf), zonked (Sl).

impractical idealistic, visionary, unworkable, impossible, pointless, preposterous.

imprecise inaccurate, inexact, vague, ill-defined, hazy.

impressionable susceptible, sensitive, formable, nonresistive, easing, mollifying, appeasing, complying, adapting.

impressive commanding, striking, exciting, powerful, imposing, awe-inspiring.

imprisoned captive, on remand, in detention, confined, interned, incarcerated, restricted, behind bars, in (Inf), inside (Inf).

improbable unlikely, uncertain, doubtful, dubious, unpromising, inauspicious, unrealistic, remote, farfetched, unexpected. *See also* questionable, unexpected.

improper incorrect, unsuitable, unfit, inappropriate, inapt, incongruous, indecorous, unseemly, unbecoming, vulgar.

improvable perfectible, ameliorable, reformable, corrigible, curable.

improved better, superior, enhanced, beautified, reformed, transformed, revised, edited, rewritten, repaired, restored, renovated, modernized, recovering, recuperating, rising, increasing, wiser. *See also* improvable, improving.

improving advancing, ameliorative, remedial, restorative, reforma-

tive, progressive, radical, extreme, civilizing, cultural, idealistic, perfectionist, Utopian, millenarian, chiliastic.

improvised makeshift, juryrigged, inventive, ad hoc, impromptu, ad-lib, extemporaneous, unrehearsed, unprepared, unpremeditated, uncalculated, catchas-catch-can (US), offhand, off-thecuff (Inf). *See also* spontaneous.

imprudent careless, unwise, foolish, reckless, unthinking.

impudent impertinent, pert, flippant, cocky, cheeky, fresh, brazen, brazen-faced, brassy, bold, unblushing, shameless.

impulsive hasty, impetuous, rash, emotional, precipitate, quick.

impure contaminated, tainted, infected, polluted, sullied, unclean.

inaccurate imprecise, mistaken, careless, defective, faulty.

inactive inert, impotent, powerless, negligent, abstaining, suspended, dormant, inoperative, deadlocked, stalemated, stationary, quiescent, immobile, motionless, still, calm, tranquil, quiet, stagnant, halfdead, dead, extinct, benumbed, frozen, paralysed, impassive, insensible, passive, apathetic, phlegmatic, dull, sluggish, leisured, relaxed, lazy, indolent, idle, fallow, unoccupied, unemployed, laid off, redundant, jobless, ostrich-like, Fabian, refraining, procrastinating, cunctative, indifferent, neutral, hands-off, blind, deaf. *See also* not working, not participating, not awake.

inadequate insufficient, deficient, lacking, scarce, meagre, scant, skimpy.

inadmissible unacceptable, inappropriate, disallowed, banned, irrelevant.

inadvisable imprudent, unwise, injudicious, impolitic, inexpedient, uncommendable.

inappropriate unfitting, unsuitable, inapposite, improper, untimely.

inarticulate unintelligible, aphasic, dysphasic, dysphemic, stammering, stuttering, paraphasic, babbling, lisping, sibilant, hissing, sighing.

inattentive thoughtless, unthinking, incurious, unmindful, forgetful, heedless, unconcerned, detached, oblivious, apathetic, listless, disregarding, distracted, unobservant. *See also* absent-minded, thoughtless, careless, perfunctory.

inaugural inauguratory, incipient, inchoative, foundational, institutionary, establishing, instigatory.

inaugurated initiated, opened, unveiled, launched, premiered.

inauspicious unfavourable, unfortunate, unlucky, adverse, ominous, accursed, jinxed; unpropitious, ill-omened, ill-starred, doomed.

incapable weak, powerless, feeble, unable, inadequate, inept.

incautious unwise, hasty, rash, impulsive, indiscreet, imprudent.

included built-in, integrated, unsegregated, unseparated, constituent, component, inherent, intrinsic, belonging, pertinent, appurtenant, admissible, allowed, eligible, classed with, related, akin, congenerous, entered, listed, noted, recorded, added, linked, joined, combined, merged.

including containing, holding, accommodating, having, allowing, considering, counting, consisting of, comprising, composed of, incorporating, all-in, comprehensive, wholesale, blanket, extensive, widespread, across-the-board, wall-to-wall, sweeping, global, expansive, broad-based, umbrella, overall, general, encyclopedic, nonexclusive, nondiscriminatory. *See also* included.

inclusive embodied, incorporated, comprehensive, encompassing.

incomparable unequalled, unrivalled, unique, beyond compare, supreme, unmatched.

incompatible conflicting, contradictory, irreconcilable, discordant, mismatched.

incompetent inadequate, incapable, unfit, useless, unable, bungling.

incomplete defective, scant, skimpy, short, insufficient, inadequate, ineffective, ineffectual, missing, omitting, lacking, wanting, needing, requiring, short of, shy of,

incomprehensible

shortened, abbreviated, abridged, truncated, curtailed, cropped, docked, lopped, maimed, mutilated, mangled, marred, spoiled, impaired, garbled, broken, fragmentary, unsatisfactory, blemished, stained, flawed, imperfect, half, partial, unfinished, developing, in progress, in embryo, in preparation, half-finished, neglected, under-developed, unprepared, unready, unripe, immature, raw, underdone, undercooked, rude, rough, crude, roughhewn, sketchy, scrappy, bitty, thin, poor, meagre, hollow, superficial, insubstantial, perfunctory, halfhearted, interrupted.

incomprehensible inexplicable, puzzling, baffling, mysterious, unfathomable, obscure.

inconsiderate thoughtless, insensitive, uncaring, unconcerned, unfeeling, unresponsive, unheedful, unmindful, unhelpful, unobliging, unaccommodating, unsympathetic, unkind, unfriendly, sullen, ungracious, inhospitable, unchristian, uncharitable, ungenerous.

inconsistent conflicting, contradictory, at odds, incompatible; changeable, variable, erratic, capricious, fickle.

inconspicuous insignificant, hazy, hidden, dim, vague, misty.

inconvenient discommodious, disadvantageous, detrimental, inexpedient, inadvisable, undesirable, uncommendable, ill-advised, ill-considered, impolitic, imprudent, injudicious, unwise, inappropriate, unfitting, misapplied, malapropos, improper, unseemly, undue, objectionable, offensive, wrong, unfit, unsuitable, ineligible, unqualified, inadmissible, unfortunate, infelicitous, inept, unapt, inopportune, unseasonable, untimely, disruptive, disturbing, unsettling, useless, unprofitable, unhelpful, hindering, untoward, adverse, unprofessional, ill-contrived, ill-planned, awkward, clumsy, cumbersome, lumbering, hulking, unwieldy, burdensome, onerous, troublesome, bothersome, annoying, irritating, irksome, boring, tiresome, vexatious, tedious. *See also* distant.

incorrect inaccurate, imprecise, false, untrue, fallacious, unsound, invalid, erroneous, mistaken, misinformed.

incorrigible intractable, hardened, obdurate, bloody-minded, irredeemable.

incorruptible honest, trustworthy, upright, just, straight.

increased enlarged, magnified, accelerated, swollen, bloated, expanded, extended, stretched, intensified, heightened, enhanced, augmented, supplemented, hiked (Inf).

increasing progressive, expanding, growing, spreading, escalating, crescent, waxing, filling, ever-increasing, cumulative, snowballing, augmentative, prolific, additional, supplementary. *See also* increased.

incredible unbelievable, far-

fetched, absurd, inconceivable, preposterous, unthinkable.

in credit creditworthy.

incredulous unbelieving, dubious, sceptical, distrustful, doubting.

incurious uninquisitive, unquestioning, trusting, credulous, gullible.
See also uninterested.

in debt pledged, bound, obliged,
committed, encumbered, mortgaged, liable, responsible, accountable, answerable, beholden, bor-
rowing, owing, unpaid, due, overdrawn, minus. *See also* unable to
pay.

indecent salacious, prurient, lewd,
lubricious, indelicate, improper,
suggestive, provocative, risqué, titillating, arousing, erotic, naughty,
blue, coarse, crude, vulgar, ribald,
strong, racy, louche, bawdy, Rabelaisian, unwholesome, insalubrious, defiling, corrupting, depraving,
impure, unclean, dirty, smutty,
filthy, scrofulous, scabrous, scata-
logical, stinking, rank, offensive,
shocking, obscene, pornographic,
uncensored, unexpurgated, fruity
(Inf).

indecisive uncertain, hesitant,
doubtful, tentative, irresolute, wavering.

indecorous unseemly, improper,
indelicate, crude, vulgar, tasteless,
rude, discourteous, impolite, gross,
coarse, boorish, churlish, uncouth,
barbaric, unrefined, unpolished,
infra dignitatem (L.), infra dig.

indefensible inexcusable, unpar-

donable, wrong, faulty, unforgivable, unjustifiable.

indefinite imprecise, indeterminate, unclear, vague, uncertain, inexact.

indelicate coarse, gross, improper,
indecent, tasteless, vulgar.

indemonstrable unverifiable, un-
provable, unconfirmable, unlikely,
improbable, unpredictable.

independent individual, self-em-
ployed, freelance, wildcat, free-
minded, maverick, individualistic,
self-reliant, self-sufficient, self-contained, self-supporting, self-moti-
vated, inner-directed, unsubjected,
freewheeling, ungoverned, anarchic, uncontrolled, uncompelled,
uninfluenced, unattached, indifferent, unconventional, breakaway,
dissenting, rationalist, humanist,
atheistic(al), nonbelieving, latitudi-
narian, bohemian, nonconforming,
eccentric, nonconformist, cowboy
(Inf).

indescribable inexpressible, unutterable, unspeakable, unmentionable.

indestructible enduring, lasting,
permanent, imperishable, immortal.

indeterminate indefinite, vague,
unclear, undefined, borderline, ambiguous, equivocal, indistinct, obscure, inaccurate, inexact, imprecise, broad, general, amorphous.

indifferent disinterested, incurious, uninquisitive, apathetic, detached, dispassionate, uninvolved,
withdrawn, aloof, carefree, fancy-

free, noncommittal, impersonal, matter-of-fact, unconcerned, uncaring, unresponsive, unaware, oblivious, insensible to, blind to, deaf to, dead to, lost to, unconscious, inert, inactive, ataractic, listless, dispirited, sluggish, inappetant, phlegmatic(al), lethargic, half-hearted, perfunctory, impassive, pococurante, blasé, easy-going, unsurprised, inexcitable, unimpressed, unaffected, unfeeling, untouched, unemotional, unmoved, unruffled, calm, lukewarm, cool, cold, frigid, frosty, cold-hearted, cold-blooded, unmoved, nonchalant, insouciant, unaffectionate, undesirous, passionless, lackadaisical, insensible, insensitive, thick-skinned, dull, deadpan, numb, benumbed, laid-back (Inf). *See also* careless, impartial, mediocre, insignificant.

indignant annoyed, angry, furious, irate, incensed.

indirect turning, curving, roundabout, winding, bending, meandering, snaking, serpentine, labyrinthine, mazy, shifting, swerving, deflected, twisting, veering, zigzag, crooked, out-of-the-way, off-course, off target, wide, lost, astray.

indiscreet foolish, rash, imprudent, reckless, heedless, hasty.

indiscriminate random, haphazard, unsystematic, mixed, assorted, unsorted, unselected, miscellaneous, motley, unorganized, confused, jumbled, muddled, intermingled, disordered, chaotic, scrambled, higgledy-piggledy (Inf).

indispensable essential, crucial, vital, necessary, key, fundamental.

indistinct blurred, confused, vague, indefinite, unclear, shadowy.

individual unique, separate, distinctive, exclusive, single, personal.

indomitable undefeated, unconquerable, unbeaten, undaunted, undiscouraged, undeterred, game, plucky, gutsy (Sl).

indulgent tolerant, liberal, favourable, permissive, compliant.

industrious sedulous, diligent, assiduous, studious, persevering, hardworking, workaholic, plodding, slogging, laborious, unflagging, tireless, indefatigable, energetic, efficient, workmanlike, businesslike, professional.

inefficient inept, incompetent, careless, incapable, weak.

inelegant dysphemistic, cacological, turgid, pompous, rhetorical, grandiloquent, formal, stiff, stilted, wooden, unfluent, ill-sounding, cacophonous, uneuphonious, jarring, grating, incorrect, solecistic, doggerel, artless, unnatural, artificial, affected, laboured, tortuous, ludicrous, grotesque.

ineligible unacceptable, unfit, unsuitable.

inept clumsy, awkward, incompetent, unskilful, inefficient; inappropriate, unsuitable, absurd, foolish.

inert inactive, passive, apathetic, indifferent, unexcitable, pacific, unaggressive, unwarlike, peaceful, unreactive, indecisive, irresolute, unresponsive, stolid, idle, lazy, indolent, slack, lax, limp, flaccid, heavy, slothful, lumpish, doltish, sluggish, slow, slumbrous (Fml), dull, numb, dormant, smouldering, latent, dead, lifeless, languid, torpid, insensible, hibernating, sleepy, immobile, unmoving, motionless, still, static, stagnant, vegetating, paralysed, quiet, quiescent, fallow, gutless (Inf). *See also* suspended.

inevitable destined, predestined, determined, predetermined, fixed, set, fated, unstoppable, ineluctable, necessary, certain, inescapable, unavoidable, inevasible, unpreventable, relentless, inflexible, inexorable, unyielding, directed, headed for. *See also* exchanged.

inexpensive cheap, low-cost, economical.

inexplicable baffling, unexplainable, incomprehensible, puzzling, mysterious.

infallible reliable, dependable, trustworthy, predictable, regular, stable, solid, secure, unshakeable, unwavering, unchanging, undeviating, steady, steadfast, firm, sound, staunch, faithful, loyal, stoical.

infatuated bewitched, besotted, fascinated, obsessed, captivated.

infectious contagious, transmittable, catching, infective, virulent.

inferior low-quality, low-grade, faulty, flawed, imperfect, defective, substandard, shoddy, punk, tawdry, trashy, rubbishy, cheap, second-class, second-rate, unsatisfactory, bad, incompetent, inefficient, unskilled, clumsy, bungled, botched, mangled, spoiled, ruined, crummy (Sl), pathetic (Inf), tacky (Inf), naff (Sl), crappy (Sl), ropy (Inf). *See also* insignificant, poor, subordinate, ordinary, defective, outclassed.

infertile infecund, fruitless, unproductive, unprolific, barren, sterile, impotent, celibate, childless, fallow, arid, dry, drought-stricken, desert, gaunt, bleak, uncultivated, stony, withered, shrivelled, dead, blasted, waste, wild, desolate, stagnant, recessionary, low-yield. *See also* rendered infertile, having no effect.

infinite boundless, limitless, bottomless, endless, interminable, recurring. *See also* immeasurable, eternal.

infirm feeble, frail, weak, doddering, failing.

inflexible unbending, unrelenting, inexorable, implacable, unyielding, intractable.

inflicting pain painful, hurtful, torturing, tormenting, brutal, cruel, sadistic.

influenced persuaded, brainwashed, converted, saved, revived, reborn, proselytized, evangelized.

influential causal, effectual, persuasive, important, significant, contributing, decisive, momentous, world-shattering, telling, prestigious, impressive, potent, powerful, interfering, mighty, forceful, superior, ruling, leading, guiding, directing, instructive, educative, reigning, commanding, authoritative, tyrannical. *See also* appealing, dominant.

informal relaxed, casual, easygoing, at home, retired, familiar, frank, candid, open, self-expressive, plain-spoken, uninhibited, unconstrained, spontaneous, willing, degage, unbuttoned (Inf). *See also* sociable, familiar, free.

informative revealing, illuminating, enlightening, explicit, clear, definite, expressive, expository, instructive, educational, advisory, cautionary, monitory, communicative, indicating, insinuating, suggesting, candid, plain-spoken, indiscreet, gossipy, big-mouthed (Sl). *See also* newsworthy, informed.

informed enlightened, alert (to), aware (of), advised (of), briefed, posted, in touch, au fait.

infuriating exasperating, annoying, vexatious, maddening.

ingenious clever, inventive, skilful, gifted, talented, resourceful.

ingenuous naive, guileless, innocent, simple, trustful, unsophisticated.

inhabited occupied, populated, lived in, indwelt, residential, tenanted, rented, leased, let, freehold, squatted, communal. *See also* native, resident.

inhabiting residential, at home, dwelling, domiciled, housed, roofed, lodged, billeted, sheltered. *See also* environmental, manorial.

in hand operational.

inhibitive introversive, conservative, embarrassing, shy, negative, foot-dragging (Inf).

inhuman cruel, barbaric, bestial, merciless, unfeeling, callous.

inhumane cruel, heartless, brutal, unkind.

iniquitous criminal, evil, immoral, sinful, base, infamous.

injected inoculated, vaccinated, implanted, impregnated, infused, perfused.

injured wounded, bruised, grazed, cut, punctured, scraped, sprained, lacerated, torn, fractured, broken, blackened.

inland landlocked, central, upstate, upcountry, midland, continental.

in love infatuated with, smitten (with), enamoured of, fond of, sweet on, keen on, mad about, set on, engaged to, wedded to, caught, hooked (Sl).

innocent virtuous, good, upright, pure, virginal, chaste, saintly, perfect, angelic, immaculate, unblemished, untainted, stainless, spotless, unsullied, undefiled, clean, pristine, white, prelapsarian, faultless, impeccable, unerring, blameless, irreprehensible, inculpable, reproachless, guiltless, uncorrupt, incorrupt, gentle, inoffensive, harmless, innocuous, safe, playful, goody-goody (Inf), clean (Sl). *See also* declared innocent, naive.

inoffensive harmless, innocent, peaceable, mild, innocuous.

insane mad, deranged, demented, abnormal, disturbed, unbalanced, unhinged, alienated, weird, peculiar, odd, anile, doited, mental (Inf), certifiable (Inf), wacky (Inf), screwy (Inf), kinky (Inf), cranky (Inf), crazy (Inf), daft (Inf), touched (Inf), cracked (Inf), crackers (Inf), crack-brained (Inf), cuckoo (Inf), dolally (Dial), bonkers (Inf), nutty (Inf), nuts (Inf), barmy (Inf), bananas (Sl), bats (Inf), batty (Inf), dotty (Inf), dippy (Sl), loopy (Sl). *See also* manic, mentally ill.

inscrutable baffling, mystifying, cryptic, enigmatic, arcane, recondite, unclear, ambiguous, indefinite, unknowable, unfathomable, unintelligible.

insectivorous anteating, pholidote, tubulidentate, edentate, toothless.

insecure anxious, uncertain, nervous, afraid; dangerous, unstable, frail, precarious.

insensitive insensible, unsusceptible, immune, unresponsive, unimpressionable, unaffected, indifferent, apathetic, impassive, unfeeling, insensate, unemotional, frigid, cold-hearted, cold-blooded, heartless, thick-skinned, impervious, proof against, rhino-hided, obtuse, blunt, tactless, unimaginative, callous, uncaring, tough, hard, blind, deaf, unaware, unconscious, imperceptive,

dull, thick (Inf). *See also* desensitized.

inseparable indivisible, indissoluble, cohesive; close, intimate, devoted, thick as thieves.

inserted introduced, introjected, insinuated, added, interpolated, intercalated, parenthetical, by-the-by, imported, infixed, impacted, planted, transplanted, grafted, embedded, tessellated, inlaid, included. *See also* injected, immersed.

insidious crafty, cunning, sly, wily, guileful.

insignificant unimportant, trivial, irrelevant, inconsequential, immaterial, boring; minimal, small, inconsiderable, diminished, small-time, unimportant, lightweight, small-town, one-horse (Inf).

insincere false, two-faced, devious, duplicitous, lying, deceitful.

insipid pallid, bland, diluted, watered-down, tasteless, half-hearted, vapid, wersh (Scot), wishy-washy (Inf).

insolent impudent, malapert, impertinent, bumptious, contumelious, flip (Inf). *See also* cheeky, audacious, arrogant, contemptuous, insulting, rude, discourteous, impudent.

insolvent in debt, owing, bankrupt, ruined, impoverished, pauperized, broken, dispossessed, stripped, fleeced, stony-broke (Sl), skint (Sl), strapped (Sl), hurting (Inf), hard-pressed (Inf), bust (Inf).

inspired animated, brilliant, exciting, thrilling, impressive.

inspiring encouraging, stimulating, uplifting, exciting, elevating.

instant instantaneous, immediate, prompt, direct, sudden.

instinctive automatic, spontaneous, reflex, innate, Pavlovian, knee-jerk (Inf).

instrumental useful, applicable, employable, utilizable, handy, helping, assisting, cooperative, advancing, promoting, aiding, supportive, subordinate, subservient, effective, efficient, effectual, efficacious, performance-oriented; vocal, choral, operatic, liturgical, hymnal, psalmic, minimalist, contrapuntal, bass, baritone, alto, tenor, soprano, treble. *See also* causal, practical.

insubstantial ethereal, rare, sublime, airy, gaseous, volatile, frothy, foamy, whipped, whisked, bubbly, effervescent, *pétillant* (Fr), sparkling, downy, feathery, cobwebby, gossamery, fluffy, soft, gentle, delicate, dainty, tender, flimsy, floaty, buoyant, unsinkable, levitative.

insufferable intolerable, unbearable, detestable.

insufficient inadequate, unsatisfactory, disappointing, unacceptable, insubstantial, limited, cramped, slender, meagre, skimpy, scanty, sketchy, deficient, incomplete, lacking, wanting, poor, inferior, incompetent, incapable, unequal to, weak, thin, watery, wersh (Scot), jejune, undernourished, underfed, niggardly, miserly, mean. *See also* unprovided, underfed, scarce.

insulting abusive, offensive, pejorative, defamatory, opprobrious, contumacious, outrageous, snubbing, slighting, rebuffing, repulsing, spurning, cutting.

integral inseparable, ineradicable, built-in, component, constituent, indivisible, integrated.

intellectual scholarly, studious, learned, academic, intelligent.

intelligent understanding, clever, learned, erudite, knowledgeable, wise, sage, sagacious, bright, smart, shrewd, astute, brilliant, alert, sharp, acute, quick-witted, keen-witted, gifted, brainy (Inf).

intelligible comprehensible, understandable, knowable, apprehensible, fathomable, penetrable, scrutable, interpretable, realizable, coherent, sane, audible, visible, luminous, unambiguous, unequivocal, univocal, meaningful, explicable, teachable, focused, clear-cut, precise, certain, positive, striking, vivid, graphic, descriptive, illustrative, explanatory, interpretative, informative. *See also* simple, recognizable.

intended meant, deliberate, intentional, voluntary, volitional, wilful, calculated, studied, planned, designed, purposeful, premeditated, aforethought, predetermined, eshatological.

intending resolute, serious, seeking, purposive, teleological, inclined, disposed, prospective, would-be, hopeful, aspiring, ambitious, hellbent (Inf). *See also* intended.

intense strong, powerful, acute, forceful, extreme; eager, ardent, fervent, passionate, keen.

intentional planned, deliberate, premeditated, studied, purposeful.

interconnected interrelated, interlocking, interlinked, interdependent, mutual, symbiotic, cooperative, two-way, bilateral, complementary, opposite.

interesting fascinating, absorbing, engaging, intriguing, amusing.

interfacial contiguous, adjacent, adjoining, meeting, abutting, liminal, interactive, confrontational, divisive, shared, common, same, cooperative, compatible, blended, dovetailed, permeated, interpenetrative, intermediary.

interior internal, central, inside, inward, inner, undersurfaced, enclosed, endemic, endodermal, subcutaneous, subcortical, intravenous, substrative, deep. *See also* internal, inland, visceral, intrinsic, internalized.

interminable endless, long, protracted, ceaseless, everlasting, boring.

internal nonexternal, subjective, personal, solipsist, conscious, subconscious, unconscious, psychoanalytic, mental, abstract.

internalized intimate, personal, private, secret, hidden, veiled, inmost, inward, self-absorbed, engrossed, egocentric, secretive, introverted.

interpreted glossed, explained, defined, illustrated, elucidated, clarified, simplified, annotated, edited, emended, amended, conflated, translated, rendered, deciphered, decoded, unscrambled, cracked, unlocked, coded, scrambled.

interpretive constructive, explanatory, explicatory, explaining, descriptive, expositive, insightful, illustrative, demonstrative, definitional, exemplary, exegetic, hermeneutic, clarifying, elucidative, illuminating, semiological, euhemeristic, demythologizing. *See also* interpreted, annotative, translational.

interrelated correlated, reciprocal, interdependent, complementary, interconnected, associated, mutual, relative, proportional, interlocked, interlinked, interallied, interassociated, interwoven, intertwined, interchanged, interacting, interworking, engaged, intermeshed, cross-referred, corresponding, agreed, similar, parallel, comparable, analogous, equal, homologous, relational, commensurate, opposite.

interrupted disturbed, disrupted, broken off, suspended; postponed, delayed, suspended, deferred, adjourned, shelved, tabled, withheld,

stopped, stayed, discontinued, abeyant, dormant, pending.

interwoven crisscross, interlaced, intertwined, webbed, braided, plaited, pleached, wreathed, reticulate, loomed, woollen, tweedy. *See also* crossing.

intimate close, cherished, dear, near, cosy, friendly; secret, private, personal; thorough, detailed, profound, exhaustive.

in time punctual, well-timed, well-judged, eleventh-hour, last-minute, deathbed.

intolerant persecuting, oppressive, racist, prejudiced, bigotted, xenophobic.

intoxicated drunk, inebriated, fuddled, tipsy.

intoxicating inebriating, temulent, stimulant, exhilarating, heady, winy, vinous, beery, spiritous, alcoholic, hard, potent, strong, proof, neat, addictive, habit-forming.

intrinsic inherent, basic, primary, fundamental, immanent, innate, inborn, inbred, deep-seated, deep-rooted, ingrained, bred-in-the-bone.

introductory introductive, initiatory, baptismal.

intuitive insightful, perceptive, sensitive, sensing, inspired; instinctive, impulsive, inspirational, clairvoyant, fey. *See also* procognitive, instinctive.

invalid ill, ailing, sick, disabled, infirm, feeble; false, untrue, baseless, null and void.

invaluable priceless, valuable, costly, precious.

invasive incursive, intrusive, trespassing, attacking, penetrating, irruptive, ingrowing, inflowing, inflooding, inpouring, inrushing.

inventive innovative, creative, original, conceptional.

inventorial glossarial, cadastral.

invertebrate protochordate, hemichordate, urochordate, cephalochordate, acraniate, coelomate, pseudocoelomate, acoelomate, metazoan, mesozoan, protozoan. *See also* echinodermal, arthropodous, molluscan, wormlike, coelenterate, spongelike, protozoan.

inverted reversed, transpositional, upside-down, head-over-heels, bottom-up, topsy-turvy, capsized, arsy-versy (Sl).

invincible unassailable, unbeatable, impregnable, indestructible.

invisible unseeable, unperceivable, imperceptible, indistinguishable, indiscernible, unnoticeable, undetectable, unrecognizable, unidentifiable, unidentified, unmarked, unapparent, inappreciable, immaterial, insubstantial, transparent, unseen, unsighted, unobserved, unwitnessed, eclipsed, latent, buried, submerged, lurking. *See also* difficult to see, private.

involuntary compulsory, impulsive, automatic, instinctive, intuitive, mechanical, autonomic, reflex.

invulnerable immune, impregnable, sacrosanct, inexpugnable, unassailable, unattackable, ungettable, unbreakable, unchallengeable, defensible, tenable, strong, proof, foolproof, fail-safe, mothproof, childproof, weatherproof, waterproof, showerproof, leakproof, rustproof, fireproof, shatterproof, bulletproof, bombproof, armoured, steel-clad, panoplied, snug, tight, seaworthy, airworthy, shrinkwrapped, vacuum-packed, freeze-dried, frozen.

inward incoming, ingoing, entering, penetrating; inner, inside, interior, private, personal.

irascible irritable, impatient, nervous, jumpy, strained, fretful, oversensitive, touchy, tetchy, thin-skinned, petulant, peevish, querulous, testy, temperamental, short-tempered, highly-strung, short, huffy, annoyed, resentful, sullen, sore, riled, nettled, ill-humoured, snappish, bellicose, waspish, sharp-tongued, tart, acerbic, sour, acid, shrewish, vixenish, crusty, ornery, prickly, peppery, hot-blooded, hot-tempered, quick-tempered, short-tempered, grumpy, gruff, cross, cantankerous, churlish, fractious, bilious, dyspeptic, contentious, quarrelsome, disputatious, argumentative, belligerent, angry, mean, bearish, grouchy (Inf), crotchety (Inf), crabby (Inf), uptight (Inf). *See also* showing irascibility.

iridescent opalescent, nacreous, pearly, semitransparent, shot, pavonine, moiré, watered, chatoyant.

irksome irritating, annoying, aggravating, tiresome, boring, troublesome.

iron-willed determined, purposeful, steadfast, resolute, adamant, unyielding, tenacious, single-minded, self-controlled.

irrational absurd, crazy, illogical, preposterous, ludicrous, nonsensical.

irrefutable certain, sure, undeniable, indisputable, invincible.

irregular nonuniform, unequal, asymmetric, uneven, rough, choppy, spotty, patchy, broken, disconnected, discontinuous, sporadic, spasmodic, halting, infrequent, intermittent, fluctuating, changeable, wavering, variable, diverse, inconsistent, erratic, inconstant, unpredictable, random, fitful, capricious, restless, desultory, unmethodically, unsystematic, unrhythmic, haphazard, disorderly, unstable, unsteady, oscillatory, wobbly, shaky, jerky, flickering, staggering, lurching, careening, veering, bumpy. *See also* unusual.

irrelevant immaterial, inappropriate, unrelated, beside the point.

irreproachable faultless, innocent, pure, perfect, guiltless, immaculate.

irresistible overpowering, compelling, potent; fascinating, alluring, seductive, tempting.

irresolute hesitating, vacillating,

irresponsible seesawing, fickle, whimsical, moody, wayward, capricious, desultory, malleable, impressionable, yielding, flighty, dizzy, giddy, scatterbrained, light-headed, light-minded, volatile, mercurial, restless, fidgety, shifty, disloyal, unfaithful, traitorous, scatty (Inf).

irresponsible careless, unreliable, untrustworthy, thoughtless.

irritable irascible, disagreeable, discontented, dissatisfied, smouldering, temperamental, bad-tempered, surly, resentful, churlish, touchy, tetchy, testy, acid, tart, vinegary, grumpy, quarrelsome, cantankerous, curmudgeonly, dyspeptic, bitter, peevish, petulant, shrewish, vixenish, cross, abrupt, brusque, gruff, frowning, unsmiling, louring, glowering, scowling, grumbling, grousing, snarling, snapping, grouchy (Inf), bitchy (Inf), bellyaching (Sl), beefing (Sl), shirty (Sl).

isolated hidden, remote, secluded, insulated, detached, dissociated.

itemized indexed, listed, coded, tabled, tabular, charted, catalogued, registered, scheduled.

iterated reiterated, retold, twice-told, recounted, related, restated, quoted, cited.

J

jaded tired, weary, fatigued, worn out; bored, glutted, gorged.

jazz syncopated, avant-garde, cool, traditional, trad, Dixieland, swinging, punk, folksy.

jealous envious, covetous, jaundiced, jaundice-eyed, green, green-eyed, yellow, yellow-eyed, lynx-eyed, sour, resentful, possessive, hostile, invidious, rival, competitive, emulative. *See also* distrustful.

jocular comical, witty, jesting, waggish, funny, humorous, droll.

joined joining, jointed, mitred, timbered, housed, flitched, mortised, dovetailed, dovetailing, cogged, cogging, trimmed, trimming, framed, framing, joisted, herringbone, beamed, boarded, boarding, two-by-four, slatted.

joint shared, combined, collective, concerted, united, common, communal, pooled, mutual, reciprocal, correlational, interrelating, interactive, communalist(ic), collectivist(ic), communist, socialist, ecumenic(al).

journalistic reportorial, reportable, editorial, newsworthy, newsy, informative, reported.

jovial jolly, cheery, convivial, gay, hearty.

jubilant elated, joyous, ecstatic, excited, exultant, glad, overjoyed.

judged selected, distinct, discrete, diagnosed, interpreted, differentiated, sorted, graded, demarcated, divided, segregated, persecuted, exploited, oppressed; on trial, sub judice.

judging discriminating, discerning, selecting, criticizing, judgmen-

labour-saving

tal, inquisitional, moralistic, sententious, approving, appreciative, disapproving, condemnatory, censorious. *See also* judicious, judged.

judicious discerning, discriminating, sensitive, accurate, right, just, fair, unbiased, dispassionate, wise, shrewd, judicial.

juicy succulent, fleshy, sappy, overripe, runny, watery, milky, lactiferous.

jurisdictional directive, judiciary, juridical, justiciable, judicatory, judicatorial, judicial, judicative, jurisdictive, jural, jurisprudential, justiciary, curial, inquisitional, forensic, Rhadamanthine, original, appellate, tribunal, magisterial, judicious, critical.

juxtaposed adjacent, near, close, tangential, contiguous, adjoining, abutting, touching, continuous, joined, connecting, intercommunicating, bordering, conterminous, coterminous, side-by-side, cheek-by-jowl, face-to-face, nose-to-nose, eyeball-to-eyeball, end-to-end, elbow-to-elbow, bumper-to-bumper, nose-to-tail. *See also* meeting.

K

kind goodly, nice, gracious, fair, virtuous, righteous, moral, honest, honourable, benevolent, helpful, good-natured, friendly, well-wishing, thoughtful, generous.

kindly compassionate, benevolent, genial, benign, cordial.

knowledgeable well-informed, omniscient, polymathic, encyclopedic, clever, intelligent, sagacious, wise, enlightened, informed, instructed, trained, cognizant, qualified, experienced, practised, versed, competent, skilled, proficient, efficient, expert, well versed, gifted, talented, good at, aware, conscious, mindful, attentive, acquainted with, conversant with, briefed, primed *au fait* (Fr), streetwise, shrewd, astute, perceptive, smart, brainy (Inf), sussed (Sl). *See also* literate, known.

known verified, proved, true, certain, discovered, explored, recognized, perceived, seen, heard of, well-known, famous, infamous, notorious, celebrated, renowned, common, public.

L

laborious strenuous, gruelling, punishing, unremitting, tiring, exhausting, backbreaking, crushing, killing, toilsome, troublesome, weary, painful, burdensome, heroic, Herculean, arduous, hard, heavy, uphill, difficult, hard-fought, hardwon, thorough, painstaking, laboured, elaborate, detailed, fussy, nit-picking (Inf).

labour-saving back-saving, time-saving, restful, reposeful, easy on, thirst-quenching.

lamentable

lamentable pitiful, tear-jerking, distressing, depressing, deplorable, regrettable.

lamenting grieving, crying, weeping, lachrymose, tearful, wailing, keening, mourning, miserable, doleful, wretched, woebegone, disconsolate, unhappy, sad, sorrowful, wet-eyed, red-eyed, plaintive, pangent, dirgelike, elegiac, threnodic, depressed, down (Sl). *See also* lamentable.

large big, enormous, huge, immense, vast, monumental.

lasting durable, enduring, long-lasting, long-lived, abiding, continuing, continuous, continual, longstanding, evergreen, long-term, lifelong; persisting, persistent, abiding, continual, continuous, surviving, perpetual. *See also* permanent.

late delayed, overdue, unpunctual, dilatory, unready, unprepared, tardy, behindhand, slow, sluggish. *See also* held up, late in the day, delaying, later, dead.

latent dormant, sleeping, hibernating, aestivating, inactive, passive, quiescent, inert, delitescent, undeveloped, potential, possible, virtual, subconscious, subliminal, submerged, underlying, archetyp(ic)al, unacknowledged, subterranean, deep. *See also* concealed, unsolved, unsaid, mysterious.

later future, distant, upcoming.

laughing giggling, tittering, laughable, comic, humorous, hilarious, side-splitting (Inf).

lavish plentiful, copious, abundant, prolific, lush, opulent.

law-breaking lawless, anarchic(al), insubordinate, insurgent, mutinous, seditious, treasonous, riotous, rebellious, revolutionary, anarchist, nihilist, terrorist, guerrilla, counter-revolutionary, insurrectionary.

layered stratified, straticulate, foliated, laminate, two-ply, three-ply, two-tiered, two-storeyed, double-decker, terraced, multistage. *See also* coated, platelike.

lazy idle, indolent, slothful, inert, inactive, languid.

leaky oozy, weeping, runny, excretory, porous, permeable, exudative, transudative.

leaping springing, vaulting, jumping, hopping, saltatory, saltant, saltatorial, skipping, prancing, bounding, bouncing, spiralling, skyrocketing.

learned wise, academic, intellectual, erudite, scholarly, profound, sagacious, enlightened, brainy (Inf).

leavening fermenting, raising, self-raising, yeasty, enzymic, diastasic, zymotic.

lecherous carnal, fleshly, voluptuous, libidinous, lustful, lickerish (Arch), concupiscent, incontinent, Paphian, sexy, hot, rampant, rutting, sex-mad, priapic, lewd, lascivious, licentious, libertine, wild, rakish, amoral, adulterous, unfaithful, dissolute, dissipated, profligate, whoremongering, debauched, depraved,

liberal

vicious, turned-on (Sl), randy (Inf), goatish (Arch).

legal lawful, licit, legitimate, valid, just, right, proper, sanctioned, allowable, permissible, permitted, authorized, licensed, warranted, legalized, legitimized, legitimatized, decriminalized, by right, de jure, legit (Sl); statutory, mandatory, compulsory, obligatory, de rigueur, regulatory, injunctive, prescriptive, procedural, administrative, official. *See also* legislative, legislated, liable to law, jurisdictional, legalistic, litigating, litigated.

legalistic litigious, disputatious, contentious, quibbling.

legislated made law, enacted, passed, decreed, ordained, codified, ratified, constitutional, statutory.

legislative nomothetic, legislatorial, legislational, decretal, nomological, jurisprudential.

legitimate legal, authentic, genuine, lawful, sanctioned, permissible.

leisure free, spare, unoccupied, recreational. *See also* leisurely.

leisurely unhurried, slow, deliberate, relaxed, easy, labour-saving, idle, inactive, resting, reposeful, leisured, unoccupied, free, available, disengaged, retired, redundant, dismissed, discharged, unemployed, jobless, non-working, fired (Inf), sacked; favour, concession, sop, humouring, consideration, leave, allowance, permission, indulgence, spoiling, gratification, kidglove treatment.

lenient lax, easy, easy-going, mild, moderate, clement, gentle, soft, tender, patient, tolerant, forbearing, long-suffering, compassionate, pitying, merciful, forgiving, reasonable, considerate, humane, benevolent, kind, gracious, charitable, accepting, magnanimous, accommodating, generous, permissive, indulgent, spoiling, kid-glove, live-and-let-live. *See also* given consideration.

lethal deadly, fatal, devastating, mortal, noxious, virulent.

lethargic apathetic, languid, dull, slow, inactive, lazy, listless.

lettered lexicographical, literal, graphic(al), printed, typed, symbolic(al), alphabetic(al), syllabic, phonogramic, phonographic, pictographic, ideographic, cuneiform, hieroglyphic(al), capital, upper-case, majuscule, uncial, lower-case, minuscule, bold, italic, sans serif, cursive, initial, monogrammatic(al), anagrammatic(al), acronymic, acrostic, voiced, vocal, vocalic, consonantal, guttural, polyphonic, polyphonous, digraphic.

liable accountable, answerable, responsible.

liberal advanced, radical, open-minded, reformist, progressive, enlightened, permissive; generous, charitable, open-handed; kind; lavish, abundant, ample, handsome, plentiful.

liberated free, emancipated, unshackled, unfettered, independent-minded, deregulated, liberalized, released, paroled, bailed, redemptive, absolving, saved, rescued, exemptible, acquitted, scot-free.

lifelike realistic, photographic, exact, faithful, graphic, vivid, eidetic, natural; verisimilar, realistic, veracious, unmistaken, naturalistic, representative.

light pale, pastel, cream-coloured, ivory, pallid, pasty, colourless, white, albino, blond, fair, flaxen, tow-headed, faded, bleached, peroxided, lightened, overexposed; unheavy, portable, handy, lightweight, featherweight, bantamweight, light-footed, weightless, unweighable, imponderable. *See also* insubstantial, lightening, leavening.

lightening unloading, off-loaded, aerating, easing, relieving, alleviating, disburdening, disencumbering.

likable favoured, admired, appreciated, popular, good, amicable, congenial, friendly, affectionate, appealing, fascinating, adorable, lovely, attractive, pleasing, endearing, captivating, infatuating, titillating, tempting, alluring, lovable, intimate. *See also* liking.

liking admiring, fascinated, devoted, empathetic, sympathetic, tending, turning, bending, leaning, predisposed, prejudiced, biased, favouring, preferring, approving, wishing, hankering, longing, yearning, loving, infatuated, desirous.

limited restricted, proscripted, prohibitive, repressive, inhibiting, no-go, off-limits (US), exclusive, definite, confined, frozen, curtailed, finite, narrow, cramped, hidebound, copyrighted, patented. *See also* furthest.

limiting bordering, fringing, extreme, polar, eventual, last.

limp soft, floppy, flabby, loose, slack, droopy.

linguistic grammatical, descriptive, structural, analytic(al), syntactic(al), phonetic, pronounced, phonological, phonemic, orthoepic, orthographic, morphophonemic, morphologic(al), diachronic, synchronic, lexicological, lexicographic(al), etymological, semantic, semasiological, glottological, glottochronological, lexicostatistical, philological, psycholingustic, geolinguistic, dialectological, onomastic, onomasiological, sociolinguistic, palaeographic(al), bilingual, multilingual, polyglot, glossological (Arch). *See also* of language, translated, lettered, worded, phrasal, grammatical.

liquefiable soluble, meltable, fusible, thawable, dissolvable, dissoluble.

liquefied dissolved, deliquescent, melted, molten, thawed, decoagulated, liquescent, liquefacient, solvent.

liquefying colliquative, thawing,

melting, fusing, dissolving, dissolutional, anticoagulent.

listed enumerated, itemized, inventoried, registered, recorded, entered, noted, filed, catalogued, taxonomic, classificatory, indexed, tabulated, charted, scheduled, programmed, timetabled. *See also* inventorial.

listless lethargic, apathetic, languid, sluggish, weary, inert.

lit illuminated, brightened, bright, lamplit, candlelit, torchlit, firelit, spotlit, floodlit, highlighted, sunlit, starlit, moonlit.

literal denotative, verbatim, textual, word-for-word, chapter-and-verse.

literate numerate, schooled, educated, erudite, scholarly, donnish, academic, intellectual, highbrow, cultured, cultivated, sophisticated, worldly, pedantic, well-qualified.

lithe lissom, supple, pliable, agile, elastic, nimble.

litigated on trial, sub judice, litigable, actionable, justiciable, disputable, arguable, suable, accusable.

litigating litigant, suing, accusing, claiming, contesting, objecting, disputing, litigious, quarrelsome, argumentative.

little small, diminutive, short, petite, squat, dumpy, dwarfish, elfin, dainty, dinky, pint-size(d), Lilliputian, miniature, mini, bantam, baby, small-scale, miniaturized, microcosmic, pocket-size(d), vest-pocket (US), duodecimo, tiny,

minute, minuscule, infinitesimal, microscopic, rudimentary, incipient, embryonic, fine, thin, slight, exiguous, tenuous, imperceptible, intangible, impalpable, negligible, indiscernible, stunted, puny, shrunk, contracted, meagre, scant, skimpy, poky, cramped, limited, snug, cosy, bijou, piddling (Inf), paltry, petty, trifling, insignificant, minimal, molecular, subatomic, microbic, amoebic, wee (Inf), teeny-weeny (Inf), titchy (Sl), tiddly (Inf), itsy-bitsy (Inf), itty-bitty (Inf), little, diminutively, daintily, slightly, minimally, tinily, minutely, finely, tenuously, inappreciably, negligibly, insignificantly. *See also* microscopically.

live alive, living, animate, vital, breathing; active, topical, burning, current, controversial; lively, energetic, dynamic, brisk, spirited.

lively animated, vivacious, spirited, energetic, vigorous, dynamic, active, sprightly, gingery (Inf).

livid black-and-blue, bruised.

living animate, vital, viable, organic, biotic, microbial, bacterial, viral.

loaded laden, holding, containing, charged, burdened, burdensome, stuffed, full, lined, padded, packed, crammed, squeezed, topped up.

loaned lent, accommodative, secured, unsecured, unsurious, extortionate, on credit.

loathsome disgusting, horrible, abhorrent, odious, repugnant, repulsive.

local

local next-door, neighbouring, nearby, provincial, parochial, diocesan, back-country, back-woods, small-town, uptown, downtown, ghettoized, slummy.

located situated, placed, positioned, sited, set, stationed, posted, established, installed, settled, fixed, emplaced, planted, ensconced. *See also* found, locational.

locational situated, positional, topographical, geographical, cartographical, navigational, geodetic, surveyed.

lofty high-and-mighty, deluded, prestigious, swanky (Inf), high-falutin(g) (Inf).

logical deductive, inductive, inferential, equivalent, consistent, compatible, necessary, sufficient, contingent, conditional, tautological, contradictory, converse, paradoxical.

lone one, single, isolated, solitary, alone, lonely.

lonely solitary, isolated, secluded, stay-at-home, unpopular, friendless, boycotted, shunned, frozen-out, outlawed, desolate, forlorn, uninvited, deserted, avoided, rejected, ostracized, exiled, banished, expelled, displaced, confined, concealed, single, celibate, divorced, incompatible, cold-shouldered (Inf).

long lengthy, tall, high, extended, prolonged, protracted, drawn out, dragged out, stretched, spun out, strung out, straggling, overlong, extensive, far-reaching, sustained, polysyllabic, sesquipedalian, interminable, endless, long-winded, verbose, shoulder-length, full-length, unabridged. *See also* elongated, longitudinal.

longitudinal lengthways, longways, endways, linear.

lookalike twin, homophyllic, matching, like, paired, cloned.

losing lost, missing, misplaced, mislaid, astray, lacking, forgotten, irrecoverable, irretrievable, incorrigible, irredeemable, hopeless, depriving, failing, squandered, depleted, stripped of, shorn of, bereft, spent, ruined. *See also* unprofitable, at a loss.

lost mislaid, vanished, gone, irretrievable; wasted, squandered, destroyed, wrecked; bewildered, confused, baffled, helpless, ignorant; absent, dreamy, preoccupied; dead, gone, obsolete, extinct; abandoned, depraved, damned.

loud noisy, booming, ringing, carrying, deafening, ear-splitting, thundering, rattling, crashing, pealing, clangorous, dinning, rackety, shrill, piercing, strident, braying, blaring, brassy, echoing, resonant, sonorous, plangent, cacophonous, shouting, yelling, whooping, bellowing, lusty, powerful, stentorian, rowdy, rumbustious, rambunctious, boisterous, vociferous, clamorous. *See also* heard.

loveable endearing, adorable, appealing, interesting, intriguing, enchanting, captivating, beguiling, de-

sirable, tempting, alluring, seductive, beautiful, winsome, sweet, winning, pleasing, engaging, graceful, angelic, divine, kissable, cuddly, popular, congenial.

lovely attractive, beautiful, handsome, pretty, graceful; delightful, gratifying, enjoyable, pleasant.

loving amorous, affectionate, demonstrative, fond, attached, devoted, kind, friendly, amicable, sympathetic, charitable, agapistic, sentimental, faithful, loyal, uxorious, motherly, paternal, fraternal, platonic, charitable, patriotic. *See also* in love, enamoured, amorous, beloved, loveable.

low short, squat, stumpy, stunted, shallow, knee-high, low-slung, flattened, knocked flat, lying down, prostrate, prone, supine, recumbent, reclining, couchant, crouched, stooped, décolleté, single-storey. *See also* lower, lowland.

lower inferior, nether, bottom, undermost, subjacent, underlying, underlaid, subscript, subcutaneous, hypodermic, subcartilaginous, subcranial.

lowered depressed, deflated, flattened, grounded, levelled, demolished, reduced, decreased, deteriorated, worse. *See also* lowering, fallen, falling, degraded, overthrown, sedentary.

lowering descendent, depressing, humiliating, demeaning, debasing.

lowland subalpine, submontane, piedmont, low-lying, flat, submerged, sunken, depressed.

lowly low, poor, mean, small, plebeian, working-class.

loyal devoted, dedicated, deferential, respectful, reverential, obedient, compliant, submissive, docile, tractable, amenable, willing; faithful, devoted, dedicated to, constant, steadfast, staunch, true, sycophantic, true-blue, leal (Scot).

lubricant lenitive, emollient, soothing, moist; oiled, greased, smooth-running, silent. *See also* lubricate, oily, unguent, smooth.

lucent luminous, radiant, refulgent, glowing, glimmering, burning, candescent, incandescent, aglow, phosphorescent, fluorescent, shining, lambent, flickering, blinking, winking, flashing, occulting, stroboscopic, illuminating, brightening, beaming. *See also* bright, lustrous, lit, sunny, starry, light, enlightened, photoelectric.

lucky fortunate, charmed, favoured, fortuitous, propitious, auspicious.

ludicrous absurd, crazy, laughable, ridiculous, preposterous, nonsensical.

luscious delicious, delectable, mouth-watering, appetizing, tasty, succulent, juicy.

lush fat, fertile, fecund, productive, prolific, abundant, plentiful, plenteous, bountiful.

lustful libidinous, lecherous, lascivious, concupiscent, randy, hot for, sexy, seductive, provocative, titillating, fanciable (Inf).

lustrous glossy, gleaming, shiny, polished, burnished, *glacé* (Fr), glassy, glistening, shimmering, opalescent, iridescent, pearly, haloed.

luxurious lavish, opulent, rich, extravagant, magnificent, plush; sensual, voluptuous, epicurean.

lying lying down, flat out, recumbent, decumbent, accumbent, prostrate, prone, procumbent, face down, supine, couchant, reclining, sprawling, spread-eagled, knocked down; untruthful, fibbing, fabricating, prevaricating, mendacious, perfidious, falsifying, propagandizing, libelling, slandering, perjuring, storytelling, equivocating, evasive, shifty, ambiguous, flimflamming (Inf).

M

mad insane, demented, lunatic, deranged, nuts (Inf), bonkers (Inf); silly, foolish, ludicrous, idiotic, absurd, senseless; frantic, hysterical, frenzied, riotous; angry, furious, incensed, fuming, raging, infuriated; fanatical, avid, ardent.

made easy facilitated, simplified, user-friendly, accessible, comprehensive.

magnanimous charitable, benevolent, humanitarian, philanthropic.

magnetic attractive, charismatic.

magnificent impressive, majestic, splendid, opulent, sumptuous, superb.

majestic stately, royal, proud, formal, solemn, stiff, starchy, dignified, grand, fine, ceremonious, palatial.

makeshift provisional, stopgap, rough-and-ready, temporary.

male masculine, manly, macho, virile, muscular, gentlemanly, chivalrous, mannish, unmanly, effeminate, gay, homosexual, laddish (Sl), butch (Sl), homo (Inf), queer (Inf).

maledictive imprecatory, damning, cursed, accursed, damned, hexed, jinxed, bewitched, unblest, execrable, banned, excommunicated, proscribed, comminatory.

malevolent ill-willed, ill-natured, ill-disposed, evil, malignant, pernicious, wicked, hating, hateful, malicious, malefic, baleful, intolerant, persecuting, oppressive, tyrannical, intimidatory, menacing, harassing, racist. *See also* cruel, callous, merciless, hostile, inconsiderate.

malicious malevolent, spiteful, vindictive, bitter, resentful, hateful.

malign malignant, evil, bad, injurious, wicked, harmful.

malignant malicious, spiteful, wicked, venomous, malign, injurious.

mammalian warm-blooded, homoiothermic, prototherian, monotrematous, metatherian, eutherian, placental.

managerial administrative, executive, organizational, directorial, leading, hegemonic, directional, guiding, steering, navigational, governing, controlling, political, official, bureaucratic, governmental, presidential, gubernatorial, legislative, judicial, authoritative, officious, dictatorial, despotic, tyrannical, supervisory, nomothetic, high-level, top-level, important. *See also* parliamentary.

manic ranting, raving, frenzied, frenetic, frantic, hysterical, demented, rabid, wild, berserk, delirious, deluded, hallucinating.

manifest revealed, disclosed, divulged, exposed, uncovered, declared, overt, public, noticeable, conspicuous, notable, apparent, visible, obvious, ostensible, open-and-shut, appearing, token, symbolic, representative, definite, recognizable, unmistakable, incontestable, pronounced, prominent, marked, striking, salient, highlighted, accentuated, patent, evident, obtrusive, flagrant, blatant, arrant, glaring, ostentatious, eye-catching, well-known, notorious, famous, infamous, showy, loud.

manly masculine, virile, courageous, brave, strong, powerful.

manorial palatial, presidential, detached, semidetached, terraced, back-to-back, duplex, split-level, single-storey, multistorey, high-rise.

many considerable, umpteen (Inf).

marked scarred, spotted, pitted, pock-marked, scabrous, scabrid.

marriageable nubile, eligible, suitable, betrothed, engaged, promised, affianced, plighted, spoken for.

married wedded, united, espoused, partnered, joined, paired, coupled, mated, newlywed, matched, one, made one, hitched (Inf), spliced (Sl), hooked (Sl).

marshy swampy, boggy, fenny, soggy, oozy, squashy, squelchy, splashy, sludgy, slushy, muddy, sodden, waterlogged, flooded.

martial naval, gladiatorial, pugilistic, mercenary, auxiliary, soldierly, brave, heroic, armed, enlisted, drafted, conscripted, recruited.

marvellous astonishing, incredible, amazing, stupendous, extraordinary, wondrous, superb, splendid, smashing (Inf), super (Inf), terrific (Inf).

massive huge, large, imposing, bulky, colossal, enormous.

masterful magistral, lordly, noble, aristocratic, magisterial, majestic, matronly, patriarchal, matriarchal, divine, royal, principal, main, major, great, parliamentary, autocratic, authoritarian, dominating, domineering, coercive, imperious, dictatorial, despotic, oppressive, executive, managerial, capitalistic, plutocratic, oligarchic, papal, pontifical, cardinal, rabbic, rabbinical, commanding, able. *See also* excellent.

material

material tangible, substantial, sensible, real, natural, massy, solid, massive, concrete, palpable, ponderable, weighty, physical, empirical, spatiotemporal, objective, impersonal, clinical, incarnate, embodied, somatic, corporal, bodily, fleshly, carnal, reincarnated, realized, materialized, worldly, earthly, unspiritual, sensual.

mathematical arithmetic(al), algebraic, geometric(al), trigonometric(al), analytic(al), topological, statistical. *See also* numerical, numerable, pictorial, logical.

matrimonial marital, conjugal, connubial, nuptial, hymeneal, spousal, premarital, concubinal, matronly, wifely, bridal, husbandly. *See also* married, marriageable, monogamous.

mature adult, grown, ripe, mellow, prepared, ready.

maturing growing, budding, pullulating, burgeoning, developing, flowering, blooming.

meagre sparse, scanty, skimpy, inadequate, insufficient, paltry; thin, skinny, emaciated, lean, scrawny; sterile, infertile, barren.

mealy branny, floury, farinaceous, furfuraceous.

mean miserly, parsimonious, ungenerous, grudging, tight, tight-fisted, close, near, money-grubbing, niggardly, penurious, penny-pinching, scrimping, cheeseparing, mingy, stingy, tight-arsed (Sl). *See also* unpleasant.

meaningful etymological, denotative, comprehensible, intelligible, unambiguous, univocal, monosemous, clear, plain, lucid, perspicuous, literal, express, explicit, pointed, declaratory, affirmative, indicative, repeated, tautological, identical, similar, synonymous, equivalent, paraphrastic, tantamount, connotative, implied, implicit, inferred, tacit, suggestive, unclear, obscure, confused, technical, professional, special, contrary, opposite, antonymous, homonymous, extended, transferred, ambiguous, multivocal, polysemous, equivocal, symbolic, figurative, metaphorical, allegorical, idiomatic, significative, importing, purporting, evocative, expressive, interpretative, telling, eloquent, allusive, meaningless, nonsensical, absurd. *See also* significant, semantic, meant.

meaningless senseless, unmeaning, irrelevant, nonsignificant, unimportant, trite, commonplace, platitudinous, hackneyed, clichéed, banal, trivial, trifling, nonsense, amphigoric, absurd, inane, foolish, fatuous, illogical, sophistic, incoherent, unintelligible, illegible, mystifying, piffling, ineffectual, ineffective, invalid, null, empty, vacuous, hollow, unexpressive, unidiomatic, unapt, rubbishy, trashy, delirious, frenzied, ranting, raving, prattling, gibbering, blithering, windy, exaggerated, Pickwickian. *See also* aimless, unmeant.

meant implied, intended, deliberate, designed, planned, destined, predestined.

measurable mensurable, quantifiable, meterable, gaugeable, calculable, computable, assessable, appraisable, estimable, determinable.

measureable quntifiable, determinable, perceptible.

measured quantified, metered, gauged, calibrated, graduated, reckoned, assessed, valued, rated, estimated, determined, surveyed, triangulated, plotted, mapped.

mechanical motorized, technological, hydraulic, electronic, powered, power-driven, labour-saving, robotic, automatic, automated, computerized, instrumental.

meddling officious, interfering, meddlesome, intrusive, nosy, prying, irritating, troublesome, dabbling, fiddling, participating, pushy (Inf).

median medial, mesial, mean, average, medium, balanced.

mediatory arbitral, diplomatic, intercessory, pacificatory, propitiatory, conciliatory, advisory; intermediary, interim, neutral, moderate, middle-of-the-road, non-committal.

medical iatric, Hippocratic, clinical, allopathic, homeopathic, surgical, osteopathic, gynaecological, obstetric, paediatric, geriatric, neurological, dermatological, urological, ophthalmological, cardiac, radiological, epidemiological, forensic, pathological, veterinary. *See also* dental, diagnostic, therapeutic.

mediocre average, passable, fair, moderate, tolerable, adequate, not bad, alright, indifferent, lukewarm, unremarkable, undistinguished, unexceptional, unnoteworthy, unspectacular, commonplace, pedestrian, prosaic, second-class, second-best, second-division, second-rate, inferior, downmarket, banal, grey, dull, run-of-the-mill, *cosi-cosi* (It), so-so (Inf), small-time (Inf).

medium average, standard, regular, median, mesial, mean, average, middle, mid-, midmost, midway, intermediate, intermediary, balanced, halfway, fifty-fifty, central, middle-of-the-road, moderate. *See also* big, fat, stocky.

meek docile, mild, modest, gentle, humble, deferential; compliant, yielding, acquiescent, tame, resigned.

meeting impinging, rubbing, brushing, grazing, glancing.

melancholy gloomy, sombre, doleful, mournful, sorrowful, downhearted.

melodious musical, tuneful, lyrical, canorous, lilting, singable, catchy, tripping, soft, sweet, dulcet, velvety, mellow, smooth, sweet-sounding, honeyed, mellifluous, Orphean, silvery, golden-toned, fine-toned, true, well-pitched, clear, chiming, full-toned, resonant, full, rich, euphonious, harmonious. *See also* harmonious.

memorable unforgettable, notable, noteworthy, remembered, unforgotten, indelible, haunting, evocative, reminiscent, nostalgic, reminding, mnemonic. *See also* remembering, memorized, memorial.

memorial commemorative, celebratory.

menacing frightening, intimidating, threatening, ominous, impending, scaring.

menstrual catamenial, monthly, menopausal, menstruating, on.

mental intellectual, rational, reasoning, thinking, conceptual, cerebral, cephalic, noetic, phrenic, psychological, logical, deductive, instinctive, intuitive. *See also* intelligent, thoughtful.

mercantile trading, exchanging, swapping, commercialistic, capitalist, wholesale, retail, exchangeable, marketable, merchantable, saleable. *See also* commercial, profitable, unprofitable, professional, contractual, corporate.

merciful compassionate, kind, clement, benevolent, magnanimous, unresentful, unrevengeful, unreproachful, placable, lenient, long-suffering, forbearing, patient, tolerant, indulgent, stoic.

merciless pitiless, ruthless, revengeful.

meritorious meriting, deserving, worthy.

merry carefree, gay, convivial, joyous, happy, gleeful; comical, funny, hilarious, humorous, amusing; tipsy, squiffy (Inf), tiddly (Inf), tight (Inf), intoxicated, inebriated.

meteorologic meteorological, synoptic, elemental, climatic, climatological. *See also* frontal, fine, windy, stormy, cloudy, warm, rainy, cool, foggy.

meticulous painstaking, fastidious, exact, precise, fussy, particular.

metrical metric, micrometric, volumetric, photometric, barometric, tachometric, optometric, psychometric, linear, cubic, mensural, mensurational, quantitative, metrological, geodetic, topographic, cartographic. *See also* measured, measurable.

miasmic mephitic, foetid, reeking, fumy, effluvial.

microscopically microcosmically, subatomically, infinitesimally, indiscernibly, imperceptibly, invisibly, intangibly, impalpably, imponderably.

middle mid, central, medial, middlemost, midmost, equidistant, midway, halfway, intermediate, lukewarm, half-and-half, even, fifty-fifty, neutral, moderate, middle-of-the-road, unextreme, noncommittal, detached, indifferent, independent, nonpartisan, nonaligned, impartial, irresolute, grey. *See also* midway, core, median, mediatory, middling.

middle-aged mature, fatherly, motherly, matronly, menopausal, climacteric, overblown, thirtysomething (Inf), fortysomething (Inf).

middling average, mediocre, ordinary, indifferent, undistinguished, fair, run-of-the-mill, so-so (Inf).

midway halfway, equidistant, mezzanine, midstream, equatorial, diametric.

mighty powerful, strong, forceful, robust, strapping, hearty, huge, massive, colossal, immense, gigantic.

mild docile, gentle, meek, placid, serene, soft.

militant militaristic, martial, belligerent, combative, hawkish, warlike, sabre-rattling, offensive; aggressive, bellicose, martial, warlike.

military martial, militant, naval, soldierly, gladiatorial, strategic, tactical, offensive, defensive, pre-emptive, aggressive, pugnacious, combative, bellicose, warlike, belligerent. See also enlisted.

milky lacteal, lacteous, lactic, lactescent, lactiferous.

millionth billionth, trillionth.

minor lesser, inferior, secondary, subordinate, paltry, trivial.

mirror-like reflecting, reflective.

misanthropic antisocial, unsociable, inhuman, cynical, egotistic, selfish, misandrous, man-hating, woman-hating, misogynous, sexist.

mischievous naughty, impish, playful, rascally, teasing; evil, bad, malignant, wicked, hurtful, harmful.

misconnected unrelated, misapplied, misreferred.

miserable unhappy, gloomy, downhearted, dejected, malancholy, wretched; mean, low, base, contemptible, squalid, shabby; poverty-stricken, destitute, poor, penniless, needy.

misinformed misled, deceived, duped, outsmarted, fooled, cheated, tricked.

misinterpreted misunderstood, mistranslated, misread, misconstrued, misconceived, mistaken, wrong, misspelt, solecistic, catachrestic, misquoted, garbled, falsified, distorted, exaggerated, inflated, misrepresented, libellous, slanderous.

misjudged misunderstood, misconstrued, misinterpreted, out, wrong, mistaken, ill-timed, ill-advised, foolish.

misjudging mistaken, wrong, muddled, fallible, gullible, misguided, misled, deluded, deceived. See also unjust, misjudged.

misleading delusory, deceitful, false, spurious, evasive.

misplaced mislaid, misput, mislocated, lost, missing, gone missing.

misrepresented biased, slanted, unrepresentative, distorted, deformed, twisted, perverted, false, untrue, wrong, incorrect, inaccurate, dissimilar, unlike, unfair, unjust, exaggerated, caricatured, parodied, grotesque, flattering, cardboard. See also misinformed.

missing lacking, wanting, wanted, deficient, minus, short, taken away, deleted, subtracted, omitted, mislaid, excluded, left out, not included.

mistaken wrong, self-contradicting, prejudiced, biased, erroneous, erring, misjudging, blundering, bungling.

mistimed misdated, anachronistic, metachronistic. *See also* too early, too late.

misty foggy, cloudy, watery, rainy, showery, drizzling, mizzly, dewy, roric.

misunderstood misconstrued, misconceived, misjudged, misread, misinterpreted, misheard.

misused abused, misemployed, misdirected, diverted, misappropriated, violated, desecrated, defiled, perverted, distorted, polluted, spoilt, unclean, ill-treated, beaten, battered, exploited, used, oppressed, mishandled, bungled, wasted. *See also* abusive.

mitigated tempered, leavened, mollified, moderated.

mixed interracial, interfaith, mingled, interspersed, interlaced, interwoven, intertwined, miscible, soluble, stirred, shaken, blended, harmonized, combined, integrated, syncretic, eclectic, fused, mashed, alloyed, merged, amalgamated, half-and-half, tempered, sophisticated, adultcrated, diluted, involved in, complicated, tangled, unsorted, disordered, jumbled, confused, chaotic, topsy-turvy, miscellaneous, random, patchy, heterogeneous, hybrid, mongrel, half-breed (Offensive), cross-bred, crossed, half-caste (Offensive), miscegenetic, interbred, intermarried, multiracial, multicultural, kaleidoscopic, phantasmagoric(al), variegated, dappled, speckled, mottled, motley, tinged, dyed, coloured, pervasive, fifty-fifty (Inf), higgledy-piggledy (Inf). *See also* mixed-up.

mixed-up muddled, jumbled, scrambled, confused, bewildered, puzzled, confounded, mistaken, forgetful.

moderate medium, equable, balanced, steady, modest, judicious, just, fair, nonviolent, harmless, gentle, mild, weak, poor, middling, mediocre, indifferent, average, unexceptional, limited, restricted, sensible, rational, reasonable, restrained, controlled, chastened, subdued, quiet, untroubled, peaceful, tranquil, low-key, temperate, sober, calm, cool, composed, so-so (Inf). *See also* politically moderate, moderating.

moderating lenitive, soothing, nonirritant, alleviative, assuaging, easing, pain-killing, analgesic, anodyne, calming, sedative, tranquillizing, narcotic, hypnotic, mesmeric, soporific, smooth, soft, bland, emollient, demulcent, lubricating, comforting, disarming, pacificatory.

modern new, novel, contemporary, latest, recent, up-to-date.

modest meek, humble, unpretentious, unpretending, unassuming,

unostentatious, unobtrusive, un-
boastful, unimposing, unimpressive,
unaspiring. *See also* blushing, bashful, shy, self-deprecating, reserved.

modified adjusted, adapted, altered, changed, varied, variational,
modulated, coordinated, conditioned, regulated, attuned, improved, reconciled, palliative, miti-
gatory, softened, moderated.

modular cellular, molecular,
atomic, integral, joined, linked, fit-
ted, built-in.

moist damp, wet, soggy, sodden,
humid, clammy, sticky, muggy,
close, dank, tacky, humectant. *See
also* misty, marshy, seeping.

monastic monachal, monkish,
nunnish, priestly, Encratite.

monetary pecuniary, financial, fiscal, numismatic, chrysological, budgetary, coined, stamped, minted,
nummular, nummary, fiduciary, devalued, depreciated, withdrawn, de-
monetized, decimal, solvent,
wealthy.

monogamous bigamous, diga-
mous, polygamous, polygynous,
polyandrous, morganatic, miscegenetic.

monotonous tedious, boring, uniform, invariable, changeless, mo-
notone, singsong, familiar, habitual,
humdrum, mundane, routine, stale,
clichéd, hackneyed, trite, yawn-
making (Inf).

monstrous hideous, grotesque,
awful, dreadful, frightful, gruesome;
abnormal, deformed, freakish, un-

natural; huge, immense, enormous,
colossal, gigantic, vast.

moral ethical, principled, high-
minded, good, decent, honourable,
honest, noble, upright, righteous,
virtuous, right-minded, right,
proper, just, fair, scrupulous,
saintly. *See also* pure, moralistic.

moralistic self-righteous, narrow-
minded, mealy-mouthed, prudish,
priggish, prim, old-maidish, smug,
sanctimonious, holier-than-thou,
pietistic, pious, puritan, Victorian,
strait-laced, grave, serious, severe,
stern, censorious, edifying, clean,
publishable, quotable, mentionable,
expurgated, bowdlerized, euphemistic, genteel, affected, squeamish, shockable.

morbid gloomy, sombre, gruesome, grisly, grim, ghastly; sick,
pathological, unhealthy, diseased.

morning matin, matutinal,
forenoon, dawn, early, fresh, dewy,
antemeridian, auroral (Arch). *See
also* noon, afternoon.

mortal human, earthly, worldly,
temporal, ephemeral; lethal, fatal,
deadly, murderous; severe, extreme,
grave, dire, awful.

motherly maternal, affectionate,
protective, gentle, loving, caring.

motionless immobile, still, inactive, unmoving, immotive, static,
stationary, stagnant, standing,
steady, poised, balanced, immovable, fixed, stiff, stuck, paralysed,
petrified, transfixed, sedentary,
stock-still, spellbound, frozen, be-

calmed, at anchor. *See also* sedentary, quiescent.

motivated persuaded, moved, influenced, induced, prompted, impelled, caused, directed, encouraged, exhorted, challenged, urged, egged on, spurred on, pressured, lobbied, prodded, goaded, provoked, stimulated, electrified, energized, animated, galvanized, inspired, inflamed, incited, roused, charmed, enticed, lured, attracted, seduced, bewitched, coaxed, flattered, spellbound, hypnotized, mesmerized.

motivational influential, directional, incentive, attractive, magnetic, persuasive, hortatory, provocative, incitive, instigative, inflammatory, hypnotic, mesmeric, irresistible, suggestive, influencing, convincing, compelling, encouraging, challenging, provoking, stimulating, electrifying, inciting, instigating, energizing, kinetic, galvanizing, inflaming, rousing, insinuating, teasing, tantalizing, alluring, tempting, inviting, fascinating. *See also* motivated, suggestible.

motiveless groundless, unintended, unmeant, noncausal, aimless, purposeless, unplanned, unmotivated, arbitrary, fortuitous, indeterminant, random, stochastic, unpredictable, haphazard, uncertain, inexplicable, unaccountable, unexpected, unreasonable, inconsistent, hit-or-miss, illogical, irrational, coincidental, accidental, chance, casual, stray, incidental, adventitious, serendipitous, aleatory, quirky, risky, fifty-fifty, toss-up, fluky (Inf), chancy (Inf), dicey (Inf).

mottled dappled, brindled, tabby, grizzled, pepper-and-salt, roan, spotted, maculate, dotted, studded, peppered, sprinkled, powdered, dusted, cloudy, blemished, fly-spotted, speckled, freckled, spotty, pimply, pockmarked.

mountainous hilly, rolling, undulating, hillocky, hummocky, orogenic, alpine, Himalayan, Andean, mountain-dwelling, hill-dwelling. *See also* orogenic.

mournful melancholy, sorrowful, sad, gloomy, piteous, unhappy.

moving motive, motor, motile, motional, mobile, motivational, locomotive, automotive, self-propelled, shifting, impelling, propelling, driving, travelling, riding, running, rushing, flowing, streaming, flying, transitional, fleeting, mercurial, restless, active, agitated, bustling, scurrying, stirring, wandering, drifting, nomadic, peripatetic, ambulant, erratic, runaway. *See also* directional.

mucilaginous gluey, glutinous, gory, mucous, snotty (Sl).

muddled jumbled, scrambled, confused, chaotic, tangled, labyrinthine, awry, askew, amiss, topsy-turvy, upside-down, higgledy-piggledy (Inf), arsy-versy (Sl), cockeyed (Sl), haywire (Inf).

muddy slushy, sludgy, squelchy,

sloppy, slabby (Arch), oozy, miry, turbid, dirty, waterlogged, marshy, silty, sedimentary.

multiple many, several, various, collective.

multiplicative multiplied, multiple, manifold, multifold, increasing, proliferative.

multitudinous numerous, legion, multiple, multifold, multifarious, manifold. *See also* many, numberless, ample, crowded.

mundane everyday, ordinary, humdrum, commonplace, banal, routine; earthly, terrestrial, physical, material.

murderous homicidal, psychopathic, pathological, genocidal, internecine, slaughterous, death-dealing, destructive, trigger-happy, cold-blooded, sanguinary, bloody, gory, bloodthirsty, cruel, savage, brutal, head-hunting, man-eating, cannibalistic, suicidal, self-destructive.

murky foggy, smoggy, dusty, smoky, misty, steamy, miasmal, cloudy, nebulous, hazy, distant, remote, vague, indistinct, unclear, low-definition, soft-focus, blurred, fuzzy, bleary, muzzy, opaque, smoked, frosted, milky, veiled, filmy, obscured, shadowy, ill-defined, indistinguishable, faint.

musical musicophile, musicianly, philharmonic. *See also* harmonic, composed, instrumental, jazz.

mutual shared, joint, common, interactive, reciprocal.

mysterious enigmatic, inscrutable, unknowable, esoteric, cabbalistic, arcane, occult, abstruse, mystifying, confusing, bewildering, puzzling, perplexing, unresolved, unintelligible, problematic, complex, intricate, labyrinthine, difficult, knotty, cryptic, hidden, concealed, camouflaged, disguised, incognito, unknown, anonymous.

N

naive naïf, artless, simple, simple-minded, ingenuous, guileless, childlike, uncontrived, unstudied, plain, homespun, unskilled, natural, primitive, ignorant, Arcadian, young, innocent, green, immature, inexperienced, trusting, gullible, uninhibited, unaffected, spontaneous, candid, frank, open, straightforward, undesigning, truthful, veracious, true, honest, sincere, honourable, aboveboard, blunt, outspoken, transparent, matter-of-fact, down-to-earth, literal-minded, modest, shy, inarticulate, unpretentious, Philistine, uncouth, vulgar.

naked bare, nude, unclothed, stripped, exposed, divested; vulnerable, unguarded, defenceless; undisguised, obvious, open, stark, plain.

narrative fictional, imaginative, kitchen-sink, factual, documentary, biographical, autobiographical, factional, mythological, epic, heroic, romantic, picaresque.

narrow slender, thin, close, tight, strait, clinging, cramped, pinched, compressed, contracted, pent, pent-up, close-fitting, figure-hugging, limited, restricted, straitened, confined, constricted, circumscribed, incommodious. *See also* fine, tapered.

nasty dirty, polluted, foul, obnoxious, vile, disgusting; lewd, blue, smutty, obscene; spiteful, evil, wicked, malicious, abusive.

national state, civic, governmental, democratic, republican, socialistic, communistic, totalitarian, public, general, communal, tribal, social, societal, cosmopolitan, international, interracial.

native indigenous, aboriginal, autochthonous, ethnic, tribal, local, metropolitan, urban, rustic, provincial.

natural artless, simple-hearted, candid, frank, blunt, open, guileless, ingenuous, honest, veracious, direct, straightforward, plain-speaking, forthright, unpretentious, unaffected, unassuming, unfeigning, unsophisticated.

naturalized internationalized, assimilated, orientalized, westernized, Americanized, Anglicized, Frenchified, Germanized, Europeanized, Africanized.

naughty mischievous, wicked, impish, misbehaved, bad, unruly; smutty, vulgar, improper, bawdy, risqué.

nauseating disgusting, revolting, sickening, repulsive, loathsome.

nautical naval, marine, seafaring, seaworthy, marine, afloat, waterborne, sailorly, able-bodied, amphibious, amphibian, seasick, natatory, buoyant. *See also* navigational.

navigational navigating, navigable, navigated, circumnavigated.

near nigh, close, proximate, proximal, side-by-side, shoulder-to-shoulder, cheek-by-jowl, hand-in-hand, arm-in-arm, elbow-to-elbow, bumper-to-bumper, intimate, inseparable, neck-and-neck, close-run, nearby, local, home, neighbouring, vicinal, next-door, next, adjoining, contiguous, immediate, nearest, closest, to hand, at hand, handy, convenient, accessible, nearer, closer, approximate, approximating, nearing, approaching, converging, convergent, forthcoming, warm (Inf), hot (Inf), get-at-able (Inf).

nearby next door, accessible, available, ready, close, adjacent, neighbouring, touching, bordering on.

neat tidy, smart, spick-and-span, trim, fastidious, spruce; clever, adept, adroit, skilful, expert, efficient; unadulterated, undiluted, pure, straight.

nebulous vague, unclear, imprecise, murky, misty, obscure, hazy, dim.

necessary essential, required, requisite, indispensable, fundamental, needed, imperative, urgent, vital.

See also obligatory, needy, inevitable, involuntary.

necessitous needy, poor, pinched, penniless, bankrupt, destitute, lacking, needing, craving, longing for, hungry, starving, deprived, disadvantaged, bust (Inf), broke (Inf), stony (Inf), skint (Sl), brassick (Sl).

needy needful, necessitous, poor, destitute, indigent, poverty-striken, hard up.

negative pessimistic, defeatist, despondent, abnegative, atheistic, agnostic, recusant, doubtful, protestant, defiant, contrary, obstructive, contradictive, contradictory, repudiative, renunciative, renunciatory, abrogative, revocatory, abjuratory, deprecative, dissociative. *See also* rejected, rebutting, nonexistent.

neglected ignored, abandoned, overlooked, forgotten, derelict.

negligent neglectful, careless, inattentive, thoughtless, unmindful, nonchalant, unconcerned, uncaring, oblivious, insouciant, disregardful, forgetful, heedless, remiss. *See also* indifferent.

negotiated mediated, arbitrated, negotiable, practicable, practical, feasible, workable, pragmatic, transferable, conveyable, exchangeable, trade-off, conditional, provisional, provisory, stipulatory, concessionary, conciliatory, compromising, collective, haggling, wrangling, treaty-making, diplomatic, communicative.

nervous edgy, on edge, anxious, agitated, jumpy, neurotic.

neurotic nervous, anxious, disordered, disturbed, highly strung, abnormal.

new brand new, newly, recent, contemporary, topical, current, up-to-date, modern, futuristic, ultramodern, postmodern, innovative, revolutionary, inventive, advanced, original, first, latest, most recent, state-of-the-art, newly produced, just out, new-made, oven-fresh, mint condition, trendy, gimmicky, neological, neophytic, in (Inf), faddish (Inf). *See also* unfamiliar, immature, inaugurated, renewed, avant-garde.

newfangled new, new-fashioned, modern, contemporary.

newsworthy front-page, headline, newsy.

next near, later, latter, proximate.

nice agreeable, pleasant, delightful, charming, pleasing, friendly; trim, fine, delicate, dainty; exact, precise, fine, meticulous, fastidious, scrupulous.

ninth ninefold, nonuple, novenary, nonary, enneadic, nonagonal, enneagonal, enneahedral.

noble aristocratic, blue-blooded, lordly, titled; distinguished, eminent, grand, superior, impressive, elevated; honourable, worthy, virtuous, generous.

noisy loud, boisterous, deafening, blaring, ear-splitting, tumultuous.

nomadic wandering, roaming, migrant, itinerant, vagrant.

no more extinct, died out, vanished, dead, passed away, all over, defunct, obsolete, past, finished, ended, annihilated, obliterated, destroyed, wiped out, kaput (Inf).

nonadhesive nonadhering, noncohesive, immiscible, decomposed, broken up, frangible, fragile, noncoherent, incoherent, nonstick, dry, smooth, slippery, unconsolidated, loose, undone, friable, crumbly, free, wide-ranging, lax, slack, relaxed, loose-fitting, baggy, flapping, flopping, floppy, dangling, hanging, peeling off, pulling off, pendulous, waving, flying, streaming, running, runny, watery, liquid, fluid. See also aloof.

nonalcoholic alcohol-free, unfermented, soft.

nonchalant airy, offhand, indifferent, unconcerned, carefree, casual.

noncommittal uncommunicative, uninformative, clamlike, tightlipped, poker-faced, vague, evasive, close, discreet, secretive, cagey (Inf), buttoned-up (Sl).

nonconforming unconventional, individual, distinct, unique, singular, peculiar, idiosyncratic, eccentric, maverick, outlandish, weird, bizarre, odd, freakish, unorthodox, heterodox, heretic(al), rebellious, freaky (Inf), nutty (Inf), wacky (Sl). See also nonconformist, unconventional, eccentric, irregular, solitary, abnormal.

nonconformist unorthodox, heterodox, heretical, iconoclastic, schismatic, schismatical, dissident, dissenting, dissentient, contumacious, recusant, radical, revolutionary, rebellious, anarchic, renegade, uncompliant, unsubmissive, recalcitrant, contrary, defiant.

nondescript indeterminate, unremarkable, dull, characterless, ordinary, mousy.

nonexistent unexisting, vacant, vacuous, empty.

nonexistent absent, missing, minus, negative, null, void, vacant, empty, blank, devoid, lacking. See also unreal, no more.

nonhuman irrational, dumb, brute, animal, instinctive, vegetable, inanimate, inorganic, mineral.

nonmaterial nonphysical, metaphysical, imaginary, illusory, ethereal, heavenly, eternal, perpetual, unworldly, otherworldly, other, unearthly, transcendent, extramundane, spiritual, celestial, supernal (Fml), religious, higher, psychic(al), immaterial, unreal, incorporeal, insubstantial, intangible, airy, without mass, disincarnated, disembodied, dematerializing, impalpable, imponderable, shadowy, ghostly. See also parapsychological, idealistic, internal.

nonresonant deadened, dulled, damped, muted, muffled, stifled, smothered, silenced, soundproof(ed), dull, heavy, flat, dead.

nonsensical foolish, silly, absurd, meaningless, senseless, idiotic,

not participating

mad, crazy, ridiculous, ludicrous, asinine, anserine, preposterous, fanciful, imaginative, fatuous, funny, jocular, humorous, droll, waggish, comic, merry, farcical, laughable, piffling (Inf).

nonstop endless, ceaseless, continuous, steady, constant, uninterrupted.

noon midday, meridian.

normal natural, in character, typical, stereotyped, conventional, orthodox, traditional, ritual, time-honoured, old-fashioned, old-world, old-line (US), permanent, lasting.

nostalgic homesick, wistful, yearning, longing, regretful.

notable noteworthy, remarkable, egregious (Arch), memorable, unforgettable, signal, first-rate, A1, gold-medal, outstanding, sterling, excellent, superior, top-rank, top-ten, top-flight, high-ranking, prestigious, conspicuous, prominent, eminent, distinguished, exalted, august, dignified, imposing, commanding, leading, impressive, formidable, powerful, influential, newsworthy, front-page, eventful, stirring, breathtaking, shattering, monumental, world-shattering, earth-shaking, seismic, epoch-making.

not awake somnolent, drowsy, dozy, sleepy, soporific, heavy-eyed, slumberous, yawning, dozing, resting, dopy, drugged, sedated, narcotized, anaesthetized, hypnotized, dormant, torpid, hibernating, aestivating, dreaming, unconscious, insensible, out cold, comatose, doped (Sl).

not bad tolerable, adequate, sufficient, fair, satisfactory, passable, respectable, standard, nice, decent, unexceptionable, indifferent, middling, mediocre, ordinary, average, sound, fresh, fifty-fifty (Inf), so-so (Inf), OK (Inf), okey-doke (Sl).

notched notchy, indented, crenate, cut, slit, split, toothed, cogged, dentate, scalloped, pinked, jagged, incisural, saw-toothed, serrated, zigzag, uneven.

not customary nonprevalent, unwonted, unpractised, unnecessary, unfashionable, bad form, tactless, gauche, vulgar, antiquated, old-fashioned, old hat, stale, defunct, outgrown, discarded, disused, unconventional, nonconformist, untraditional, unprecedented, avant-garde, original, experimental, odd, strange, unusual, uncommon, non-U (Inf).

noted renowned, famous, celebrated, acclaimed, distinguished, illustrious.

notorious infamous, disreputable, scandalous, disgraceful, ignominious; obvious, flagrant, blatant, overt, open.

not participating lazy, idle, indolent, slothful, work-shy, bone idle, loafing, lolling, parasitic, slack, lax, slow, dilatory, dawdling, tardy, procrastinating, laggard, sluggish, lethargic, languid, dull, listless, tor-

not the real thing

pid, apathetic, indifferent, uninterested, phlegmatic, impassive.

not the real thing artificial, synthetic, man-made, simulated, imitation, mock, pretend, dummy, sham, fake, false, spurious, specious, phony, bogus, counterfeit, so-called, put-on, quasi, pseudo (Inf).

not wanted unrequired, unneeded, unnecessary, unsold, unbought, remaindered, remaining, left-over, superfluous, redundant, otiose, vacant, free, dispensed with, waived, shunned, unemployed, laid off, redundant, superannuated, retired, idle, inactive, fired (Inf), sacked (Inf).

not working unemployed, unengaged, laid off, redundant, on strike, jobless, resting, free, broken down, unused, fallow, idle, disengaged, unoccupied.

nourishing nutritious, alimentary, wholesome, beneficial, sustaining, healthy.

novel unique, different, personal, individual, one-off, unparalleled, unprecedented, unheard-of, offbeat, sui generis, inimitable, incomparable, new, fresh, avant-garde, revolutionary, transcendent, unmatched.

nude naked, bare, unclothed, stripped, exposed, starkers (Inf).

null void, nonexistent, missing, lacking, gone, vanished.

numberless innumerable, countless, incalculable, myriad, immeasurable, uncounted, untold, infinite, endless, limitless, boundless, inexhaustible.

numerable enumerable, denumerable, countable, quantifiable, measurable, mensurable, calculable, computable, soluble, insoluble, decidable, undecidable.

numerical numeric, numerary, numerative, numerate, digital, figurate; positive, negative, even, odd, integral, whole, digital, fractional, decimal, denary, binary, ternary. *See also* odd, fractional.

numerous many, abundant, copious, plentiful, manifold.

O

obdurate obstinate, hard-hearted, unfeeling, inflexible, harsh, relentless.

obedient compliant, complaisant, acquiescent, deferential, obsequious, dutiful, conforming, law-abiding, willing, meek, submissive, passive, yielding, docile, resigned, disciplined, biddable, subservient, servile, slavish, tractable, amenable, pliant, manageable, malleable, tame, trained. *See also* loyal, obeisant.

obeisant worshipping, reverential, kneeling, humble, respectful, courteous.

obese fat, corpulent, stout, overweight, fleshy, tubby.

objectionable awkward, unattractive, ungracious, discomforting, impolite, uncivil, discourteous, unchivalrous, unkind, uncouth, impertinent, rude, boorish, mean, cantankerous, obnoxious, quarrelsome, crabbed, aggressive, bellicose, beastly (Inf), bloody-minded (Inf).

obligatory mandatory, compulsory, binding, incumbent on, inescapable, unavoidable, unconditional, categorical, peremptory, imperative.

oblique skew, skewed, deviating, divergent, skewed, diagonal, deflected, indirect, sidelong, transverse, sideways, cater-cornered (US), kitty-cornered (US), crooked, convoluted, digressive, meandering, tangent, bevelled, twisted, turning, bending, zigzag, inclining, sloping, slanting, pitched, tilting, leaning, listing, off-course, off-target, skewwhiff (Inf). *See also* devious.

obliterated erased, expunged, eliminated, deleted, effaced, concealed, crossed out, rubbed out, vaporized, liquidated, extirpated, cancelled, edited, censored, destroyed, eradicated, annihilated, demolished, exterminated, buried, forgotten, unrecorded.

oblivious abstracted, detached, withdrawn, (self-)absorbed, introspective, distracted, preoccupied, blind, deaf, unaware, depersonalized, catatonic, senseless, insensible, unconscious, rapturous, ecstatic, hypnotic, trance-like, spaced-out (Sl). *See also* blank, unthinking, forgotten.

obnoxious foul, disgusting, abominable, offensive, repulsive, vile.

obscene dirty, filthy, rude, indecent, risqué, ribald, smutty, scatological, pornographic, blue, adult, salacious, prurient, lewd, lascivious, licentious, scabrous.

obscure unclear, obfuscatory, unintelligible, incomprehensible, opaque, cloudy, foggy, fuzzy, murky, obsidian, difficult, Johnsonian, ornamental, purple, tortuous, convoluted, involved, complex, confused, gnostic, muddled, indistinct, vague, uncertain, imprecise, inexact, inaccurate, indefinite, abstract, indirect, allusive, ambiguous, Cimmerian, cabalistic, equivocal, shapeless, amorphous, mysterious, enigmatic, cryptic, abstruse, esoteric, arcane, recondite, profound, overcompressed, elliptical, diffuse, jibbering, mumbo-jumbo.

observant heeding, watchful, regarding, attentive, careful of, conscientious, diligent, meticulous, scrupulous, fastidious, punctual, literal, pedantic, exact, accurate, reliable, responsible, dependable, dutiful, constant, compliant, conforming, obedient, adhering to, faithful, devout, religious, orthodox, traditional, conventional, loyal, true, honourable.

obsolete dated, archaic, passé, ancient, old-fashioned, outmoded.

obstinate stubborn, obdurate, refractory, recalcitrant, headstrong,

obstreperous pig-headed, mulish, pertinacious, wilful, self-willed, froward (Arch), *entêté* (Fr), awkward, dog-in-the-manger, bloody-minded (Inf). *See also* refractory, unyielding, set.

obstreperous boisterous, loud, riotous, rowdy, unruly.

obstructive restrictive, preventative, awkward.

obvious conspicuous, evident, clear, overt, open, plain.

occasional temporary, provisional, interim, passing, pro tem; sporadic, intermittent, infrequent.

occult cryptic, paranormal, supersensible, superphysical, supernatural, hermetic, symbolic, anagogic(al), latent, covert, enigmatic, arcane, esoteric, obscure, secret, mysterious, encoded, cabbalistic, runic. *See also* witchlike, psychic, divinatory, spiritual, bewitched.

occupied full, engaged, unavailable, inhabited, used, lived-in; absorbed, preoccupied, engrossed, busy, employed, entertained.

oceanic nautical, tidal, briny, billowing, swelling, surging, breaking, rolling, choppy, turbulent, marine, maritime; ocean-going, seaworthy, seafaring, submarine; subaquatic, thalassic, pelagic, estuarine, littoral, sublittoral, intertidal, abyssal, terriginous. *See also* oceanographic(al).

oceanographic(al) thalassographic(al), hydrographic(al), bathymetric(al).

odd impair, even, pair, cardinal, ordinal, imaginary, real, rational, irrational, arithmetical, geometrical, algorithmic, digital, round, whole, prime, positive, negative.

odious loathsome, horrible, offensive, repugnant, disgusting, abominable.

offensive unpleasant, revolting, disgusting, loathsome, nasty, repugnant; insulting, abusive, annoying, insolent, rude, impertinent; aggressive, invading, attacking.

offered inviting, propositional, sale-price, persuasive, advertised, illegal, bribed, cheap, reduced, requested, available, on hire, to let. *See also* voluntary, sacrificial.

offhand casual, curt, abrupt, brusque, careless, nonchalant.

official formal, legitimate, proper, authentic, licensed, sanctioned.

officious overzealous, interfering, intrusive, meddling, opinionated, forward, pushy (Inf).

oily unctuous, greasy, waxy, slippery, slithery, unctuous, unguinous, oleaginous, oleic, fatty, adipose, pinguid, lardy, blubbery, tallowy, suety, sebaceous, rich, buttery, butyraceous, soapy, saponaceous, mucoid. *See also* unguent, lubricant, resinous, basted, lubricated.

old elderly, aged, venerable, veteran, senior, patriarchal, mature, mellow, ripe, grey-haired, white-haired, grizzled, hoary, decrepit, senile, senescent, doddering. *See also* olden, former, historic, primal.

olden antiquarian, antique, ancient,

timeworn, archaic, outdated, moth-eaten, musty, crumbling, mouldering, stale, time-honoured, rooted, established, traditional, age-old, ancestral, immemorial, antediluvian, adamic, old-world, prewar, venerable, vintage, classic.

ominous menacing, foreboding, sinister, threatening, portentous, fateful.

one single, solo, mono, monadic, atomic, individual, solitary, sole, lone. *See also* one-sided, whole, singular, solo, alone, single.

onerous oppressive, burdensome, exacting, difficult, laborious, hard, heavy.

one-sided unilateral, uniplanar, one-way, unidirectional, one-size, one-piece, unisex, unicellular, unipolar, unicameral, monolingual, monochromatic.

on fire alight, flaming, burning, ablaze, flaring, inflammable, flammable, combustible, incendiary, igneous, caustic, thermonuclear, volcanic, pyrogenic, frazzled (Inf).

on form fit, able, capable, healthy, salubrious, hale, hearty.

ongoing continuing, inexorable, irreversible, onward, oncoming, proceeding, moving, profluent, flowing on, unbroken.

on-line off-line, user-friendly, erasable, rewritable, read-only, write-enabled.

opaque nontransparent, nontranslucent, dense, thick, solid, impenetrable, impermeable, impervi-ous, light-tight, dark, black, windowless, blank, covered, coated. *See also* shady, mirror-like, inscrutable, unintelligent.

open wide-open, unclosed, uncovered, unfolded, exposed, visible, ajar, split, torn, cracked, creviced, cleft, fissured, breached, gaping, open-mouthed; candid, frank, explicit, plain-speaking, clear, crystal-clear, truthful, honest, veracious, free, unreserved, forthright, straightforward, blunt, outspoken, emphatic, bold, no-nonsense, daring, brazen, immodest, shameless, impudent, defiant, barefaced, flaunting. *See also* opened up, holed, open, beginning.

open-air outdoor, out-of-door, alfresco.

opened up unblocked, unlocked, unbarred, unfastened, unsealed, uncovered, uncorked, unobstructed, patent, clear, evident, obvious, manifest, unimpeded, unhindered, unrestricted, accessible, open-door, available, vacant, unenclosed, unprotected, extended, bare, open-plan.

operational functional, going, working, usable, running, active. *See also* workable, operative.

operative in force, relevant, significant, important, crucial, critical, key, influential, efficacious, efficient, effective; working, switched on, armed, in force, valid, established.

opinionated dogmatic.

opportune timely, appropriate, convenient, suitable, fitting, auspicious.

opposing resistant, obstructive, hindering, confrontational, disapproving, antipathetic, antagonistic, hostile, defiant, contentious, rival, inimical.

opposite diametric(al), other, contrapositive, antithetic(al), antipodal, contrary, contrariwise, contrasting, reverse, inverse, obverse, converse, confronting, oncoming, face-to-face, eyeball-to-eyeball, polarized. *See also* opposing.

oppositional opposing, hostile, antagonistic, inimical, unfriendly, unfavourable, unpropitious, adverse, contrary, counteractive, cross, antipathetic(al), averse, disapproving, alien, repugnant. *See also* discordant, contrary, uncooperative.

oppressive overweening, overbearing, hubristic.

optimistic hopeful, cheerful, confident, positive, expectant, idealistic.

opulent luxurious, lavish, sumptuous, palatial, splendid, first-class, de luxe, expensive, diamond-studded, gilded, glittering, plush (Inf), ritzy (Sl), glitzy (Sl).

oral verbal, spoken, vocal.

orange reddish-yellow, ochreous, amber, saffron, apricot, peach, golden, old-gold, or, carroty, Titian, ginger, tan, bronze, brassy, flame-coloured, coppery.

oratorical rhetorical, declamatory, demagogic, demagogical. *See also* vocative.

orbital rotatory, revolutionary, circuitous, circulatory, turning, roundabout, indirect, oblique, meandering, ambagious (Arch), deviating, circumnavigable, circumambient, circumlocutory. *See also* circular, orbiting.

orbiting wheeling, circling, spiralling, turning, spinning, gyrating.

ordered organized, formalized, arranged, arrayed, disposed, composed, structured, schematic, systematic, symmetrical, balanced, ordained. *See also* grouped, hierarchical, orderly, well-ordered, habitual, harmonious, disciplined.

orderly tidy, neat, clean, smooth, straight, correct, trim, spruce, dapper, smart, sleek, slick, groomed, kempt, shipshape, dinky (Inf); regular, balanced, uniform, even, steady, level, flat, ordinary, everyday, typical, routine, continual, constant, methodical, metrical, consistent, normal, legal, customary, traditional.

ordinary middling, average, median, everyday, commonplace, mediocre, middle-of-the-road, moderate, unheroic, only passable, tolerable, bearable, so-so (Inf), wet (Inf).

organic organismal, organological, morphologic(al), anatomic(al), formal.

organizational methodical, systematic, schematic, rational, formational.

organized methodized, systematized, rationalized, planned, prearranged.

original experimental, inventive, creative, innovative, novel, modern, new, unfamiliar, strange, avant-garde, venturesome, daring, enterprising, reckless, risky, chancy. *See also* novel, authentic.

ornamental showy, ornate, decorated, garnished, attractive.

ornate elaborate, fancy, decorated, adorned, garnished, trimmed, embellished, beautified, gilded, coloured, rich, luxuriant, florid, flowery, precious, euphuistic, euphemistic, extravagant, overstated, exaggerated, hyperbolic, affected, pompous, pretentious, ostentatious, flamboyant, showy, meretricious, frothy, fussy, overloaded, stiff, stilted, pedantic, ponderous, Latinate, sesquipedalian, Johnsonian, diffuse, circumlocutory, convoluted, tortuous, rhetorical, declamatory, oratorical, eloquent, grandiloquent, magniloquent, lofty, high-flown, loud, brassy, ringing, ranting, orotund, high-pitched, grandiose, stately, bombastic, fustian, inflated, tumid, turgid, antithetical, alliterative, metaphorical, figurative, highfalutin (Inf).

ornithological avicultural.

orogenic orographic, orogenetic, orological, orometric.

oscillating swinging, fluctuating, alternating, reciprocal, back-and-forth, to-and-fro, up-and-down, see-saw, periodic(al), harmonic, libratory, nutational. *See also* vibrating, vacillating, rocking, waving.

ostensible seeming, deceptive, specious, illusory, visionary, dream-like, chimerical, imaginary, hallucinatory.

ostentatious showy, plumed, crested, fine, grand, fashionable, flaunting.

otological audiological, otolaryngological, otorhinolaryngological, ENT (ear, nose, and throat), otalgic, otoscopic.

outclassed outshone, bested, worsted, trounced, beaten, defeated, humiliated, humbled, ruined.

outdated old-fashioned, archaic, outmoded, obsolete.

outer outward, superficial, surface, external, exterior, visual, reflected, visible.

outflowing outpouring, effluent, effusive, extravasated, expended, spent.

outgoing outward-bound, going, departing, leaving, forthcoming, issuing, egressive, emerging, coming out, arising, surfacing, erupting, volcanic, explosive, expulsive, emanating, transeunt, transient. *See also* outflowing, leaky.

outlandish unconventional, barbarous, alien, exotic, strange, weird.

outlined summarized, brief, impressionistic, representative, emblematic, sample, random, descrip-

outrageous

tive, delineative, depictive, thumb-nail, skeletal, abridged, abbreviated, circumscriptive, projectional, peripheral, marginal.

outrageous horrible, shocking, atrocious, beastly, scandalous, vile; extravagant, excessive, immoderate, preposterous.

outside outward, out-of-doors, open-air, alfresco, outermost, outlying, extramural.

outspoken straightforward, frank, direct, plain-spoken, candid, curt, bluff, abrupt.

outstanding distinguished, celebrated, eminent, great, impressive, notable; owing, due, payable, unpaid, pending.

outward surface, facial, superficial, displayed, projected, assumed.

over gone, gone forever, bygone, finished, exhausted, ended, done, spent, completed, irrecoverable, extinct.

overambitious rash, overloaded, overextended.

overbearing domineering, oppressive, superior, officious, high-handed, autocratic.

overcast cloudy, louring, glowering, dismal.

overestimated overvalued, overrated, overpriced, dear, expensive, misjudged, exaggerated, overpraised.

overestimating overconfident, rash, overoptimistic, overenthusiastic, hubristic, arrogant. *See also* overestimated.

overindulgent immoderate, uncontrolled, unrestrained, undisciplined, abandoned, inordinate, excessive, incontinent, concupiscent, intemperate, drunk, crapulent, addicted, greedy, gluttonous, gourmandizing, extravagant, wasteful, prodigal.

overjoyed delighted, jubilant, elated, thrilled, over the moon (Inf).

overlooked disregarded, blotted (out), wiped away, swept clean.

overrated exaggerated, overestimated, overvalued.

overrun overspread, overgrown, overflowing, brimming, flooding, inundated, infested, beset, teeming, swarming, plagued, encroaching, trespassing, intrusive, invasive. *See also* excessive, exaggerated, surpassing, out of reach.

oversensitive touchy, irritable, irascible, thin-skinned, highly strung, temperamental, nervy, jumpy.

overthrown overturned, overset, upset, toppled, subverted, suppressed, oppressed, subversive, revolutionary.

overwrought on edge, agitated, tense, keyed up, excited, frantic.

owed unpaid, unsettled, in arrears, outstanding, payable, chargeable, redeemable, coming to.

owing due, unpaid, outstanding, overdue, in arrears.

P

pacificatory conciliatory, placatory, propitiatory, appeasing, irenic, dove-like, friendly, disarming, satisfying, calming, soothing, emollient, lenitive, mediatory, negotiated, pacifiable, satisfied, happy, content.

packed crammed, full, crowded, brimful, stuffed, jammed.

paid liquidated, debt-free, cleared, settled, discharged.

painful sore, hurting, distressing, chronic, acute, stinging, tingling, smarting, cramping, lancinating, aching, tender, raw, throbbing, biting, gnawing, gripping, stabbing, shooting, grinding, splitting, pounding, agonizing, purgatorial, excruciating, racking; harrowing, burning, searing, scalding, traumatic, extreme, unbearable. *See also* injured, feeling pain, inflicting pain.

painless effortless, easy, simple, pain-free.

painstaking meticulous, careful, scrupulous, conscientious, assiduous, thorough.

palatable tasty, mouthwatering, appetizing, delicious, luscious, delectable.

palatial opulent, spacious, stately, grand, imposing, magnificent.

pale pallid, sallow, waxen, ashen, livid, ghastly.

paltry petty, minor, trifling, puny, insignificant, derisory.

panting wheezing, snorting, winded.

parallel equidistant, concentric, co-extensive, nonconvergent, nondivergent, antiparallel. *See also* correlated.

parapsychological extrasensory, supersensible, precognitive, clairvoyant, telepathic, psychokinetic, psychic(al), occult, spiritual, supernatural, animist, astral, phantom.

parched dry, arid, thirsty, withered, shrivelled, scorched.

parliamentary congressional, senatorial, legislative, deliberative, unicameral, bicameral, conciliar, convocational, ecclesiastical, synodal, canonical, decretal.

parlous dangerous, risky, hazardous, dire.

parsimonious tight-fisted, mean, miserly, stingy, penny-pinching, niggardly.

partial broken, fragmented, in smithereens, brashy, crumbly, incomplete, limbless, headless, imperfect, inadequate, insufficient, scrappy, bitty, piecemeal, unfinished, fractional, aliquot, proportional, partitive, segmental, sectional, compartmental, departmental, divided, molecular, atomic, elemental, sliced, diced, minced, ground, shredded, wispy.

particular specific, definite, determined, stipulated, indicated, named, fixed, pinned down, distinct, singular, single, individual.

passing overtaking, moving, proceeding, transferring, transducing, crossing, traversing, transitional. *See also* penetrating.

passionate intense, effusive, ardent, fervent, zealous, vehement, rapturous, ecstatic, fiery, heated, inflamed, excitable, impetuous, hotheaded, temperamental, touchy, volatile, mercurial, unstable, melodramatic, hysterical, obsessed, jealous, envious, fanatical, manic, raving, raging, OTT (Sl).

passive compliant, submissive, docile, resigned, inactive, inert.

past historical, old, prehistoric, protohistoric, ancient, early, elder, primitive, primal, primeval. *See also* over, antiquarian, former, retrospective.

pastoral rural, rustic, idyllic, country; clerical, ministerial.

patchy sketchy, bitty, erratic, fitful, irregular.

paternal fatherly, protective, solicitous.

pathetic touching, plaintive, poignant, sad, tender, emotional; meagre, paltry, inadequate, pitiful, contemptible.

payable due, owed, remittable, refundable, redeemable.

paying disbursing, expending, spending. *See also* paid, payable, profitable, receiving pay, paying in return.

peaceful quiet, tranquil, serene, still, calm, halcyon, piping, palmy, golden, harmonious, peacelike, dovelike, innocent, mild, easy-going, good-natured, agreeable, tolerant, peaceable, law-abiding, nonaggressive, pacifist, nonviolent, passive, civilian, neutral, nonaligned, conciliatory, placatory, irenic.

pealing chiming, repeating.

pedantic strict, rigid, severe, rigorous, literal-minded, close, authoritative, cogent, weighty, forceful, legal, lawful, legitimate.

peeling shedding, sloughy, exuvial, exfoliatory, leafless, desquamative, ecdysial, moulting, unfledged, unfeathered, plucked.

penetrating infiltrating, transudating, permeating, percolating, osmotic, intervening.

penitent repentant, contrite, remorseful, regretful, lamenting, sorry, apologetic, sorrowful, rueful, ashamed, self-condemning, compunctious, guilty, conscience-stricken, confessing, reformed, converted, born-again. *See also* penitential.

penitential atoning, self-punishing, humiliated.

perfect finished, completed, fulfilled, polished, ripened, ready, matured, exact, just right, ideal, best, flawless, faultless, impeccable, infallible, indefectible, correct, precise, accurate, spot on, irreproachable, immaculate, unsoiled, spotless, blemish-free, uncontaminated, pure, blameless, exemplary, innocent, impeccant, saintly, sound, unbroken, uncracked, undamaged, unmarred, unspoiled, unscathed, unscarred, airtight, watertight, intact, whole, entire, absolute, utter, total, excellent, sublime, superb, dazzling, brilliant, masterly, expert, proficient, skilled, consummate, supreme, transcendent, unsurpassable, unequalled, unmatched, unrivalled, peerless, top, number-one, archetypal, classical, Augustan, A-OK (Inf), A1 (Inf). *See also* perfectionist.

perfectionist purist, pedantic, precise, punctilious, meticulous, fastidious, scrupulous, particular, exacting, demanding, fussy.

perfunctory casual, lackadaisical, desultory, superficial.

periodic cyclic, repetitive, annual, yearly, biannual, biennial, monthly, weekly, daily, hourly; intermittent, sporadic, discontinuous, fitful, irregular.

periodical regular, repetitive, iterative, returning, recurrent, quinquennial, millennial, cyclic, seasonal, yearly, annual, biennial, monthly, weekly, daily. *See also* periodic.

perjurious perjured, libellous, slanderous, defamatory, misrepresented, trumped-up, planted (Inf), cooked-up (Inf), put-up (Inf), framed (Sl).

permanent lasting, unchanging, everlasting, perpetual, persistent, persevering, continuing, constant, changeless, invariable, unalterable, immutable, unfailing, dependable, reliable, steadfast, sustained, perennial, evergreen, abiding, enduring, surviving, subsisting, durable, stable, fixed, established, entrenched, longstanding, indestructible, conserved, preserved, imperishable, unbreakable, inviolable, immortal, undying, eternal, firm, solid, steady, rock-steady, immovable, rigid, static, stationary. *See also* conservative.

permitted allowed, authorized, warranted, sanctioned, licensed, legal, lawful, licit, decriminalized, chartered, patent, above board, legitimate, acceptable, worthwhile, approved, passed, unconditional, without strings, legit (Sl) permitting.

permitting permissive, admissible, allowing, printable, tolerant, lenient, indulgent, loose, lax, overindulgent, irresolute, unassertive, conniving.

perpendicular orthogonal, right-angled, square, normal, rectangular.

perpetual incessant, continual, ceaseless, never-ending, eternal, enduring.

perplexing puzzling, baffling, bewildering, muddling, mysterious, weird.

persevering persistent, tenacious, sedulous, assiduous, dogged, determined, resolute, stubborn, obstinate, enduring, staunch, faithful, diligent, surviving, patient, plodding, slogging away, industrious, strenuous. *See also* steady, indomitable.

persistent determined, dogged, persevering, resolute, stubborn, obstinate; constant, perpetual, unrelenting, incessant.

personable appealing, enchanting, agreeable, charming, becoming presentable, tidy (Inf), trim, attractive, peachy, blooming, rosy, elegant, tasteful.

personal private, intimate, exclusive, individual, confidential.

persuadable credulous, receptive, tractable, docile, inspired, motivated, incited, spurred on, encouraged, egged on, induced, pressured.

persuasive influential, impressive, convincing, cogent, hortatory, didactic, protreptic, directive, compelling, forceful, effective, winning, inducing, incentive, motivating, encouraging, stimulating, challenging, rousing, provocative, teasing, tantalizing, tempting, alluring, attractive, inviting, magnetic, fascinating, bewitching, hypnotic, mesmeric, charismatic, irresistible, addictive. *See also* persuadable.

pertinent appropriate, fitting, apt, proper, seemly, suitable.

perturbed alarmed, agitated, flustered, disturbed, ruffled, unsettled.

pervasive extensive, widespread, rife, prevalent, universal, common.

perverted abnormal, aberrant, deviant, unnatural, warped, wicked.

pessimistic gloomy, despondent, despairing, glum, depressed.

petrographic petrographical, petrological, petrogenic, lithic, igneous, magmatic, volcanic, plutonic, pyroclastic, intrusive, extrusive, sedimentary, stratified, clastic, detrital, metamorphic, foliated.

petty unimportant, trivial, insignificant, paltry, minor; mean, stingy, grudging, spiteful, narrowminded.

petulant bad-tempered, cross, peevish, querulous, sulky, fretful.

phenomenal sensational, marvellous, exceptional, wonderful, extraordinary, fantastic.

philanthropic humanitarian, benevolent, beneficent, humane, charitable, altruistic, aid-giving, alms-giving, generous, munificent, kind, compassionate, gracious, bighearted, public spirited, idealistic, enlightened, reforming, visionary, liberal, utilitarian, socialistic, communistic.

philistine uncultured, crass, lowbrow, uneducated, bourgeois, boorish.

philosophical learned, erudite, rational, logical, thoughtful, wise; calm, patient, cool, resigned, stoical, unruffled.

phlegmatic indifferent, apathetic, impassive, cold, stoical, unemotional.

phonetic phonic, tonic, tonal, nasal, twangy, throaty, guttural, aspirate.

phoney bogus, sham, fake, false, affected.

photoelectric photoconductive, photoemissive, photometric, photo-

sensitive, phototropic, photophobic, spectral, photic, optic.

photographic photogenic, camera-shy, photosensitive.

phrasal phraseological, clausal, sentential, collocating, locutionary, metaphoric(al), circumlocutory, periphrastic, diffuse, paraphrastic, phraseographic, epitaphic.

physical classical, mechanical, dynamic, static, kinetic, kinematic, hydrodynamic, aerodynamic, acoustic(al), ultrasonic, subsonic, optical, thermal, calorific, thermodynamic, cryogenic, electrical, magnetic, electrodynamic, atomic, crystallographic, spectroscopic, spectrometric, quantum, statistical, relativistic.

physiological metabolic, anabolic, catabolic, alimentary, respiratory, aerobic, anaerobic, photosynthetic, secretory, excretory, reproductive, locomotory.

pictorial diagrammatic, graphic, tabular, calligraphic, linear, optical, illusionistic, photographic, iconic. *See also* sculptural, artistic, realist.

picturesque beautiful, attractive, colourful, vivid, graphic, artistic.

piquant pungent, aromatic, flavourful, appetizing, stinging, biting, hot, peppery, seasoned, spiced, herby, savoury, tangy, tart, sharp, sour, bitter, minty, highly seasoned, spicy, salty, strong, smoky, cured, kippered, pickled, soused, gamy, racy. *See also* stimulating.

piteous lamentable, miserable,

poignant, moving, affecting, woeful.

pitiful heart-rending, heart-breaking, pathetic, sad, distressing, grievous, touching, moving, tear-jerking, affecting, ruthful (Arch), self-pitying.

pitiless unpitying, unfeeling, unmoved, unresponsive, impassive, uncaring, obdurate, unsympathetic, heartless, hardhearted, cold, coldhearted, stony-hearted, hard, harsh, severe, flinty, tough, callous, ruthless, cruel, soulless, brutal, coldblooded, sadistic, barbarous, remorseless, vengeful, vindictive, unforgiving. *See also* inflexible.

pitying sympathetic, comforting, consoling, commiserative, condolent, understanding, compassionate, caring, tenderhearted, gentle, kind, kindhearted, softhearted, warmhearted, benevolent, gracious, generous, clement, yielding, lenient, forbearant, charitable, humane, merciful, forgiving. *See also* pitiful.

placid tranquil, calm, serene, gentle, quiet, composed.

plain clear, distinct, obvious, lucid, evident, manifest; simple, ordinary, pure, unpretentious, everyday, modest; ugly, unattractive, ordinary, unpretentious; blunt, candid, frank, outspoken, forthright; austere, severe, bare, restrained, unadorned, basic; flat, even, level, smooth, plane.

planned intended, intentional, rational, meant, premeditated, contrived, designed, organized, schematic, systematic, orderly, methodical, worked out, prepared, strategic, tactical, under discussion, under consideration, in draft, in proof, drawn up. *See also* planning.

planning scheming, cunning, contriving, resourceful, ingenious, purposeful, involved, in deep, intriguing, plotting, conspiratorial, Machiavellian, wheeler-dealing (Inf).

plantlike vegetable, vegetal, vegetative, herbal, herbaceous, grassy, leafy, verdant, overgrown, weedy. *See also* plants, botanical.

platelike leaflike, foliate, lamellar, placoid, membranous, pellicular, filmy, scummy, drossy, scaly, furfuraceous, squamous, flaky, scurfy, flocculent.

plausible probable, possible, reasonable, credible, believable, persuasive.

playful frisky, frolicsome, lively, merry, mischievous, spirited.

pleasant comfortable, easeful, restful, relaxing, soothing, comforting, warm, congenial, agreeable, likable, nice, pleasing, satisfying, gratifying, refreshing, enjoyable, convivial, delectable, charming, delightful, idyllic, Elysian, paradisiacal, luscious, opulent, luxuriant, exquisite, sumptuous, de luxe, lush, welcome, inviting, snug, cosy, soft, cuddly, heart-warming, lovable, blissful, palatable, delicious, mouthwatering, ambrosial, sweet, succu-

lent, juicy, perfumed, euphonious, dulcet, titillating, seductive, sensual, erotic, carnal, voluptuous, scrumptious (Inf), cushy (Inf). *See also* pleased; likable, comfortable, tasty, pleasure-loving.

pleased relaxed, comfortable, warm, cosy, content, happy, at ease, delighted, sensual, profligate, voluptuous, licentious, hedonistic, fun-loving, wanton, sybaritic, excited, titillated, gratified, satisfied, mollycoddled, cosseted, pampered, spoiled, euphoric, chuffed (Sl), gruntled (Brit), high (Sl).

pleasing agreeable, gratifying, pleasant, charming, attractive, winning.

pleasure-loving hedonistic, epicurean, gourmet, gourmand, self-indulgent, voluptuous.

plebian common, vulgar, coarse, unrefined, proletarian, working-class.

plentiful ample, superfluous, redundant, openhanded, generous, bountiful, lavish, liberal, extravagant, prodigal, wholesale, unsparing, unmeasured, endless, inexhaustible, bottomless, great, luxuriant, riotous, lush, rank, fat, fertile, prolific, profuse, abundant, copious, overflowing, superabundant, rich, opulent, affluent.

pliable flexible, supple, pliant, lithe, plastic, malleable; adaptable, responsive, compliant, receptive, docile, yielding.

pliant giving, yielding, melting,

flexible, bendable, stretchable, elastic, lithe, willowy, supple, lissom, loose-limbed, springy, acrobatic, athletic, plastic, extensile, ductile, tractile, adaptable, malleable, mouldable, shapable, impressible, waxy, doughy, pasty, putty-like.

plucky brave, valiant, courageous, daring, spirited, bold.

plural multiple, many, several, some, upwards of, more, most, majority, numerous, multitudinous. See also various, multiplicative.

poetic lyrical, rhyming, metrical.

poignant moving, sad, painful, distressing, touching, plaintive; sharp, cutting, acute, pointed, caustic, piercing.

pointless futile, senseless, silly, stupid, vain, irrelevant, ineffectual.

poised calm, serene, dignified, graceful, composed, self-confident; ready, waiting, prepared.

poisonous toxic, venomous, deadly, lethal, fatal, infectious.

polished varnished, burnished, waxed, enamelled, lacquered, glazed, glacé, gleaming, shiny, glossy, glassy, mirror-like, slippery, skiddy, slithery, buttery, lubricated, oily, greasy, soapy.

polite courteous, respectful, genteel, refined, polished, cultivated.

political politicized, party-minded, partisan, bipartisan, affiliated, associated, right-wing, true-blue, left-wing, leftist, popular, middle-of-the-road, liberal, independent, non-partisan, green, radical, socialistic, communistic, factional, sectional, sectarian, separatist, particular, nationalistic, red (Inf).

pompous stuffy, self-important, grandiloquent, bombastic, turgid, pontificating, windy, long-drawn-out.

ponderous onerous, heavy-handed, cumbersome, weighed down, burdensome, taxed, saddled, overburdened, overloaded, overladen, oppressive, taxing, overbalanced, top-heavy, unwieldy, pressing, incumbent on, pressurized, handicapped.

poor impecunious, penniless, moneyless, penurious, poverty-stricken, lowpaid, underprivileged, deprived, needy, indigent, wanting, straitened, hand-to-mouth, destitute, necessitous; worthless, bad, shoddy, substandard, subnormal, tatty, cheap, scratch, makeshift, jerry-built, patchy, crummy (Sl), crappy (Sl), duff (Inf); mean, wretched, miserable, sad, woeful, pitiful, grievous, lamentable, deplorable, contemptible, despicable, scruffy, shabby, grubby, nauseating, revolting, disgusting, hateful, coarse, vulgar, reprehensible, disgraceful, shameful; rotten, decaying, putrid, stinking, foul, corrupt, stale, mouldy, diseased, poisoned, measly (Inf), lousy (Inf), grotty (Sl), gungy (Inf), yucky (Sl). See also insolvent, beggarly, inadequate.

popular beloved, liked, sought after, welcome, entertained, feted.

portable

portable movable, handy, convenient, light, manageable, compact.

positive certain, absolute, decisive, definite, actual, clear-cut; assertive, cocksure, forceful, resolute; constructive, practical, useful, progressive; utter, perfect, complete, out-and-out.

possessed owned, held, belonging to, on hand, in store, exclusive, unshared, monopolized by.

possessing possessory, owning, landowning, landed, property-owning, having, holding, enjoying, proprietorial, occupying, squatting, exclusive, unshared, monopolistic. *See also* possessed.

possible potential, imaginable, thinkable, credible, believable, feasible, admissible, viable, tenable, reasonable, practical, doable, workable, performable, operable, achievable, attainable, realizable, likely, accessible, approachable, reachable, available, flexible, able, capable. *See also* potential.

post-mortem post-obit, posthumous, funereal, embalmed, mummified, fossilized.

potent forceful, powerful, puissant (Arch), mighty, redoubtable, formidable, great, high-powered, overwhelming, superior, compelling, convincing, persuasive, effective, cogent, telling, trenchant, weighty, clear-cut, distinct, unmistakable, marked, urgent, pressing, severe, intense, vehement, extreme, drastic, Draconian, thoroughgoing, well-founded, firm, staunch, fervent, fierce.

potential possible, promising, undeveloped, future, prospective, eventual, virtual, dormant.

powdery dusty, pulverulent, scobiform, dirty, sooty, chalky, calcareous, flocculent. *See also* mealy, grainy, pulverized, crumbly, pulverizable.

powered charged, combustible, inflammable, flammable, explosive, incendiary, carbonaceous, carboniferous, coaly, bituminous, lignitic, coal-fired, gaseous, gas-fired, electric, hydroelectric, electrical, woody, ligneous, wood-burning, oil-fired, thermal, nuclear, thermonuclear, geothermal, solar, solar-powered.

powerful potent, mighty, virile, strong, puissant (Arch), great, prevailing, prevalent, predominant, superior, influential, omnipotent, almighty, empowered, endowed, authoritative, sovereign, hegemonic, plenipotentiary, competent, capable, fit, able, gifted, talented, qualified, equal to, up to, effectual, efficient, proficient, forceful, compelling, charismatic, compulsive, cogent; athletic, muscular, brawny, burly, sinewy, strapping, weather-beaten, lean, wiry, stringy, robust, enduring, untiring, unflagging, indefatigable, tenacious, resilient, hardy, stalwart, rough, brutal, vicious, bullying. *See also* operative, full of energy, charged, powered.

powerless unable, incapable, unauthorized, invalid, illegal, disfranchised, inoperative, unemployed, switched off, suspended, deactivated, in abeyance, mothballed, broken down, deposed, disqualified, unfit, inept, good-for-nothing, unworkable, worthless, useless, ineffective, inefficient, incompetent, dud (Inf), duff (Inf), kaput (Sl). *See also* unprotected, impotent, unsexed.

practical realistic, pragmatic, expedient, sensible, matter-of-fact, nononsense, no-frills, down-to-earth, businesslike, hard-headed, level-headed, sound, functional, utilitarian, useable, serviceable, workable, operative.

pragmatic sensible, practical, down-to-earth, efficient, realistic.

praiseworthy laudable, commendable, worthy, estimable, creditable, admirable, unimpeachable, meritorious, deserving.

precarious hazardous, risky, dangerous, dubious, insecure, perilous.

preceding antecedent, anterior, precessional, leading, first, earliest, pre-emptive. *See also* prior, primary, precursory, preparatory.

precious cherished, beloved, prized, treasured, esteemed, valued; costly, rare, dear, priceless, valuable; affected, pretentious, over-refined, twee (Inf).

precise exact, definite, accurate, specific, clear-cut, correct.

precocious advanced, forward, quick, clever, premature.

precognitive *a priori*, unmediated, second-sighted, clairvoyant, divinatory, telepathic, extrasensory, presentient.

precursory preliminary, initial, introductory, precursive, preceding.

predatory rapacious, voracious, ravenous, greedy, plundering, marauding.

predetermined destined, predestined, fated, doomed, appointed, foreordained, preordained, decreed. *See also* deliberate.

predictable foreseeable, probable, possible, potential, likely, certain, sure; unsurprising, unimpressive, customary, ordinary, common, expected, straightforward, run-of-the-mill, usual, plain.

predicted foretold, forecast, foreseeable.

predicting foretelling, forewarning, presentient, prescient, foreseeing, clairvoyant, fortune-telling, weather-wise, prophetic, oracular, mantic, vatic, fatidic, apocalyptic, sibylline, premonitory, foreboding, cautionary, heralding, prefiguring, precursory, signifying. *See also* predicted, presageful.

predominant ruling, superior, prevailing, leading, principal, chief.

preferable favoured, chosen, better, best, worthier, superior.

prejudiced contemptuous, class conscious, despising, undemocratic, xenophobic, racially prejudiced, anti-semitic, sexist, ageist, feminist, (male) chauvinist.

preliminary initial, introductory, first, opening, test, prior.

premature precipitate, precocious, forward, beforehand, prevenient, preparatory, prophetic, foresighted, anticipatory, expectative, impetuous, hasty, overhasty, too soon, pre-emptive, half-cocked (Inf), half-baked (Inf).

preoccupied absorbed, engrossed, intent, rapt, unaware, oblivious.

preparatory foundational, developmental, leading, guiding, piloting, exploratory, reconnoitring, founding, discovering, innovatory, avant-garde, pioneering, trailblazing, ground-breaking. *See also* developing, prepared, in hand, developed, ready-made.

prepared ready, alert, vigilant, mobilized, standing by, all set, teed up, keyed up, spoiling for, trained, qualified, experienced, practised, well-rehearsed, organized, tuned, primed, briefed, instructed, tutored, forewarned, forearmed, in harness, armed, equipped, furnished, well-appointed, groomed, accoutred, dressed.

preposterous ludicrous, ridiculous, absurd, foolish, outrageous, senseless.

presageful portentous, significant, fateful, augural, auspicial, haruspical, propitious, promising, fortunate, favourable, ominous, inauspicious, unfavourable.

present existent, extant, real, actual, material, solid, manifest, omnipresent, ubiquitous, infinite, everywhere, pervasive, diffusive, penetrating, permeating, suffusive, ghostly, spectral, haunted. *See also* attendant, resident, available, occasional, available.

preserved kept, alive, fresh, undecayed, desiccated, dried, frozen, pickled, marinated, salted, corned, soused, smoked, cured, canned, tinned, potted, bottled, mummified, embalmed, stuffed, mothballed, stored, conserved, protected, saved, treasured, cherished.

preserving conserving, protecting, prophylactic, preventive, salubrious, desiccated, redemptive, energy-saving, ecological, environment-friendly, conservational, green. *See also* preserved.

prestigious dignified, august, high-flying, stylish, commanding, patronizing, impressive, mighty, high-falutin(g) (Inf).

presumptive usurpative, violative, arrogative, familiar, impertinent.

pretending dissembling, dissimulating, play-acting, masquerading, feigning, bluffing, affecting, attitudinizing, posturing, posing, seeming, apparent, so-called, ostensible.

pretentious deceptive, showy, hypocritical, insincere, meretricious, pretending, posing, posturing, play-acting, dissembling, feigning, bluffing, unnatural, false, phoney, hollow, affected, sanctimonious, mealy-mouthed, artificial, false-faced, tokenistic, unctuous, sweet-talking (Inf).

pretty beautiful, good-looking, attractive, lovely, pleasing, charming.

prevailing prevalent, widespread, common, popular, accepted, predominant, dominant, public, communal, unrestricted.

priced valued, rated, assessed, worth. *See also* chargeable.

priceless expensive, precious, rare, dear, unique, treasured.

priestly ecclesiastic(al), sacerdotal, hieratic(al), clerical, ministerial, churchly, pastoral, canonical, papal, pontifical, episcopal, rabbinic, prelatic, presbyteral, hierophantic, druidic, hierocratic, parochial, diocesan.

prim demure, proper, strait-laced, prudish, stuffy, starchy (Inf).

primal primordial, primitive, primeval, early, antediluvian, prelapsarian, Precambrian, glacial, prehistoric, Palaeolithic, Stone-Age.

primary senior, superior, supreme, pre-eminent, leading, first, foremost, headmost, chief, elder.

primate primatial, prosimian, anthropoid, simian, pongid, hominid.

prime primal, primordial, primeval, primitive, aboriginal, earliest, original, pristine.

primeval primitive, ancient.

primitive first, early, original, ancient, primeval, primordial; crude, rude, rough, unsophisticated, savage, rudimentary.

principal chief, main, paramount, leading, first, major, key.

prior former, ex, late, erstwhile, one-time, previous, last, earlier, foregoing, above-mentioned, aforementioned, aforenamed, aforesaid.

private internal, inward, hidden, concealed, covert, secret, clandestine, disguised, camouflaged, screened, masked, covered, veiled, recondite, dark, obscure, obstructed, backstage, in camera.

privileged advantaged, favoured, indulged, entitled, immune.

prized cherished, treasured, valued, esteemed, appreciated.

probable likely, expected, undoubted, indubitable, unquestionable, apparent, ostensible, evident, presumable, predictive, prone, liable, apt, anticipated, prospective, tending, drifting. *See also* plausible.

problematic puzzling, baffling, confusing, perplexing, troubling, obfuscating, demanding, exacting, challenging, tough, complex, complicated, intricate, delicate, convoluted, involved, confused, labyrinthine, skilled, specialized, technical, abstruse, recondite, esoteric, impenetrable, obscure, unclear, unintelligible, illegible, indecipherable, knotty (Inf), tricky (Inf), thorny (Inf), ticklish (Inf), sticky

(Inf), hairy (Inf), pernickety (Inf), crabbed (Inf), cramped (Inf).

procrastinating postponing, delaying, sluggish, lazy, neglectful, negligent, remiss.

prodigious huge, vast, gigantic, enormous, immense, colossal; amazing, phenomenal, striking, marvellous, wonderful, fabulous.

produced created, man-made, synthetic, artificial, manufactured, processed, ready-made, machine-made, mass-produced, handmade, homemade, homespun, tailor-made, architect-designed, custom-built, invented, imagined, devised, worked out, discovered, begotten, bred, hatched, sown, grown, raised, reared, educated.

productive creative, innovative, inventive, original, formative, structural, constructive, architectonic, manufacturing, industrial, developed, mechanized, automated, computerized, robotic, postindustrial, developing, agricultural, fertile, fruitful, fecund, prolific, rich, profitable, remunerative, lucrative, paying, high-yielding, interest-bearing, worthwhile, high-tech (Inf), low-tech (Inf). *See also* produced.

profane irreverant, sinful, pagan, godless, heathen, wicked; unholy, temporal, worldly, lay, unconsecrated; coarse, crude, obscene, vulgar, foul.

professional vocational, occupational, industrial.

proficient efficient, competent, ac-

complished, expert, handy, skilled, deft, versatile, dexterous, adroit, talented, gifted, masterful, wicked (Sl).

profitable remunerative, lucrative, paying, gainful, productive, fruitful, beneficial, advantageous, salutary, edifying, worthwhile, valuable; money-making.

profound wise, learned, erudite, intellectual, philosophical, recondite; deep, cavernous, bottomless, abyssal, yawning; extreme, absolute, utter, intense, keen, sincere.

progressive increasing, growing, advancing, ongoing; dynamic, modern, radical, enlightened, liberal.

prohibitive repressive, preventive, restraining, suppressive, forbidding; exorbitant, extortionate, steep, excessive.

projectile trajectile, jaculatory, ejective, ballistic, missile, expulsive, explosive.

projecting overhanging, jutting, sticking out, beetle-browed.

prominent conspicuous, obvious, obtrusive, noticeable, striking, pronounced, marked; projecting, bulging, protruding, jutting; distinguished, eminent, celebrated, famous, important, renowned, foremost.

promiscuous debauched, wanton, loose, abandoned, licentious, profligate; careless, casual, heedless, uncritical, irresponsible, indiscriminate.

promised pledged, bound, committed, testimonial, sworn, on oath, adjuratory, votive, affirmative, assured, professed, engaged, betrothed, spoken for. *See also* guaranteeing, auspicious, future.

prompt instant, rapid, speedy, immediate, punctual; alert, eager, willing, ready.

propertied proprietary, possessing, freehold, leasehold, copyhold, movable, immovable, real, allotted, territorial, landed, praedial, manorial, seignorial, feudal, feodal, allodial, patrimonial, hereditary, testamentary, limited, assessed, collateral, secured, tangible, intangible, fixed, frozen, liquid, net, endowed, dowered, established, copyrighted, patented.

propitious fortunate, promising, opportune, timely, encouraging, bright.

propulsive propellant, pulsive, motive, driving, shoving, pushing. *See also* projectile.

prosaic dull, dreary, boring, mundane, ordinary, unimaginative, banal.

prosperous successful, thriving, flourishing, booming, well-to-do, well-off, rising, upwardly mobile, profiteering, famous, affluent, rich, opulent, wealthy, luxurious, fat, comfortable, cosy, at ease, bullish, fortunate, lucky, palmy, halcyon, golden, rosy, blissful, blessed, favourable, promising, auspicious, propitious, well-heeled (Inf).

protected shielded, enclosed, wrapped, packaged, boxed, crated, encased, bound, sheathed, swathed, bandaged, hidden, concealed, screened, masked, veiled, shrouded, cloaked, robed, hooded, camouflaged, disguised, walled in.

protective defensive, vigilant, guarding, shielding, watchful, jealous.

protesting opposing, dissenting, dissatisfied, disapproving, negative, negating, hostile, critical, discontent, malcontent, unconsenting, deprecatory, recalcitrant, refractory, challenging, noncooperative, noncompliant, nonconformist, disobedient, angry, contrary, defiant, recusant, counteractive, denying, contradictive, repudiated, clamourous, hissing, booing, jeering, bolshie (Inf), bloody-minded (Inf). *See also* law-breaking.

prototypical original, exemplary, dummy, paradigmatic, generic, model, custom-built, ready-made, tailor-made, designer.

protracted prolonged, extended, lengthened, drawn-out, interminable, unceasing, unremitting, unrelenting, persistent, unfailing, inexhaustible, without respite, nonstop, endless, enduring, lasting, everlasting.

protuberant protrudent, swelling, sticking out, proud, jutting out, bumpy, beaked. *See also* eminent, conspicuous.

proud self-important, self-confident, self-esteeming, self-regarding, spirited, courageous, house-proud, supercilious, hoity-toity, high-hatted, honourable. *See also* unapproachable, oppressive, conceited, prestigious, stately, fulfilled, ostentatious, boastful, prejudiced.

proved authenticated, ascertained, verified, validated, certified, demonstrated, confirmed, determined, established, attested, substantiated, corroborated.

proven shown, substantiated, confirmed, verified, determined, ascertained, settled, ratified, corroborated, borne out, justified, affirmed, attested, evidential, probative, probatory, corroborative, relevant.

proverbial aphoristic, gnomic, epigrammatic, axiomatic, banal, clichéd, platitudinous, commonplace, trite, hackneyed, stock, stereotyped, sententious, moralistic, preceptive, witty, pithy, enigmatic, oracular.

provisional supplied, provided, furnished, equipped, all found, all-in, well-appointed, catered, offered, given, staffed, prepared, ready, stocked, victualled.

provisioning supplying, providing, furnishing, equipping, catering, commissarial, self-service, takeaway, sufficing, sufficient, available, in stock, on tap. *See also* provisional.

provocative annoying, insulting, inciting, exasperating, provoking, stimulating; tempting, inviting, sexy (Inf), alluring, seductive.

prudent judicious, wise, cautious, canny, practical, considerate.

prying officious, meddlesome, meddling, prurient, gossipy, snooping (Inf), snoopy (Inf), nosy (Inf).

psychic subconscious, transcendental, cosmic, telepathic, telekinetic, psychokinetic, telergic, telaesthetic, radiaesthetic, extrasensory, spiritualistic, mediumistic, psychosensory, parapsychological, pseudopsychological.

psychological psychiatric, neuropsychiatric, psychotherapeutic, psychoanalytical, psychodiagnostic, psychometric, psychopathological, psychosocial, psychosomatic, psychophysical, psychobiological, psychoneurological, psychosexual, psychogenic, psychogenetic, psychotechnical, psychogeriatric, psychopharmacological. *See also* subconscious.

published printed, circulating, current, open, public, revealed, disclosed, exposed, announced, declared, proclaimed, ventilated, aired, communicated, disseminated, distributed, circularized, broadcast, televised. *See also* well-known, publishing.

publishing declaratory, notificatory.

puerile infantile, childish, petty, trivial, juvenile, petty.

pugnacious aggressive, belligerent, quarrelsome, contentious, argumentative, petulant.

pulpy spongy, doughy, squashy,

stodgy, soggy, mushy, flabby, creamy, soupy, starchy, amylaceous.

pulverized powdered, ground, granulated, disintegrated, crushed, grated, shredded, sifted, pestled, comminuted, triturated, levigated, sharded.

punctilious fussy, meticulous, precise, correct, scrupulous, particular.

punctual prompt, exact, precise, strict, timely.

punishable liable, amerceable, mulctable, condemned.

punished disciplined, castigated, imprisoned, fined, beaten, tortured, executed, gated (Sl).

punishing hard, arduous, strenuous, exhausting, gruelling, laborious, back-breaking, demanding, taxing, torturous, painful.

punitive punishing, penalizing, capital, corporal, disciplinary, corrective, instructive, castigatory, admonitory, vindictive, retributive, revengeful, retaliatory. *See also* punished, punishing, punishable.

puny weak, feeble, delicate, small, tiny, insignificant.

pure unadulterated, undiluted, unpolluted, uncontaminated, faultless, perfect, sinless, immaculate, spotless, purified, refined, snowy, white, innocent, modest, bashful, blushing, coy, shy, chaste, undefiled, unfallen, virgin, vestal, maidenly, untouched, unwedded, celibate, continent, temperate, Platonic, sublimated, sexless, cold, frigid.

purified cleansed, spick-and-span, shining, polished, scrubbed, snow-white, dainty, nice, deodorized, disinfected, aseptic, antiseptic, sterilized, sterile, kosher (Judaism), halal.

purifying cleansing, purificatory, lustral, hygienic, sterilizing, germicidal, sanitary, disinfectant, detergent, purging, ablutionary.

purple purplish, purply, lavender, lilac, mauve, purple-red, fuchsia, magenta, maroon, plum-coloured, damson-coloured, puce, amaranthine, hyacinthine, heliotrope, violet, violaceous, amethystine, purpure, aubergine, mulberry, murrey (Arch), purple-blue, indigo. *See also* livid, furious.

purposive functional, teleological, aiming, functioning, targeting, intentional, proposed, aimed, schematic, designed, planned, reasoned, significant, meaningful.

pursued sought, followed, chased, hounded, hunted.

pursuing seeking, searching, questing, following, chasing, in pursuit. *See also* hunting, pursued.

purulent suppurative, festering, pussy, mattering, running.

putrid putrescent, decaying, rotting, rotten, decomposed, high, off, gamy, rancid, sour, tainted.

puzzling bewildering, baffling, mystifying, perplexing, incomprehensible, enigmatic.

quadrilateral

Q

quadrilateral four-sided, square, rectangular, quadrate, tetrahedral, foursquare.

qualified capable, able, eligible, suitable, suited, well-adapted, acceptable, appropriate, fit, prepared, ready, apt, worthy, deserved, merited, competent, efficient, professional, businesslike, proficient, equipped, endowed, talented, gifted, masterful, expert, skilled, experienced, practised, versed. *See also* authorized, modified, conditional.

quantitative measured, weighed, counted, sized, ample, high, deep, long, wide, massive, voluminous, thick, thin, heavy, light, bunched, packed, sparse, mountainous, increased, added, extended, greater, majority, most, many, any, about, approximate, plural, infinite, all, total, whole, entire, enough, small, some, certain, limited, rationed, finite, few, smaller, least, numbered, fractional, variable, average.

quarrelsome argumentative, cross, fractious, irritable, touchy, testy.

querulous fretful, petulant, peevish, cross, testy, whining.

questionable doubtful, uncertain, moot, at issue, debatable, controversial, borderline, arguable, disputable, equivocal, suspicious, dubious, implausible, unlikely, improbable, chancy, risky, unreliable, unverifiable, untrustworthy, deceptive, ambiguous, shady, spurious.

questioned asked, interrogated, cross-examined, quizzed, examined, analysed, researched, challenged, investigated, inspected, scrutinized, reviewed, surveyed, studied, probed, polled, canvassed, sought, grilled (Inf), pumped (Inf).

questioning requesting, pleading, inquiring, interrogative, curious, inquisitive, elenctic, investigative, examining, fact-finding, knowledge-seeking, exploratory, analytic, interpellant, probing, searching, researching, questing, prying, introspective, wondering, doubting. *See also* problematic, questionable, sceptical, questioned.

quibbling cavilling, captious, hair-splitting, nit-picking, shuffling, hedging, equivocal, prevaricating, pettifogging, pussyfooting (Inf).

quiescent silent, still, hushed, insensible, soundless, placid, tranquil, calm, serene, peaceful, restful, composed, contemplative, smooth, unruffled, untroubled, unperturbed, unagitated, unhurried, unstirring, stolid, stoic, impassive, inexcitable, imperturbable, pacific, halcyon, undisturbed, sequestered, leisured, reposing.

quiet noiseless, inaudible, hushed, silent, low; calm, untroubled, tranquil, serene, restful, placid; secluded, secret, private, isolated; simple, plain, modest; shy, retiring, gentle, docile.

quintessential constitutional, structural, organic, peerless, singular, unique, consummate, archetypical.

R

rabbit-like rabbity, lagomorphic, leporine.

racial ethnic, Caucasian, Caucasoid, White, Nordic, Alpine, Aryan, albinic, albinistic, albiniotic, Negroid, Black, Nilotic, Afro-Caribbean, Afro-American, Anglo-African, Melanesian, Polynesian, Australasian, Mongoloid, Oriental, Asian, Anglo-Indian, mixed, mulatto, octaroon, quadroon, half-caste (Offensive), half-breed (Offensive), indigenous, native, aboriginal, Indian, Amerindian.

radiating radial, rayed, spoked.

rainless fair, hot, sunny, fine, cloudless.

rainy pluvial, showery, wet, drizzly, torrential.

raised lifted, upraised, elevated, levitated, erected, set up, escalated, upreared, uplifted, upcast, upbuoyed, attolent, supportive, upstanding, vertical, hoisted, heaved, mounted, lobbed, thrown, blown up, swollen. *See also* exalted.

ranging travelling, free-range, unconfined, untethered, unfettered, manoeuvrable.

ranked hierarchic, classed, classified, ordered, rated, given status.

raw

rarefied expansive, extensive, extending, attenuated, dilative, etherealized, thinning, diluted, weak, adulterated, watered-down, cut.

rash reckless, hasty, impetuous, precipitate, headlong, breakneck, imprudent, improvident, injudicious, indiscreet, inconsiderate, thoughtless, ill-considered, inattentive, negligent, slapdash, hit-and-miss, careless, heedless, regardless, incautious, uncircumspect, unwary, irresponsible, wild, impulsive, capricious, frivolous, flippant, couldn't-care-less, devil-may-care, free-and-easy, happy-go-lucky, foolhardy, foolish, harebrained, hot-headed, madcap, daredevil, death-defying, danger-loving, risk-taking, adventurous, daring, bold, audacious, overconfident, impatient, desperate, do-or-die, trigger-happy (Inf).

rational reasonable, coherent, logical, intelligible, lucid, clear-headed, balanced, level-headed, stable, steady, sound, sensible, commonsensical, intelligent.

rattling clattering, chattering, sputtering, clicking, ticking, knocking.

ravenous famished, hungry, starved, voracious, rapacious, greedy.

raw unripe, unseasoned, immature, callow, green, inexperienced, unskilled, inexpert, untrained, untried, untested, unsophisticated, naive, ingenuous, artless, innocent, credulous, gullible, gauche, awkward.

reactive reacting, responsive, retortive, antiphonal, reflex, knee-jerk, reactionary, retroactive, recalcitrant, revulsive.

ready-made cut-and-dried, ready-to-wear, prefabricated, processed, convenience, oven-ready, ready-to-cook, instant, predigested.

real actual, occurring, existing, entelechial, true, factual, de facto, valid, historical, material, corporeal, tangible, solid, substantial. *See also* realistic, practical, realizable.

realist naturalist, photorealist, verist, socialist realist, regionalist, precisionist, purist, classical, neoclassical, romantic, neoromantic, impressionist, neoimpressionist, postimpressionist, pointillist, divisionist, minimalist, primitive, naive, Fauvist, vorticist, concrete, constructivist, cubist, expressionist, neoexpressionist, figurative, symbolist, Dadaist, abstract, eclectic, mannerist, postmodernist, rayonist, Orphistic, suprematist, synchronic, synthetic, analytic, Renaissance, Baroque, rococo, Gothic, Hellenistic, Etruscan, Celtic, Byzantine, Bohemian.

realistic natural, lifelike, truthful, authentic, genuine, faithful, graphic.

realizable achievable, attainable, practicable, plausible, feasible, possible, probable, likely.

rear back, hind, hindermost, last, end, postern, posterior, mizzen, dorsal, lumbar, tail, continued, supplemental, anal, caudal, latter, lower. *See also* bred.

rearranged reordered, reorganized, restructured, realigned, adjusted.

reasonable sensible, practical, judicious, advisable, logical, rational; fair, just, acceptable, tolerable, modest, proper.

reasoning reasonable, rational, thinking, intellectual, intelligent, understanding, perceptive, knowledgeable, judgmental, wise, sensible, sane. *See also* rational, argumentative, causal.

rebutting refuting, rejecting, prohibiting, refusing, denying, forswearing, rejoining, retorting, objecting, opposing, obstructing, deprecating, dissenting, doubting, questioning, challenging, contradicting, countering, disagreeing, impugning, disaffirming, gainsaying (Arch).

receding recessive, retreating, retractile, regressive, declining, ebbing, refluent, backsliding, lapsing, relapsing.

receivable takable, gettable, collectable, compensatory, pensionary, hereditary, primogenitary.

received accepted, taken, acquired, gained, collected, secured, inherited, admitted, heard, read, seen, acknowledged, welcomed, entertained, baptized, christened, confirmed.

receiving recipient, taking, accepting, wage-earning, salaried, paid, compensated, pensioned, awarded, rewarded, given, allotted. *See also* receptive, received, receivable.

recent current, contemporary, new, modern, up-to-date, fresh.

receptive recipient, open, accessible, welcoming, hospitable, inviting.

reciprocal interacting, interchangeable, interplaying, give-and-take, compromising, exchanged, changed, bartered, swapped, trade-off, alternative, balancing, seesaw, compensatory, retaliatory, reacting, recoiling, requited, counteracting. *See also* interconnected, correlative.

reckless hasty, imprudent, rash, thoughtless, impetuous, impulsive.

recognizable distinguishable, identifiable, distinct, defined, unmistakable, knowable.

recoiling rebounding, resilient, springy, bouncing, bounding, elastic, resonant, vibrating, reverberative, reflective, repercussive, backfiring. *See also* reactive.

recorded documented, chronicled, logged, noted, inscribed, written down, on paper, printed, entered, registered, enrolled, filed, indexed, listed, copied, photographed, photocopied, input, taped, videotaped, filmed, official, documentary.

recreational entertaining, amusing, competitive.

recurrent regular, periodic, cyclical, returning, recurring, reappearing, ubiquitous, haunting, contin-

ual, continuous, constant, incessant, ceaseless, unremitting.

red pink, coral, shell-pink, flesh-coloured, peach-coloured, salmon-pink, shocking pink, damask, carnation, rosy, roseate, cherry, cerise, blood-red, carmine, crimson, cramoisy (Arch), scarlet, Turkey red, vermilion, vermeil, gules, brick-red, pillarbox red, flame-coloured, ruby, wine-coloured, beetroot-red, fuchsia, cyclamen, magenta, maroon, murrey (Arch), oxblood, rust-coloured, rufous, russet. *See also* red-faced, red-haired, bloody.

red-faced red-cheeked, rosy-cheeked, glowing, blooming, flushing, blushing, rubescent (Fml), ruddy, sanguine, rubicund, florid, blowzy, rouged, reddened, flushed, sunburnt, hectic, feverish, fiery, red-hot.

red-haired ginger-haired, carroty, sandy, Titian, auburn, chestnut.

reduced decreased, minus, curtailed, mutilated, headless, decapitated, docked, chopped, lopped, severed, limbless, shortened, condensed, abridged, abbreviated, cut-price, cut-rate (US), discounted, devalued, diminished, lessened, decimated, eroded, corroded, worn.

redundant superfluous, surplus, excessive, unwanted, extra, unnecessary.

refined elegant, graceful, tasteful, dignified, polished, delicate, U(Inf), well-finished, well-bred, urbane,

refractory

well-mannered, well-spoken, courteous, distingué, ladylike, gentlemanly, genteel, civilized, cosmopolitan, sophisticated, discriminating, fastidious, sensitive, artistic, aesthetic, appreciative, critical, refined.

refractory recalcitrant, wayward, arbitrary, perverse, contrary, contumacious, disobedient, unruly, restive, unmanageable, intractable, uncontrollable, ungovernable, unpersuadable, incorrigible, irrepressible, stiff-necked, hard-mouthed, indocile, cross-grained, crotchety, irascible.

refreshed cool, braced, stimulated, exhilarated, invigorated, enlivened, fortified, revitalized, recovered, revived, restored, rested, perked up.

refreshing bracing, stimulating, exhilarating, invigorating, fortifying, revitalizing, fresh, cool, cold, comforting, relieving, recreative, reviving, restorative, tonic. *See also* refreshed.

refused uncooperative, unconsenting, uncompliant, resistant, negative, recalcitrant, unwilling, nonaccepting, turned down, turned away, thrown out, ejected, excluded, withheld, retained, strike-bound, deaf to. *See also* dissenting, abnegating.

refusing unconsenting, unreconciled, unconvinced, dissenting, adverse, opposed, opting out, disagreeing.

refutable confutable, disprovable,

defeasible, weak, faulty, flawed, unfounded, groundless, unsound, objectionable, inconclusive. *See also* refuting.

refuting confuting, confounding, contradictory, counteractive, retaliatory, answering, responding, contravening, rebutting, repudiating, renouncing, abnegating, disclaiming, disowning, discrediting, exploding, disproving, negating, invalidating, overturning, destroying.

regional areal, spatial, geographical, topographic, territorial, zonal, longitudinal, latitudinal, highland, lowland, peninsular, insular, tropical, subtropical, continental, eastern, western, northern, southern, Occidental, Oriental, antipodean. *See also* national, local.

regressive recessive, reversionary, retroverse, retrograde, restitutive, compensatory, retrospective, reflexive, reactive, retroactive, atavistic, recidivist. *See also* reversed, reversible.

regrettable distressing, lamentable, disappointing, sad, shameful.

regular frequent, periodic, recurrent, repeating, repetitive, tidal, reciprocal, alternating, to-and-fro, oscillatory, revolving, returning, timed, isochronal, phasic, serial, rhythmic, measured, swinging, steady, stable, clockwork, beating, ticking, throbbing, pulsating, undulating, constant, even, symmetrical, consistent, level, flat, featureless.

See also cyclic, anniversary, orderly.

rejected refused, denied, refuted, declined, turned down, unacceptable, rebutted, disobeyed, disavowed, disallowed, prohibited, obstructed, contravened, invalidated, declined, vetoed, disbelieved, disowned, disclaimed, relinquished, renounced, negated, deprecated, repudiated, repealed, rescinded, retracted, reversed, recanted, cancelled, nullified, annulled, countermanded, challenged, questioned, contested, disproved.

rejoicing celebratory, jubilant, exultant, triumphant, glorious, ecstatic, euphoric, happy, joyful, cheery, merry, jolly, revelling, applauding, cheering, high (Sl). *See also* laughing.

related relevant, pertinent, germane, apposite, connected, associated, affiliated, allied, linked, bonded, kindred, cognate, agnate, akin to, consanguineous, wedded, bound, joined, tied, twinned, paired, involved, implicated, merged, combined, added, attached, accompanied, spliced (Inf). *See also* interrelated, ranked.

relative respective, related, analogous, comparative, related, allied; appropriate, relevant, pertinent, applicable, apposite, germane.

relaxed comfortable, painfree, carefree, troublefree, leisurely, unhurried, gentle.

relegated demoted, downgraded, dismissed, discharged, laid off, sacked.

reliable sure, certain, honest, trustworthy, sound, stable.

relieved calmed, restored, refreshed, eased, comforted, soothed, consoled, reassured, mollified, appeased, relaxed, sedated, assuaged, cured. *See also* relieving.

relieving helping, refreshing, restorative, comforting, consoling, reassuring, relaxing, easing, calming, soothing, balsamic, curative, remedial, assuaging, palliative, sedative, hypnotic.

religious pious, devout, holy, godly, saintly, seraphic, cherubic, transcendent, spiritual, mystic, other-worldly, churchgoing, practising, strict, faithful, orthodox, reverent, worshipful, prayerful, reverential, God-fearing, theopathic, humble, self-sacrificing, monastic, anchoretic, ascetic, ardent, unctuous, zealous, overreligious, priest-ridden, formalistic, Pharisaic, ritualistic, churchy, holier-than-thou, self-righteous, sanctimonious, fervent, preachy, canting, Bible-worshipping, fundamentalist, evangelical, crusading, militant, missionary, fanatical, witch-hunting, bigoted, Bible-bashing (Sl). *See also* priestly, theological.

relinquished surrendered, dropped, waived, forgone, scrapped, jettisoned, castaway, forsaken, apostatical, abandoned, derelict, deserted, stranded, jilted, cancelled, void, invalid, discontinued, abolished.

reluctant resistant, protesting, sulky, dissenting, sceptical, atheistic.

remaining residual, resultant, left, hereditary, patrimonial, vestigial, precipitated, deposited, sedimentary, surviving, bereft, widowed, orphaned, abandoned, discarded, rejected, cast-off. *See also* surplus.

remedial corrective, therapeutic, medicinal, analeptic, curative, first-aid, restorative, helpful, beneficial, healing, curing, hygienic, sanitary, salubrious, salutiferous, panacean, all-healing, soothing, paregoric, balsamic, demulcent, emollient, palliative, lenitive, anodyne, analgesic, narcotic, hypnotic, anaesthetic, insensible, peptic, digestive, purging, cleansing, cathartic, emetic, vomitory, laxative, antidotal, counteracting, theriacal, prophylactic, preventive, disinfectant, antiseptic, antipyretic, febrifugal, tonic, sttimulative, dietetic, alimentary, nutritive. *See also* medical.

remembering retrospective, mindful.

remote far, out-of-the-way, distant, isolated, inaccessible, secluded; foreign, alien, outside, extraneous; slight, faint, slim, slender, unlikely; standoffish, aloof, cool, unfriendly, detached, withdrawn.

removed extracted, extricated, uprooted, ripped, torn, wrested, pulled, drawn, plucked.

renewed renovated, restored, refurbished, regenerated, rejuvenated, refreshed, freshened up, touched up, repainted, resurrected, revived, re-vivified, remade, changed, reconstructed, redesigned, modernized, new-look, updated.

renowned famous, celebrated, eminent, distinguished, notable, well-known.

repairable restorable, mendable, rectifiable, recoverable, retrievable, redeemable, curable, operable, treatable, medicable.

repaired mended, patched up, fixed, right, correct, restored, reconditioned, renovated, redecorated, remade, rebuilt, reconstructed, reconstituted, refurbished, re-equipped, refitted, redone, rectified, reinforced, improved, like new, renewed, reborn, redeemed, saved, resuscitated, revived, renascent, resurgent, phoenix-like, reclaimed, recovered, salvaged. *See also* repairable, cured, restorative.

repeated duplicated, doubled, reproduced, replicated, echoed, mirrored, imitative, parrotlike, plagiarized. *See also* iterated, reprinted, repetitious, monotonous, recurrent, reverberatory.

repercussive causal, resultant, knock-on, consequential, reverberatory.

repetitious duplicative, reproductive, doubling, echoing, iterative, reiterant, tautological, redundant, otiose, pleonastic, recapitulative, harping, stuck-in-a-groove, wordy, prolix.

replaced overthrown, deposed, supplanted, transferred, removed, banished, expelled, deported, exiled, ostracized, evicted, evacuated, unhoused, homeless, rootless.

reprehensible errant, culpable, blameworthy, shameful, delinquent, unworthy.

representational depictive, delineatory, portraying, symbolic, emblematic, figurative, typical, quintessential, archetypal, characteristic, exemplary, evocative, descriptive, illustrative, graphic, pictorial, hieroglyphic, reflecting, similar, like, imitative, iconic, diagrammatic, vivid, realistic, naturalistic, true-to-life, impressionistic, abstract, nonrepresentational, surrealistic, artistic, photogenic, photographic.

representing iconic, pictorial, emblematic, symbolic, figurative, diagrammatic, representational, realistic, true-to-life, photographic, artistic, primitive, naive, impressionistic, surrealistic, abstract.

reprinted reissued, remade, replayed, reshown, revived, restored, renewed, reborn, reincarnated, reheated, recycled, reprocessed, rehashed (Inf).

reproduced printed, duplicated, copied, repeated, renewed, re-created, reborn, renascent, resurgent, resurrectional, reappearing. *See also* reproductive.

reproductive generative, procreative, originative, seminal, spermatic, germinal, genetic, sexual, genital, vulvar, clitoral, vaginal, cervical, ovarian, penile, phallic, scrotal, in season, on heat, pregnant, impregnated, fertilized, fecundated, breeding, broody, enceinte, gravid, expecting, parturient, in labour, antenatal, perinatal, postnatal, puerperal, obstetric, viviparous, oviparous, parthenogenetic, pregers (Sl).

reptilian reptiliform, cold-blooded, poikilothermic, lizardlike, saurian, lacertilian, turtlelike, chelonian, crocodilian, scaly, squamous. *See also* snakelike, amphibian.

repulsive repellent, repugnant, offensive, noisome, off-putting, antipathetic, ugly, abhorrent, obnoxious, disgusting, nauseating, sickening, foul, loathsome, horrible, appalling, hideous, obscene. *See also* abducent, defensive.

reputable creditworthy, respected, honoured, emeritus, popular, distinguished, eminent, approved, renowned, famous, fabled, above board. *See also* reputed.

reputed alleged, supposed.

requesting asking, insistent, urgent, inviting, desired, petitioned, round-robin, invocational, incantational, adjuratory, entreating, beseeching, propositional, proposable, offered, required, courting, wooing. *See also* demanding, begging.

required essential, necessary,

needed, vital, indispensable, compulsory, obligatory, requisite, prerequisite, demanded, ordered, requested, desired, wanted, on call, earmarked, reserved, booked, lacking, missing, absent. *See also* necessitous, demanding.

resentful offended, insulted, affronted, hurt, pained, put-out, indignant, reproachful, bitter, virulent, acrimonious, sharp, acid, splenetic, acerbic, caustic, irritated, vexed, wrought-up, discontented, disapproving, displeased, provoked, riled, worked-up, annoyed, aggravated, exasperated, piqued, peeved, nettled, stung, sore, grudging, malicious, jealous, envious, bileful, spiteful, ill-humoured, impatient, shirty (Sl). *See also* angry.

reserved restrained, reticent, constrained, backward, retiring, reluctant, unseen, unheard, quiet.

resident dwelling, settled, domiciled, colonial, colonized, naturalized.

resigned accepting, acquiescent, stoical, sanguine, phlegmatic, indifferent.

resigning abdicating, retiring, past, former, one-time, sometime, late, emeritus, pensioned off, forced out, outgoing, renunciatory. *See also* resigned.

resilient elastic, reflexive.

resinous rosiny, bituminous, pitchy, tarry, asphaltic, varnished, japanned, myrrhy, masticic, gummy.

resistant renitent, withstanding, reluctant, refusing, striking, unwilling, noncooperative, opposing, objecting, challenging, deprecative, protesting, dissenting, defiant, rebuffing, repulsing, repellent, obstructive, hard-headed (US), hard-shell (US), hard-core, hard-nosed (Inf). *See also* obstinate, resisting, desisting.

resisting unsubmissive, undefeated, unsubdued, unbowed, unquelled, unbeatable, invincible, bulletproof, self-defensive, revolutionary, rebellious, mutinous, insurgent, reactionary, terrorist, anarchist.

resolute resolved, determined, decided, decisive, deliberate, single-minded, concentrated, purposeful, intent, (dead) set, obsessed, hell-bent (Inf). *See also* tenacious, strong-willed, undaunted, steady.

resonant reverberating, reboant, stentorian, resounding, rebounding, hollow, echoing, vibrating, pulsating, carrying, lingering, persisting, humming, whirring, buzzing. *See also* ringing, deep.

respectable reputable, upright, worthy, venerable, estimable, praiseworthy, laudable.

respected esteemed, honoured, revered, reverenced, admired, appreciated, valued, prized, time-honoured, prestigious.

respectful regardful, considerate, attentive, honorific, ceremonious, appreciative. *See also* showing respect, reverent, in a respectful

reversed

stance, respected, respectable, awe-inspiring.

restful placid, calm, quiet, relaxing, soothing, serene.

restless feverish, fevered, fidgety, itchy, unquiet, unpeaceful, twitchy, excited, flustered, fussing, fluttering, fluttery.

restorative reparative, analeptic, reviving, recuperative, curative, sanative, healing, medicated, remedial, redemptive.

restoring restitutive, restorable, redemptive, redeeming, atoning, refunding, compensatory, indemnificatory, reparative.

restrained calm, controlled, reticent, constrained, curbed, repressed; discreet, tasteful, unobtrusive, subdued.

restraining constrained, suppressive, oppressive, strict, coercive, slow, preventive, under control, prohibitive, conditional, restrictive, tied down, in check, injunctive, interdictive, severe, disciplined, punished, authoritative, pressurized, censored, banned, stifling, limiting, required, constrictive, narrow, cramped, circumscriptive, exclusive, copyrighted, rationed, frozen, rate-capped, monopolistic, interventional, protective, embargoed. *See also* self-restrained, detained.

retained stuck firm, fast, held, bound, glued, gummed, grasped, gripped, clasped, clutched, pinioned, pinned, stapled, strangled, detained, imprisoned, penned, walled in, fenced in, contained, circumscribed, saved, kept (back), withheld, refused, preserved.

retaliatory retaliative, retributive, punitive, recriminatory, reciprocal, revengeful, vindictive, vengeful, rightly served.

retentive retaining, tenacious, cohesive, adhesive, costive, constipated, clogged, indissoluble, firm, sticky, gluey, gummy, prehensile, tight-fisted, parsimonious, grasping, gripping, clinging, clasping, vice-like, strangling, throttling, restraining, gooey (*Inf*). *See also* retained.

reticent reserved, silent, mum, tight-lipped, taciturn, quiet.

retiring demure, coy, shy, reserved, bashful, unassuming.

retractive ductile.

retroactive nostalgic, reactionary, backward-looking, retrospective.

retrospective retroactive, diachronic, remembering, reminiscing, backward-looking.

returning homing, homeward-bound.

revelatory expository, explicatory, explanatory, interpretive, apocalyptic, manifesting, epiphanic.

reverberatory resonant, vibrational, oscillatory, rhythmical, beating, pulsating, throbbing, drumming, hammering, chiming, chanting, rhyming, alliterative, assonant.

reverent venerative, admiring, adoring, worshipping, adulatory, deifying, idolizing, awestruck.

reversed regressed, retracted, recanted, retreated, retired, reverted, reacted, recoiled, backfired, returned, restored, reinstated, revived, resumed, recovered, retrieved, recycled, replied, retorted, answered, responded, refuted.

reversible returnable, restorable, recoverable, retrievable, recyclable, refutable.

revolting repulsive, obnoxious, repugnant, offensive, abhorrent, nauseating.

rewarded recognized, credited, acknowledged, acclaimed, praised.

rewarding satisfying, paying, profitable, money-making, lucrative, remunerative, gainful. *See also* rewarded, compensatory, giving.

rheumy weeping, pussy, purulent, suppurating, sanious, ichorous, phlegmy, humoral, serous, chylific, tearlike, lachrymal.

ribald bawdy, rabelaisian, provocative, immoral, blue, unmentionable, unquotable, unprintable, filthy, obscene, smutty, barbarius, lewd, indecent, scatological.

rich wealthy, opulent, well-off, prosperous, affluent, loaded (Inf); fertile, productive, plentiful, abundant, copious, prolific; full, well-stocked, abounding, profuse; expensive, costly, dear, extravagant, valuable, precious; succulent, luscious, juicy, creamy, spicy; bright, deep, intense, vivid, resonant, sonorous.

ridiculing mocking, derisive, sarcastic, ironic, satirical, imitating, burlesque, caricatural, parodic.

ridiculous preposterous, daft, nutty (Inf), laughable, priceless, absurd, asinine, foolish, funny, comical, clownish, droll, eccentric, bizarre, zany, humourous, witty, comic, farcical, slapstick, clownish, hilarious, rib-tickling (Inf), side-splitting (Inf), risible, fatuous, burlesque, knock-about, derisory, rum (Inf).

right fair, just, equitable, equal, impartial, fair-minded, open-minded, square, unbiased, disinterested, even-handed, objective, neutral, unprejudiced. *See also* correct, in the right, moral, right-minded, all right.

right-minded decent, law-abiding, sporting, sportsmanlike.

rigid austere, inflexible, stiff, harsh, severe, stern.

rigorous challenging, demanding, harsh, austere, exacting, firm; bad, extreme, severe, bleak, harsh, inclement.

ringing tintinnabular, pealing, tolling, sounding, chiming, tinkling, jingling, pinging, clanging, loud.

rising mounting, buoyant, rampant, rearing, bullish, escalating, uprising, upgoing, upcoming, ascendant, ascensional, anabatic, soaring, zooming, rocketing, lifting, gaining height, light, floating, airborne.

ritualistic ceremonial, festive, impetrational, petitionary, invocational, supplicatory, liturgical, hymnological, hymnographical, comminatory, laudational, doxological, sacramental, sacral, oblational, libational, chrismal, sacrificial, nuptial, matrimonial, penitential, funereal, baptismal, symbolic, eucharistic, transubstantial, totemistic, fetishistic, cannibalistic. *See also* worshipping.

rocking rolling, reeling, lurching, careening, pitching, shaking, dancing, tossing, staggering, swaying.

romantic loving, passionate, tender, fond, amorous; colourful, exotic, glamorous, picturesque; idealistic, dreamy, visionary, fantastic.

roofed pitched, hipped, imbricate, domed, pendentive.

rotary orbital, pivotal, trochilic, circumrotatory, circumgyratory, gyratory, centrifugal, centripetal, circling, cyclic, circulatory, torsional, vortical, cyclonic, turbinated, vertiginous, dizzy, giddy, tornadic, whirlwindy.

rotating revolving, gyrating, turning, orbiting, swivelling, pivoting, whirling, spinning, swirling, twirling, reeling, wheeling, rolling, trolling, bowling. *See also* rotary.

rotten corrupt, bad, decaying, putrid, mouldy, fetid; despicable, mean, low, base, vile, nasty.

rough rough-hewn, roughcast, unsmooth, textured, undulatory, wrinkled, crinkled, crinkly, crumpled, rugose, uneven, corrugated, nonuniform, irregular, ruffled, muricate, inequal, rugged,

ragged, unsifted; rasping, grating, grinding, chafing, fretting, galling. *See also* coarse, barbed, bumpy, unfinished.

round rotund, orbicular, gibbous, spherical, globose, convex, egg-shaped, ovoid, cylindrical, tubular, conical, bell-shaped, bulbous, spherelike, hemispherical. *See also* well-rounded.

rude disrespectful, contemptuous, derisive, bluff, brash, barefaced.

rudimentary rudimental, basic, elementary, fundamental.

ruling authoritative, commanding, influential, controlling, powerful, dominant, supreme, masterful, reigning, sovereign.

ruthless callous, brutal, fierce, harsh, heartless, pitiless

S

sacrificial martyred, consecrated, oblatory, contributory, donated, propitiatory, conciliatory, expiatory.

sad unhappy, sorrowful, crestfallen, downhearted, heavyhearted, distressed, miserable, wretched, forlorn, languishing, tormented, woebegone, tearful, doleful, dolorous, mournful, pining, heartbroken, disconsolate, inconsolable, desolate, grief-stricken, ululant. *See also* depressed, distressing.

safe secure, protected, guarded, defended, assured, sure, certain, sound, snug, spared, preserved, intact, undamaged, unharmed, uninjured, unhurt, unscathed, garrisoned, well-defended, insured, covered, immunized, vaccinated, inoculated, disinfected, salubrious, hygienic, in harbour, clear, unaccused, unthreatened, unmolested, unexposed, sheltered, shielded, screened, patronized, imprisoned, reliable, dependable, trustworthy, guaranteed, warranted, benign, innocent, tame, harmless, innocuous, unthreatening, risk-free, unhazardous, nonflammable, nontoxic, unpolluted, edible, drinkable, potable. *See also* invulnerable, tutelary.

saleable vendible, marketable, merchantable, available. *See also* sold.

salivating spitting, coughing, spluttering, slobbering, slavering, dribbling, drooling, frothing, foaming, rheumy, watery, mucous, expectorant.

same idem (L), selfsame, identical, isotrophic, indistinguishable, undifferentiated, repetitious, unvarying, repeated, redundant, tautologic(al), verbatim, united, solid, one, homogeneous, merging, absorbed, coalescent, assimilated, agreed, consubstantial, homoousian. *See also* equivalent, lookalike, duplicate, equal, regular.

sane normal, sober, together (Inf). *See also* rational.

satisfactory sufficient, enough,

adequate, acceptable, passable, tolerable, fair, so-so (Inf), OK (Inf).

satisfied fulfilled, gratified, thankful, content, serene, uncomplaining, undemanding, secure, safe, happy, pleased, satiated, full, comfortable, smug, complacent. *See also* satisfying, satisfactory.

satisfying fulfilling, gratifying, pleasing, pacifying, comforting, satiating, filling, ample.

scant sparse, meagre, few.

scarce rare, infrequent, sparse, few, short, unavailable, unobtainable, unprocurable, nonexistent.

sceptical doubting, Pyrrhonist, agnostic, distrustful, journalistic, scientific, criminal, philosophical, legal, experimental, conjectural, guessing, hesitating.

scornful contemptuous, contumelious, sarcastic, ridiculing, mocking, scoffing, sneering, derisive.

sculptural marmoreal, monumental, graven, moulded, plastic, glyptic, anaglyptic, ceroplastic, toreutic.

seasonable appropriate, suitable, convenient, timely, well-timed, welcome, providential, opportune.

seasonal equinoctial, solstitial. *See also* spring, summer, autumn, winter, seasonable, seasoned, mitigated, in season.

seasoned hardened, toughened, matured, inured, accustomed.

secluded private, isolated, quiet, remote, deserted, desolate, hidden, cloistered, sequestered, uninhabited.

secondary minor, incidental, by-side, subsidiary, peripheral, low-level.

secret private, privy, intimate, confidential, closed, classified, sealed, isolated, unrevealed, undisclosed, undivulged, unspoken, untold, top-secret, classified, restricted, censored, suppressed, off-the-record, hush-hush (Inf). *See also* secretive, mysterious.

secretive silent, close, reticent, surreptitious, stealthy, furtive, sly, clandestine, covert, undercover, underhand, conspiratorial, cabalistic, cloak-and-dagger (Inf).

secretory exudative, transudatory, emissive, excretory, emanative, glandular, merocrine, eccrine, apocrine, holocrine, secreting, lactating, lactiferous, lacrimatory, crying, weeping, sebaceous, sebiferous, sweating, sudatory, salivating. *See also* of a secretion, inducing secretion.

secure safe, sure, protective, sheltered, invulnerable, impregnable, immune, safeguarded, shielded, deterrent. *See also* guaranteed, accomplished, fast.

sedentary stay-at-home, housebound, shut-in (US), home-loving, domesticated, supine, bedridden, disabled, idle, unemployed, inert, dormant, passive, latent, languid, apathetic, indifferent, indolent, phlegmatic, sluggish, vegetating, unaroused, suspended, abeyant, sleeping, slumbering, smouldering, groggy, heavy, leaden, dull, flat, slack, tame, dead, lifeless, catatonic, numb, dopey (Inf).

seedy shabby, tatty, tacky, down-at-heel, moth-eaten, dog-eared.

seeing sighted, sharp-eyed, eagle-eyed, hawk-eyed, staring, glaring, goggle-eyed, pop-eyed, noticing, watching, looking, observant, watchful, vigilant, aware, perceptive, clear-sighted, far-sighted, perspicacious, discerning, imaginative, visionary.

seeping dripping, percolating, splashed, spattered, weeping, tearful, dribbling, drivelling, drooling, sweating, perspiring.

selecting choosing, deciding, decisive, eclectic, optional, discretional, volitional, exercising choice, selective, particular, discriminating, discerning, showing preference, preferential, favouring, choosy (Inf), picky (Inf). *See also* chosen, elective.

self-abasing self-effacing, deferent, self-submitting, diminished, self-abnegating, dispirited, self-doubting, self-deprecating, condescending, submitting.

self-absorbed self-obsessed, self-devoted, self-worshipping, self-loving, narcissistic, vain, self-centred, egotistic, selfish.

self-admiring narcissistic, smug, supercilious, vainglorious.

self-assured self-confident, controlling, domineering, superior, lordly, powerful, autocratic, imperious, high-handed, authorized, commissioned, appointed, mandated, bossy (Inf).

self-deprecating self-effacing, self-doubting, unambitious, deprecating, self-distrustful.

self-existent self-existing, uncreated, god-like, divine.

self-indulgent self-gratifying, pleasure-seeking, hedonistic, sybaritic, epicurean, sensual, voluptuous, carnal. *See also* dissipated, overindulgent, self-absorbed.

self-interested selfish, egotistic(al), egocentric, solipsistic, self-centred.

selfish self-indulgent, self-interested, self-seeking, possessive, covetous, jealous, envious, avaricious, acquisitive, materialistic, ambitious, greedy, monopolistic, opportunistic, individualistic, ungenerous, uncharitable, stingy, miserly, niggardly, mean, mean-spirited, parsimonious, cold-hearted, money-grubbing (Inf). *See also* egoistic.

self-reliant confident, unafraid, unfearing, steadfast, persevering, tenacious, dogged, determined, resolute, intrepid.

self-restrained self-controlled, self-disciplined, self-denying, restrictive, strict, repressive, prohibited, renunciative, relinquished, restrained, refraining, forbearing, abstaining, abstemious, celibate, continent, chaste, pure, puritanic(al), temperate, sober, teetotal, dieting, fasting, Lenten, ascetic, plain, frugal, economical, parsimonious, stinting, sparing, costive, self-sufficient, strait-laced (Inf), uptight (Inf). *See also* moderate, calm.

self-satisfied complacent, contented, smug.

semantic semasiological, semiotic, linguistic, philological, verbal, lexical.

semiliquid semifluid, emulsive, colloidal, sticky, pasty, slimy, incrassate, inspissate, viscous, viscid, gooey (Inf), gunky (Inf), gungy (Inf). *See also* muddy, pulpy, juicy, thick, gelatinous, mucilaginous.

semi-skilled semi-literate, semi-schooled, lay, amateur, inexperienced, unqualified, quack, shallow, superficial, dilettante, half-baked (Inf).

semitransparent translucent, milky, pearly, misty, smoky, tinted, stained, frosted, opalescent, semi-opaque.

sensate perceptible, tactile, palpable, tangible, audible, visible, noticeable.

sensible sensitive, aware, sentient, feeling, percipient. *See also* conscious, susceptible, sensate, exciting, sensory.

sensitive sympathetic, empathetic, feeling, caring, fond, cordial, friendly, amicable, warm, soft-hearted, tender, romantic, nostalgic, sentimental, bathetic, maudlin, mawkish, sloppy (Inf); emotional, tearful, overcome, overwhelmed, overwrought, highly strung. *See also* oversensitive, sore, accurate.

sensory nervous, neurological.

separable severable, partiable, divisible, fissionable, scissile, tearable, dissolvable, resolvable (image), discernible, distinguishable, breakable, biodegradable.

separate disunited, disjointed, disjunctive, dislocated, divorced, disconnected, unplugged, unstuck, untied, undone, unzipped, loosened, liberated, released, expelled, ejected, unfettered, unchained, free, discontinuous, partitioned, bipartite, multipartite, dichotomous, dividing, halved, quartered, dismembered, disembowelled, cut, torn, severed, ruptured. *See also* apart, unjoined, disagreeable, separable.

separated discrete, disintegrated, fragmented, decomposed, broken-up, split-up.

sequential succeeding, successional, following, serial, consecutive, sequacious, continuous, progressive. *See also* alternating, next, consequent, additional, rear.

serious solemn, grave, weighty, important, significant, heavy, intense, solid, impressive, lofty, elevated, sublime, grand, majestic.

servile slavish, deferential, compliant, subservient, menial, abject, submissive, dependent. *See also* sycophantic.

serving attending, helping, ministering, aiding, obedient, menial, subject, servile, in captivity, below stairs.

set habituated, hidebound, conservative, obscurantist, reactionary, blimpish, unteachable, impervious, blind, deaf, opinionated, dogmatic, hard-line, hard-shelled (US), pedantic, obsessed, bigoted, fanatical, dry (Inf), blinkered (Inf).

seventh sevenfold, septuple, septuplicate, septenary, septennial, heptadic, heptagonal, heptangular, heptahedral, heptatonic.

severe strict, rigorous, harsh, hard, uncompromising, unbending, stubborn, obstinate, hard-headed (US), stern, rigid, firm, inflexible, uncharitable, Draconian, exacting, pedantic, formal, orthodox, fundamental, fastidious, stringent, censorious, regimented, disciplined, rugged, tough, hardhearted, intolerant, inquisitorial, bigoted, inclement, callous, pitiless, merciless, unsparing, unforgiving, inhumane, cruel, brutal, coercive, oppressive, repressive, exploitative, undemocratic, militaristic, authoritarian, totalitarian, despotic, dictatorial, autocratic, Fascist, tyrannical, domineering, dominating, heavy-handed, bossy (Inf). *See also* suppressed, unadorned.

shady obscure, dark, murky, dirty, grimy, dusty, dull, lustreless, matt, muddy, turbid, cloudy, milky, fuzzy, blurred, vague, dim, hazy, smoky, foggy, misty, clouded, obfuscated, opaline, frosted, smoked, filmy, semiopaque.

shaky shaking, quaky, quaking, quivery, quivering, quavery, quavering, unsteady, doddering, shivery, shivering, aguey, shuddering, juddering, wobbly, successive, succussatory, vibratory, vibrating, pulsating, throbbing.

shallow shoal, reefy, ankle-deep. *See also* superficial.

shapeless formless, amorphous, unfinished, undefined, indefinite, undeveloped, incomplete, raw, uncut, vague, obscure, unclear, shadowed, fuzzy, blurred, hazy, misty, ill-defined, featureless.

sharp pointed, needle-like, acicular, mucronate, acuminate, spearlike, lanceolate, lance-shaped, hastate, arrow-like, sagittal, unblunted, tapered, tapering, fastigiate, conic(al), pyramidal, convergent, spindle-shaped, fusiform, wedge-shaped, spiked, sharp-edged, toothed.

sharp-edged honed, razor-edged, knife-edged, cultrate, keen-edged, double-edged, cutting, swordlike, ensiform, saw-edged.

shed moulted, shaven, scalped, flayed, skinned.

shoddy shabby, scruffy, base, low, mean, poor, paltry, poky, mangy, scummy, tacky, gaudy, tawdry, tatty, trashy, twopenny, second-rate, inferior, low quality, useless, unsaleable, unmarketable, valueless, worthless, shopsoiled, crummy (Sl), tinpot (Sl), lousy (Sl).

short deficient, needy, wanting, lacking, scarce, missing, amiss, minus, inadequate, insufficient, un-

reached, unfulfilled, unfinished, incomplete, half-done; diminutive, little, stubby, stumpy, thickset, stocky, dumpy, squat, stunted, low, snub, retroussé, pug-nosed, transient, brief, skimpy, scanty, curt, terse, concise, succinct, synoptic, summary, compendious. *See also* defective, shortened, abrupt.

shortened abbreviated, abridged, condensed, compressed, digested, abstracted, capsulized, encapsulated, epitomized, elliptical, elided, foreshortened, cut, sawn-off, truncated, curtailed, curtal, docked, bobbed, clipped, trimmed, cropped, pruned, mown, sheared, shorn, shaved, polled, decapitated.

showy ostentatious, demonstrative, pretentious, shameless.

shrill high-pitched, sharp, acute, ear-piercing, squeaky, creaky, tinny, reedy, piping, whistling, bleeping.

shy timid, diffident, self-conscious, retiring, timorous, embarrassed, frightened, mouselike, shrinking, unimportant, inarticulate, stammering.

sick ill, unwell, poorly, indisposed, off-colour, wasting away, queasy, feverish, headachy, confined, quarantined, bedridden, prostrate, hospitalized, taken ill, comatose, serious, critical, chronic, incurable, terminal, inoperable, moribund, groggy (Inf).

side sidelong, oblique, lateral, flanking, skirting, facing, right, left, far, near, two-sided, many-sided, multifaceted, bilateral, quadrilateral, collateral.

signalling telegraphic, heliographic(al), semaphoric(al), flashing, warning, summoning, ringing, bleeping, shouting, hailing, proclaiming, publishing, announcing, inviting, calling, commanding.

significant consequential, serious, important, weighty, substantial, pithy, meaty, of moment.

signifying indicative, significative, identifying, directional, pointing, connotative, denotative, signalizing, disclosing, revealing, explanatory, betraying, telltale, signalling, symbolic, semiotic, symptomatic, diagnostic, expressive, implicative, demonstrative, meaningful, suggestive, evidential, representative, nominal, diagrammatic, typical, characteristic, individual, special, interpretive, prophetic, presageful, ominous. *See also* gestural, signalling.

silent quiet, inaudible, noiseless, soundless, taciturn, mute, mum, tight-lipped, dumb, voiceless, aphonic, aphasic, speechless, dumbfounded, wordless, hushed, still, stilly (Arch), calm, peaceful, quiescent, soft, faint, muted, soundproof, unspoken, tacit, solemn, awful, deathlike.

similar same, synonymous, symmetrical, akin, like, alike, resembling, allied, connected, related, matching, corresponding, analogous, equivalent, comparable, com-

simultaneous

mensurable, parallel, identical, approximate, near, close, quasi, connatural, homogeneous, assonant, alliterative, rhyming, favouring, following. *See also* simulated, lifelike.

simple clear, plain, explicit, articulate, distinct, direct, straightforward, downright, forthright, uncomplicated, easy, obvious, self-explanatory, self-evident, readable, legible, *lisible* (Fr), explained, interpreted, popularized, exoteric, apodictic, limpid, transparent, lucid, perspicuous; plain, basic, ordinary, common, everyday, workaday, homy, homespun, humble, lowly, austere, severe, Spartan, spare, ascetic, stark, bald, bare, naked, classic, neat, uncluttered, clear, clean, pure, unadulterated, uncomplicated, unpretentious, unaffected, unassuming, modest, chaste, unsensational, restrained, sober, serious, dry, stodgy, tedious, boring, humdrum, mundane, usual, vernacular, matter-of-fact, prosaic, quotidian, mundane, unimaginative, uninspired, unpoetical, common-or-garden. *See also* unadorned, natural.

simulated artificial, false, imitation, cultured, ersatz, synthetic, aped, mimicked, imitated, mocked, phoney, counterfeit, copied, duplicated, replicated, spurious, pseudo (Inf).

simultaneous coeval, contemporary, coexistent, coeternal, concomitant, coincident, concurrent, photo-finish, accompanying,

twinned. *See also* synchronized, equal.

sinful wicked, illegal, criminal, trespassing, transgressing, heinous, mortal, deadly, murderous.

singing warbling, carolling, tweeting, twittering, twittery, chattering.

single unmarried, divorced, separated, widowed, chaste, celibate.

singular individual, special, particular, distinct, unique, only-begotten, one-off, once-in-a-lifetime.

situated positioned, located, set, placed, sited, seated, stationed, orientated, pointed, appointed, employed, posted, occupational. *See also* situational, circumstantial.

situational directional, topographical, geographical, local.

sixth sixfold, sextuple, sextuplicate, sexennial, sexpartite, hexadic, hexagonal, hexangular, hexahedral, hexatonic.

skeletal bony, osteal, osseous, ossiferous, ossicular, ossified.

skilful able, proficient, competent, efficient, talented, gifted, excellent, superb, topnotch, topflight, apt, adroit, dexterous, deft, adept, slick, agile, sure-footed, nimble, green-fingered, clever, quick-witted, shrewd, cunning, smart, intelligent, diplomatic, wise, versatile, adaptable, ingenious, resourceful, panurgic, sound, masterful, magisterial, accomplished, first-rate (Inf), A1 (Inf), ace (Inf), crack (Inf), wizard (Inf). *See also* gifted, expert, well-made.

skirting skirted, edged, fringed, valanced.

sleepy somnolent, dopy, drowsy, fuzzy, woozy (Inf).

slimming dieting, reducing, slenderizing, weight-watching, calorie-counting.

slow ambling, strolling, sauntering, lumbering, snail-paced, faltering, flagging, creeping, crawling, dragging, waddling, slouching, shuffling, plodding, clumsy, limping, halting, hobbling, shambling, tottering, staggering. *See also* unhurried, hesitant, delayed.

small tiny, infinitesimal, insignificant.

smaller contracted, shrunk, Sanforized (Tm), compressed, compact, condensed, concentrated, boiled-down, miniaturized, scaled-down, squeezed, tightened, pressed, crushed, pinched, rolled-up, curled-up, huddled, clenched, cramped, constricted, coarctate, limited, restricted, circumscribed, strangled, deflated, flat, collapsed, telescoped, shortened, abbreviated, curtailed, abridged, stunted, pruned, trimmed, clipped, shorn, narrowed, drawn-in, closed-up, gathered, smocked, tucked, puckered, puckered up, pursed, knitted, wrinkled, shrivelled, shrivelled-up, withered, wizened, seared, wasted, consumptive, emaciated, thin, slim, decreased, reduced. *See also* contracting.

smoky smoggy, steamy, vaporing, cloudy, misty, foggy.

smooth streamlined, frictionless, even, flush, sleek, bald, clean-shaven, hairless, glabrous, smooth-haired, combed, brushed, groomed, silken, satiny, velvety, smooth-skinned, peachlike; slick, sleek, slippery, slithery, slimy. *See also* uniform, soothing, polished, smooth-mannered.

smooth-mannered well-mannered, suave, sophisticated, urbane, glib, slick, sleek, sycophantic, unctuous, ingratiating, creepy (Inf), smarmy (Inf).

snakelike snaky, serpentine, serpentiform, ophidian, ophiomorphic, colubrine, colubriform, anguine, viperish.

sober clear-headed, abstinent, abstemious, temperate, teetotal (TT), prohibitionist, unfuddled (Inf), dry (Inf). *See also* nonalcoholic.

sociable affable, social-minded, communal, collective, common, public, civic, companionable, amicable, amiable, affable, clubbish, communicative, friendly, courteous, civil, urbane, easy-going, free-and-easy, party-minded, cordial, genial, witty, amusing, charming, charismatic, extrovert, gregarious, outgoing, hearty, lively, hail-fellow-well-met, convivial, jolly, jovial, merry, cheerful, smiling, welcoming, warm, affectionate, hospitable, neighbourly, inviting, matey (Inf), pally (Inf). *See also* popular, festive.

social hospitable, congenial, gala, festive, celebratory.

soft nonrigid, flaccid, limp, rubbery, flabby, floppy, flimsy, unstrung, relaxed, slack, lax, loose, sprung, fluid. *See also* pliant, smooth, compressible, softhearted, impressionable.

softhearted warm-hearted, sympathetic, compassionate, gentle, tender, kind, delicate, mild, easygoing, relaxed, lenient, lax, complaisant, mellow.

sold in demand, popular, sought after.

solemn grave, serious, thoughtful, pensive, sedate, staid, sober, stern, severe, unsmiling, straight-faced, grim, poker-faced, stony-faced, deadpan, humourless, sombre, dour, sullen, glum, long-faced, frowning. *See also* earnest, important.

solicitous caring, concerned, protective, considerate, mindful, indulgent, attentive, courteous, gallant.

solitary standoffish, unsociable, antisocial, lone, reclusive, isolated, aloof.

solo one-man, one-woman, independent, single-handed, alone, unaided, unassisted, unaccompanied, unchaperoned.

solved soluble, resultant, issuing, resolved, concluded, discovered, worked out, unscrambled, cleared up, sorted out, decoded, interpreted, interpretational, explanatory, explained, reasoned, contrived, measured, planned, remedial, antidotal.

solvent

solvent sound, solid, credit-worthy; dissolving.

soothing peaceful, still, quiet, calm, dead, quiescent.

sore painful, raw, tender, allergic, sensitized, ticklish, itchy, tingling.

sound able-bodied, strong, fit, well, healthy, recovered.

spaced interspaced, interstitial, separate, parted, removed, intervallic, discontinuous. *See also* cracked.

spacious roomy, airy, lofty, capacious, voluminous, commodious, cavernous, sizeable, ample, vast, great, immense, enormous, outsized, expansive, extended, long, broad, wide, deep, high, amplitudinous.

sparse scant, light, thin, little, minimal, meagre, exiguous, measly, niggardly, infrequent, occasional, sporadic, intermittent, rare, uncommon, scarce, strung out, widely spaced, dispersed, scattered, sprinkled, dotted about, underpopulated, low-density, understaffed.
See also rarefied.

spatial dimensional, proportional, two-dimensional, surface, radial, superficial, flat, cubic, volumetric, stereoscopic, space-time, spatiotemporal. *See also* extensive, spacious.

speaking articulate, fluent, talkative, loquacious, voluble, outspoken, well-spoken.

speculative introspective, meditative, profound, deliberative, pondered, musing, inventive, dreamy, notional, conceptual, fanciful, theoretical, conjectural, suppositional.

speech oral, verbal, lingual, linguistic, vocal, spoken, voiced, vocalized, pronounced, enunciated. *See also* phonetic, speaking, eloquent.

speechless inarticulate, mute, dumb, tongue-tied, taciturn, reticent, silent, silenced, gagged, choked, dumbfounded, struck dumb, mum (Inf), stum (Sl), gobsmacked (Sl).

spendthrift extravagant, profligate, prodigal.

spiked star-shaped, stellate, barbed, spiny, acanthoid, prickly, pricky, bristly, hispid, awned, stinging, thorny, brambly, briery, thistly.

spiritual immaterial, incorporeal, intangible, disembodied, ethereal, airy, elemental, ghostly, spectral, shadowy, phantasmal, unearthly, otherworldly, astral, alien, extraterrestrial, extramundane, supramundane, transmundane, unworldly, eerie, weird, eldritch, uncanny, strange, creepy (Inf), spooky (Inf).

splenetic rancorous, bilious, sarcastic, harsh, crabbed, bitter, morose, sullen, grumpy.

spongelike poriferan, poriferous, spongy, fibrous, calcareous.

spontaneous sudden, snap, spur-of-the-moment, unprompted, unmotivated, unprovoked, unforced, voluntary, willing, unguarded, incautious, rash, impetuous, impulsive, natural, instinctive, involuntary, automatic, kneejerk, intuitive, untaught, emotional; ad hoc, extemporized, improvised, impromptu, ad lib, unrehearsed, snap, uncontrived, unstudied.

sporting competitive, agonistic, sportive, sporty, athletic, gymnastic, acrobatic.

sprawled straggling, drifting, astray, wandering, loose.

spring vernal, flowery, sappy, juicy, young.

spun twisted, braided, twined, plaited, extruded. *See also* woven, treated.

spurious bogus, ungenuine, unauthentic, unreal, apocryphal, forged, artificial, factitious, hollow, humbug, specious, sophistic, casuistic, charlatan, quackish, imposturous, illegitimate, phoney (Inf).

stabilized unchanged, unaltered, settled, transfixed, stereotyped, anchored, moored, tethered, tied, chained, grounded, stranded, rooted, established, ingrained, entrenched, engraved, balanced.

stable steady, steadfast, solid, sound, firm, stiff, secure, strong, durable, permanent, consistent, reliable, constant, dependable, predictable, unchangeable, unvarying, inalterable, irrevocable, irreversible, restful, quiet, calm, immobile, immovable, aground, well-founded, frozen, hard, inflexible, unshakable, incontrovertible, indisputable, indefeasible, homeostatic, equal, immutable, invariable, incommutable,

intransmutable, indissoluble, imperishable, inextinguishable, invulnerable, indestructible, ineradicable, indelible, evergreen, enduring, perpetual, rocklike. *See also* stabilized, determined.

starry starbright, star-spangled, star-studded.

stated declared, asserted, pronounced, professed, uttered, proclaimed, affirmed, attested, alleged, announced, released, read, submitted, admitted, confessed, avowed, disclosed.

stately lofty, condescending, aristocratic, noble, majestic, imposing, grand, venerable, sedate, solemn, grave, sombre, worthy, august, pompous, high-and-mighty, highnosed, regal, lordly, princely, royal, kingly, queenly, statuesque, elevated, imperious, authoritative, high-handed.

steady constant, firm, solid, immovable, unchangeable, staunch, reliable, dependable, self-controlled, self-possessed; unfaltering, unwavering, unflagging, undrooping, unwearied, untiring, indefatigable, vigilant, unfailing, unremitting, constant, continual, unceasing, renewed, iterated, reiterated, repeated.

stimulating interesting, intriguing, titillating, exciting, lively, restorative, medicinal, provocative, spirited, arch, thought-provoking, poignant.

stinking smelly, reeking, noisome,

offensive, malodorous, foul-smelling, mephitic, miasmic, over-powering, unwholesome, sweaty, unwashed, fetid, frowsty, frowzy, musty, unventilated, fusty, fuggy, stale, rank, olid, graveolent, gassy, asphyxiating, sulphurous, ammoniacal, whiffy (Inf), niffy (Inf), pongy (Inf). *See also* putrid.

stocky stout, thickset, heavyset, squat, square, well-built, burly, strapping, lusty, brawny, beefy, meaty, heavy, chunky, hefty, hulking, lumbering, lumpish, elephantine.

stolen purloined, pilfered, thieving, burglarious, brigandish, kleptomaniac, larcenous, ill-gotten, kidnapped, hijacked, skyjacking, poaching, predatory, buccannering, privateering, piratelike, raiding, plunderous, looting, pillaging, spoliatory, marauding, foraging, ravaging, grave-robbing, body-snatching (Inf), sticky-fingered (Inf), hot (Sl), rip-off (Sl). *See also* fraudulent.

stopped plugged, capped, corked, dammed, staunched, bandaged, blocked, obstructed, occluded, blocked up, clogged, clogged up, impenetrable, impassable, bunged up, stuffed up, constipated, costive, constricted, congested, choked up, full, stuffed, packed, jammed.

stored amassed, accumulated, heaped, abundant, plentiful, stacked, loaded, stowed (away), packed (away), hoarded, held, saved, unused, unspent, unex-

pended, banked, funded, invested, available, spare, supernumerary, preserved, conserved, bottled, pickled.

stormy inclement, tempestuous, thundery.

straight linear, rectilinear, perpendicular, horizontal, vertical, true, right, plumb, rigid, uncurled, unbent, direct. *See also* straightforward, continuous, traditional, honourable.

straightforward simple, direct, plain, clear, uncomplicated.

strange odd, weird, abnormal, unexpected, bizarre, quaint, eccentric, oddball (Inf).

strengthened toughened, reinforced, fortified, well-armed, well-protected, protective, hard-wearing, heavy-duty, well-built, stout, substantial, durable, tough, resistant, restored, revived, braced, buttressed.

strident harsh, raucous, discordant, grating, jarring, flat, inharmonious, unmelodious, unmusical, twangy, metallic, penetrating, loud, clamorous, cacophonous, dissonant, ear-splitting, squawky, howling, ululant, brassy, braying, blaring. *See also* hoarse, shrill.

striped striate, banded, barred, lined, streaked, marbled, veined, jaspé, reticulate, panelled, paned.

strong-willed uncompromising, unbending, inflexible, unyielding, intransigent, adamant, obstinate, stubborn, relentless, ruthless, mer-

subversive

ciless, inexorable, implacable, stern, grim, hard, cast-iron, steely.

structural constructional, edificial, architectural, architectonic, superstructural, substructural, foundational, mechanical, fabricated, precast, prestressed.

stupid dim, dull, dense, thick, unintelligent, obtuse, doltish, dim-witted.

styled phrased, worded, expressed, put; tailored, sartorial, tailor-made, bespoke, made-to-measure, designer, ready-made, ready-to-wear, snazzy (Inf). *See also* stylish, inelegant.

stylish elegant, graceful, chic, sophisticated, fashionable.

subconscious subliminal, unconscious, repressed, suppressed, inhibited, restrained, blocked, controlled.

subject subjecting, subjugated, browbeaten, henpecked, inferior, lower, substitute, subordinate, junior, dependent, symbiotic(al), apprenticed, subservient, obedient, servile, employed, employable, captive, in harness, unfree, compulsory, involuntary, indentured, enslaving, feudal. *See also* dominating.

submissive subservient, obedient, resigned, disinterested.

submitting surrendering, quiet, meek, humble, tame, docile, unresisting, law-abiding, peaceful, subservient, servile, menial, lowly, abject, obedient, slavish, unconcerned, fatalistic, resigned, subdued, acqui-

escent, concessionary, assenting, pliant, accommodating, malleable, biddable, tractable, amenable, agreeable, soft, weak-kneed, bending, crouching, crawling, cringing, prostrate, boot-licking, sycophantic, toadying, humble, masochistic.

subordinate minor, inferior, junior, dependent, subsidiary, subject, subservient, humble, tributary, ancillary, auxiliary, untouchable, criminal.

substitute alternate, acting, deputy, proxy, reserve, replacement, equivalent, lookalike, soundalike, surrogate, second, additional, stopgap, makeshift, temporary, provisional. *See also* substituted.

substituted exchanged, switched, swapped, replaced, deputized, supplanted, superseded, compensated.

substitutive substitutable, alternative, surrogate, foster, stand-in, back-up, relief, locum, reserve.

subtle delicate, restrained, elegant, refined, tasteful, discriminating, fastidious, pastel.

subtracted removed, deducted, excepted, abstracted, withdrawn, extracted, excluded, expelled, ejected, eliminated, eradicated, deleted, erased, obliterated. *See also* subtractive, reduced.

subtractive reductive, extirpative, deductive, abstract, removable, eradicable.

subversive seditious, conspiratorial, factional, anarchic, treasonable, revolutionary, rebellious, mutinous, breakaway, schismatic, insurgent, insurrectional.

succeeding successional, following, next, proximate, close, near, sequential, consecutive, ordered, arranged, second, another, every, alternate, subsequent, consequent, ensuing, pursuant, late, latter, last. *See also* subordinate.

successful winning, wealthy, prosperous, fruitful, thriving, flourishing, favourable, famous, efficacious, effective, masterly, best-selling, chart-topping, best-ever, lucky, fortunate, never-failing, surefire, surefooted, certain, rising, crowning. *See also* rewarding, victorious.

sufficient enough, adequate, satisfactory, acceptable, sufficing, self-sufficient, complete, competent, equal to, fitting, suitable, satisfying, contenting, measured, commensurate, hand-to-mouth, makeshift, provisional. *See also* plentiful, filled.

suggestible susceptible, receptive, impressible, tractable, malleable, adaptable, docile, compliant, willing, easily led.

suitable fit, fitting, apt, appropriate, relevant, pertinent.

sullen sulky, surly, serious, pouting, melancholy, atrabilious, moody, morose, glum, grim, stern, dour, sour, gloomy, sombre, dismal, dark, black, dejected, depressed, cheerless, ill-humoured, ill-natured, blue, saturnine. *See also* irritable, overcast.

summary brief, short, curt, brusque, terse, concise, pithy, compendious, succinct, compact, pointed, epigrammatic, laconic, irreducible. *See also* shortened.

summer aestival, midsummer.

sunny daylight, cloudless, clear.

superficial surface, one-dimensional, cursory, hasty, slight, light, skin-deep, thin, flat, trivial, trifling, lightweight, unimportant, petty, meaningless, empty, flimsy, frivolous, foolish, idle, silly.

superfluous supererogatory, excess, extra, spare, surplus, leftover, remaining, nonessential, luxury, unnecessary, needless, rambling, circuitous, tautologous, otiose, pleonastic, redundant, overmanned, overstaffed.

superior greater, better, finer, higher, over, super, above, surpassing, eclipsing, overtopping, arch, exceeding, leading, outclassing, ahead, above average, ascendent, preferred, favourite, top-drawer, capping (Inf). *See also* dominant, best, excellent.

supplementary auxiliary, subsidiary, ancillary, accessory, subservient.

supportable bearable, tolerable, endurable, sufferable, acceptable, manageable, passable, average, so-so (Inf).

supported confirmed, corroborated, substantiated, ratified, authenticated, attested, validated, verified, certified, established, assured, endorsed, supported, backed, reinforced.

supporting supportive, backing, advocating, championing, recommending, in favour, for, pro.

supportive retaining, foundational, ground, basal, upholding, sustaining, maintaining, helpful, encouraging, kindly, sympathetic, empathetic, understanding, reassuring, cooperative, corroborative, collaborative, benevolent, patronal, well-disposed, favourable, contributory, stipendiary, advocatory, preferential, intercessional, auxiliary, subsidiary, ancillary, substitute, discipular, attending, guardian. *See also* supportable.

supposed assumed, presumed, premised, postulated, surmised, conjectured, guessed, hypothesized, understood, taken, proposed, suggested, mooted, topical, given, granted, assented, suppositive, putative, inferred, deduced, pretended, alleged, reputed, so-called, titular, quasi, unreal, abstract, fanciful, imagined, fabled, untrue, supposable, assumable, presumable, surmisable, imaginable.

suppositional assumptive, presumptive, notional, conjectural, guessing, intuitive, propositional, hypothetical, theoretical, postulatory, putative, unverified, moot, armchair, speculative, blue-sky (US), gratuitous, suggestive, hinting, allusive, stimulating, thought-provoking, academic, guesstimating (Inf). *See also* supposed, meant.

suppressed oppressed, repressed, subjugated, persecuted, coerced, harassed, censored, expurgated, exploited, victimized, tyrannized, tortured, executed.

surpassing over-extended, overlong.

surplus net, unused, outcast, left over, unwanted, outstanding, owed, carried over, extra, spare, excess, overabundant, overloaded, redundant, superfluous, pleonastic, otiose.

surprised unprepared, unsuspecting, unaware, startled, ambushed, trapped. *See also* amazed, surprising.

surprising unexpected, unanticipated, unforeseen, unpredictable, sudden, unannounced, amazing, astounding, astonishing, staggering, shocking, serendipitous, unusual, unprecedented, abnormal, freakish, odd, peculiar, freaky (Sl).

surrounded encircled, enveloped, wrapped, enfolded, encompassed, girded, circumscribed, circumambient, roundabout, hemmed-in, enclosed.

surrounding environmental, neighbourhood, background, outlying, perimetric, peripheral, suburban. *See also* surrounded, atmospheric.

susceptible impressionable, perceptive, responsive, over-sensitive, allergic, thin-skinned, delicate, tender, touchy, irritable, tetchy, jumpy, excited, temperamental, agitated, irritated, thrilled, stirred, hyperactive, hot-blooded, carnal, epicurean, sensuous, aesthetic.

suspended hanging, dangling, swinging, sagging, pendulous, pendent, pensile; pending, in abeyance, switched off, on hold, on ice, in reserve, abrogated, deactivated, powerless. *See also* projecting, interrupted.

sweaty sudatory, sudoric, diaphoretic, sweating, perspiring, clammy, sticky, wilting, glowing.

sweet saccharine, cloying, sickly, honeyed, sugared, treacly, syrupy, ambrosial, nectared, candied, crystallized, glazed, iced, bittersweet, sweet-and-sour. *See also* pleasant.

swift fast, quick, rapid, fleet, speedy, high-velocity, daring, dashing, snappy, round, smart, expeditious, hustling, hurrying, hasty, double-quick, rapid-fire, alacritous, prompt, sudden, early, immediate, instantaneous, express, meteoric, jet-propelled, supersonic, hypersonic, ultrasonic, electric, high-geared, streamlined, running, runaway, charging, racing, galloping, cantering, light-footed, nimble, agile, volant (Fml), winged, flying, hurtling, whirling, rattling, headlong, tempestuous, pelting, breakneck, precipitate, expeditious, darting, flashing, nifty (Inf), zippy (Inf), whizzing (Inf), spanking (Inf), all-out (Inf), flat-out (Inf), ton-up (Inf), scorching, souped-up (Sl), hotted-

up (Sl). *See also* mentally quick, accelerating.

sycophantic obsequious, flattering, fawning, grovelling, toadying, sponging, parasitic, cringing, footlicking, bootlicking, back-scratching, apple-polishing, hand-shaking, time-serving, obeisant, prostrate, mealy-mouthed, crawling, ingratiating, truckling, soft-soaping, smarmy, whining, free-loading, cringing, cowering, snivelling, leechlike, beggarly, hangdog, kow-towing, bowing, scraping, crawling, sneaking, creepy, unctuous, soapy, oily, slimy, arse-licking (Sl), brown-nosing (Sl).

symmetrical uniform, balanced, proportional, harmonious, counter-balanced, equal, equilateral, even-sided, bisymmetric(al), isosceles, congruent, correspondent, correlational, coordinate, interdependent, interacting, reciprocal, enantiomorphic, chiastic. *See also* even.

synchronized isochronal, timed, phased, in time, in step.

T

taciturn quiet, reserved, reticent, withdrawn, shy, uncommunicative, unforthcoming, diffident, reserved, tight-lipped, antisocial, unsociable, sullen, self-contained, mum (Sl), shtoom (Sl). *See also* silent, sparing with words.

taking avaricious, greedy, grasp-

ing, rapacious, predatory, possessive, acquisitive, acquiring, inheriting, assaulted, raped, appropriated,
requisitionary, acquisitional, retrievable, tax-raising, expropriatory,
confiscatory, commandeering, annexed, deductive, asset-stripped,
plundered, extortionate, deceptive,
manipulative, thieving, rip-off (Sl).

talkative loquacious, voluble, garrulous, verbose, wordy, prolix,
long-winded, chattering, babbling,
gabbling, jabbering, jibbering, fluent, glib, multiloquent, eloquent,
gassy (Inf), gabby (Inf). *See also*
effusive.

tall lanky, rangy, leggy, long-
legged, long-limbed, long-necked,
giant, gigantic, colossal, statuesque,
monumental, Amazonian,
Olympian, knee-high, shoulder-
high, gangling (Inf), gangly (Inf).

tame domesticated, broken, obedient, disciplined, submissive, subdued; docile, gentle, meek,
tractable, fearless; boring, dull, tedious, bland, prosaic, flat.

tangible palpable, evident, perceptible, material, physical, actual.

tapered tapering, convergent, attenuated, attenuate, pointed, peaked,
conical, cone-shaped, wedge-
shaped, fusiform.

tasteful cultivated, refined, discriminating, elegant, vulgar.

tasteless bland, insipid,
plain, tame, dull, rapid, weak, thin,
feeble, flat, stale, dry, arid, humdrum, monotonous, nondescript, un-

exciting, uninviting, lifeless,
flavourless, unsalted, unseasoned,
watered down, diluted, adulterated,
unappetizing, banal, trite, uninspired, boring, jejune, unsatisfying,
indifferent, characterless, wishy-
wash (Inf). *See also* coarse.

tasty palatable, delicious, edible,
esculent, comestible, sapid,
savoury, appetizing, inviting, rel-
ishable, delectable, dainty, epicurean, flavourful, ambrosial,
potable, drinkable, toothsome,
mouthwatering, succulent, sharp,
unpleasant, unpalatable, acid, spicy,
sweet, sour, tart, bitter, pungent,
salty, scrumptious (Inf), yummy
(Sl), moreish (Inf). *See also* tasteful.

taunting jeering, mocking, flout-
ing, scoffing, scorning, jibing,
sneering, hissing, booing, catcalling, hooting, bantering, chaffing,
teasing, barracking (Inf).

tawdry flashy, gaudy, vulgar,
showy, cheap, tasteless.

tax-free duty-free, post-free, zero-
rated.

taxonomic systematic, biosys-
tematic, cladistic, generic, specific,
subspecific.

tearful weepy (Inf), crying, lachrymose, sorrowful, pitiful, distressed.

tedious boring, irksome, monotonous, dreary, dull, humdrum.

temporal time-based, time-related,
temporary. *See also* lasting through
time, periodic, occasional, between
times, of known date.

temporary fleeting, passing, transient, momentary, brief, short-lived.

tempting inviting, seductive, attractive, alluring, enticing, appetizing.

tenacious persevering, persistent, dogged, zealous, thorough, all-consuming, earnest, serious, insistent, pressing, urgent, driving, forceful, energetic, vigorous, hard-hitting, desperate, all out, whole-hearted, committed, devoted, dedicated, tireless, indefatigable, whole-hog (Sl), gung-ho (Inf).

tender gentle, loving, caring, warm, compassionate, humane; delicate, soft, fragile, weak; immature, green, young, raw, unripe, new; touchy, risky, difficult, sensitive, ticklish; painful, inflamed, sore, aching, bruised.

tense edgy, jumpy, nervous, keyed up, strained, wound up (Inf); taut, tight, rigid, stiff, stretched; exciting, stressful, nerve-racking.

tentative experimental, trial, pilot, testing, searching, inquiring, probationary, on approval, on appro (Inf).

tenth tenfold, decuple, decimal, denary, decennial, decagonal, decahedral.

tepid lukewarm, cool, indifferent, apathetic.

terrestrial global, atmospheric, hydrospheric, geospheric, continental, topographic(al), subterranean, underground.

terrible awful, bad, dire, horrible, horrifying, dreadful, frightful.

terrific amazing, superb, marvellous, breathtaking, outstanding, excellent; dreadful, fearful, severe, enormous, huge, intense.

terrified horrified, appalled, petrified, frightened, scared, terrorized.

tested tried, researched, determined, verified, checked, essayed, ventured, estimated, risked, chanced.

thanking blessing, praising, crediting, cognizant of, acknowledging.

thankless unrewarding, useless, fruitless, unprofitable.

theological religious, divine, patristic, physicotheological, ontotheological, hierological, hagiological, soteriological, Christological, eschatological, doctrinal, ecclesiological, canonical, scriptural, metaphysical.

theoretical notional, abstract, putative, conceptual, perceptual, philosophical, hypothetical, conjectural, speculative, suppositional, propositional, suggestive, indicative, suspected, assumed, presumed, estimated, guesstimated (Inf). See also ideational, purposive, ideal.

therapeutic medicinal, preventive, prophylactic, remedial, curative.

thick broad, wide, deep, massive, substantial, bulky, ample, chunky, heavy, stout, buxom, endomorphic, fat, corpulent, obese, overweight, well-fed, plump, portly, round, rotund, flabby, chubby, podgy, tubby, potbellied, solid, padded, swollen,

tied

incrassate, stocky, sturdy, thickset, barrel-chested, bull-necked, thick-lipped, thick-stemmed, thick-skinned, pachydermatous; stupid, unintelligent.

thick-witted slow-witted, dull, dense, stupid, obtuse, dim, dumb, boneheaded (Sl) thick (Sl).

thin slender, slim, svelte, gracile, sylphlike, willowy, twiggy, slight, small-framed, leptosomic, ectomorphic, narrow-waisted, wasp-waisted, flat-chested, girlish, boyish, spindle-legged, thin-faced, hatchet-faced, lantern-jawed, lean, spare, wiry, bony, rangy, lanky, gawky, underweight, skinny, scrawny, scraggy, puny, gangling, weedy (Inf). *See also* emaciated, slimming, fine, thinned, scant.

thinned diluted, watered-down, watery, runny, weak, rarefied, attenuated, flattened, pressed.

thirsty dry, parched, drouthy (Scot).

thorough scrupulous, painstaking, careful, conscientious, assiduous, exhaustive; thoroughgoing, absolute, complete, total, unmitigated, utter.

thoughtful attentive, meditative, cogitative, contemplative, reflective, speculative, pensive, introspective; judicious, profound. *See also* concentrating, speculative, reasoning.

thoughtless inconsiderate, uncaring, mindless, unthinking, unreflective, inane, fatuous, vacuous, vacant, blank, empty-headed, absent-minded, abstracted, fallow, oblivious, ignorant, foolish, carefree, easygoing, happy-go-lucky, devil-may-care. *See also* instinctive, inconsiderate, unthought.

thousandth millenary, millenarian, millenial, thousandfold.

three triple, triplex, triadic, trinal, trine, triform, trimorphic, ternary, trinary, triune, treble, triplicate, threefold, trifold, cubed, third, tertiary. *See also* three-sided, trisected.

three-sided triangular, trigonal, trilateral, trihedral, deltoid, fan-shaped, three-pointed, three-pronged, trident, tridentate, tricorn, three-leaved, trifoliate, three-legged, tripedal, tripodic, three-ply, three-way, three-dimensional (3-D), tridimensional, trilingual, trimetric, triennial, trimestral.

thrifty economical, conserving, saving, labour-saving, time-saving, money-saving, canny, careful, prudent, economizing, sparing, frugal, spartan, austere, meagre, scrimpy, cheeseparing.

tidied tidy, neat, straightened out, cleared up, untangled, disentangled, unravelled, unsnarled.

tidy neat, methodical, orderly, trim, spick-and-span, shipshape; considerable, substantial, ample, big, sizable.

tied bound, knotted, lashed, hitched, yoked, spliced, stitched, interwoven, plaited, secured, fastened, attached, adhering, cohesive, glued,

tight secure, wedged, jammed, immovable.

tight taut, stiff, stretched, stable, compact; sealed, impervious, hermetic; mean, tight-fisted, stingy, miserly; near, close, well-matched; drunk, tipsy, inebriated, intoxicated.

timekeeping horological, chronometric, chronographic, chronologic, annalistic, diaristic, calendrical, chronogrammatic, temporal.

timeless eternal, sempiternal (Fml), ageless, dateless, immortal, undying, lasting, everlasting, continuous, perpetual, unceasing. *See also* changeless.

timely opportune, seasonable, providential, propitious, auspicious, appropriate, apropos, suitable, suited, befitting, convenient, heaven-sent, welcome, favourable, fortunate, lucky, happy, felicitous. *See also* critical, in time.

timid tremulous, nervy, jumpy, jittery, panicky, faint-hearted, cowardly, squeamish, weak, pusillanimous, spineless, insipid, ineffectual, wimpish (Sl), wet (Inf), wishy-washy (Inf).

tiny small, wee, dwarfish, pygmy, little, minute.

tired fatigued, sleepy, drowsy, weary, exhausted, worn out.

tiresome irksome, tedious, boring, monotonous, dull, trying.

tolerable bearable, endurable, supportable, acceptable; adequate, average, middling, passable, mediocre, so-so (Inf).

tolerant broad-minded, liberal, unprejudiced, fair, lenient, easy-going.

toothed fanged, tusked, horned, corniculate, cornute, odontoid, dentiform, denticulate, cusped, muricate, serrated, notched, emarginate, comblike, pectinate, snagged, craggy, rough, jagged.

toothless edentate, teethless, biteless.

top tiptop, uppermost, highest, ultimate, maximum, consummate, climactic, culminating, crowning, meridian, polar, head, leading, chief, capital, supreme, paramount, summital, zenithal, apical, vertical. *See also* topped.

topical current, present, immediate, contemporary, up-to-date, up-to-the-minute, timely, happening (Sl). *See also* focused, problematic, local.

topped capped, crowned, tipped, crested, headed, covered, roofed, iced, frosted.

total whole, entire, utter, complete, outright, unqualified.

touchable palpable, tangible, solid, concrete, material, real, substantial, perceptible, attainable, handy, reachable, getable, sensory, tactical, tactile, sensuous, touch-sensitive, sensitive, tender, get-at-able (Inf). *See also* touching, handed.

touching adjacent, adjoining, meeting, contiguous, bordering, abutting, intersecting, glancing, colliding, crashing, overlapping, interfacing, connecting, hand-in-hand, hand-in-glove.

tough strong, firm, solid, unbreakable, adamant, indestructible, shatterproof, resistant, starchy, boned, stark, stiff, rigid, inflexible, inelastic, unsprung, unrelaxed, tight, taut, tense. *See also* toughened, hard, powerful, mentally tough.

toughened case-hardened, tanned, hardened, tempered, annealed, vulcanized, strengthened.

toxic poisonous, mephitic, pestilent, germ-laden, venomous, poisoned, gathering, festering, septic, pussy, purulent, suppurating, lethal, deadly.

tractional pulling, drawing, hauling, tugging, towing, attracting, drawn. *See also* retractive, magnetic.

traditional conventional, conservative, moderate, old-fashioned, cautious, heterosexual, square (Inf).

tragic tragi-comic, comic, farcical, type-cast, miscast, hammy (Inf).

tranquil calm, quiet, peaceful, serene, still, unperturbed.

transferable transmittable, transmissible, communicable, contagious, infectious, transfusable, importable, metastatic(al), metathetic(al), shifting, conveyable, mailable, consignable, conductive, exchangeable, negotiable, removable, portable, transportable, transposable, carriageable, roadworthy, airworthy, seaworthy.

transferring exchangeable, nego-

tiable, conveyed, made over, assigned, consignable, devisable, bequeathing, bestowable, inheritable.

transformative mutative, transmutative, transubstantial, metamorphic, metamorphous, metabolic, convertive.

transient fleeting, flying, fugitive, quick, ephemeral, perishable, unstable, brief, short, shortlived, evanescent, volatile, disappearing, fading, decaying, passing, transitory, meteoric, momentary, sudden. *See also* impermanent.

translated rendering, word-for-word, paraphrased, reworded, restated, transliterated, abridged, edited, redacted, hermeneutic(al), exegetic(al), epigraphic(al), ciphered, deciphered, decoded.

translational paraphrastic, metaphrastic, polyglot, multilingual, bilingual, synonymous, equivalent, literal, word-for-word, verbatim, faithful, free, loose.

translucent see-through, revealing, diaphanous, lucent, gauzy, open-textured, sheer, thin, flimsy, filmy, fine, insubstantial, vaporous.

transparent clear, limpid, pellucid, colourless, crystalline, glassy, vitreous, hyaline, transpicuous, dioptric, refractive, nonreflective, watery, liquid, clarified, pure, cloudless. *See also* translucent, semitransparent, easily seen through.

transportable movable, portable, roadworthy, airworthy, seaworthy,

trapped door-to-door, commercial, shipped, freight, private, forwarded, loaded, unloaded, bussed, commuting, passenger, express, short-range, long-range, supersonic, waterborne, towed, navigated, inland, ocean-going, merchant, piped, pumped, consigned.

trapped snared, ginned, ambushed, mined, kidnapped, hijacked, baited, trawled, hooked, netted, meshed, webbed.

treacherous false-hearted, duplicitous, faithless, inconstant, double-dealing, betraying, treasonous, perfidious, dangerous.

treated washed, bleached, dyed, coloured, dyed-in-the-wool, dyed-in-the-yarn, tie-dyed, coated, flame-proof, preshrunk, Sanforized (Tm), waterproof, showerproof, drip-dry, crease-resistant, rubberized, vulcanized.

treelike arboreal, arboraceous, arborescent, dendritic, dendroid, dendriform, palmate, palmaceous, branching, slender, willowy, shrubby, bushy, gnarled, coniferous, evergreen, piny, resinous. *See also* woody, wooded, arboricultural.

tremendous vast, immense, massive, formidable, enormous, awesome; marvellous, amazing, fantastic, incredible, extraordinary, exceptional.

tricky difficult, complicated, ticklish, delicate, knotty, problematic.

trisected tripartite, three-part, trichotomous, trifid, trifurcated.

trite ordinary, banal, commonplace, corny (Inf), unoriginal, hackneyed.

triumphant victorious, successful, winning, exultant, jubilant, undefeated.

trivial petty, trifling, nugatory, piffling, piddling, pettifogging, frivolous, puerile, childish, featherbrained, foolish, insubstantial, superficial, shallow, small, tiny, token, nominal, small-time, light-weight, cheap, twopenny-halfpenny, inferior, bad, poor, shoddy, jerry-built, tawdry, rubbishy, trashy, pulp, worthless, second-rate, mediocre, commonplace, parochial, nit-picking (Inf), footling (Inf).

troubled beset, worried, anxious, perturbed, bothered, vexed, annoyed, puzzled, confused, baffled, perplexed, bewildered, mystified, nonplussed, inconvenienced, put out, harassed, plagued, distressed, embarrassed, deadlocked, snookered, in difficulties, stumped (Inf), stuck (Inf).

troublesome demanding, contrary, perverse, wayward, unmanageable, beyond control, stubborn, obstinate, obdurate, headstrong, intractable, refractory, badly behaved, naughty, disobedient, disruptive, obstreperous, critical, fault-finding, censorious, disapproving, grudging, discontented, fussy, fastidious, finicky, particular, bloody-minded (Inf), stroppy (Inf), moody (Inf), nit-

unaccustomed

picking (Inf), pedantic, pernickety (Inf).

truant absentee, defected, deserted.

true veritable, veracious, factual, right, unmistaken, unfictitious, honest-to-goodness, honest-to-God, gospel, Biblical, revealed. *See also* existing, truistic, truthful, authentic, proved, accurate, uniform, literal, pedantic, lifelike, faithful.

truistic intrinsic, primary, axiomatic, aphoristic, platitudinous, proverbial, preceptive, principled.

trustworthy dependable, reliable, responsible, true, steadfast, honourable.

truthful frank, veracious, honest, veridical, undisguised, unexaggerated, objective, unbiased, candid, sincere, open, openhearted, forthright, straightforward, direct, blunt, unflattering, plain, bald, outspoken, ingenuous, naive, artless, guileless, simple, unpretending, unpretentious, unassuming, unaffected, downright.

turbulent choppy, rough, bumpy, bouncy, pitching, rolling, stormy, tempestuous, boiling, seething, fuming, effervescent.

twentieth vigesimal, vicenary, vicennial.

two dual, double, duple, duplex, binary, dyadic, twofold, bifold, paired, coupled, twinned, matched, mated, doubled, squared, two abreast, second, secondary. *See also* two-sided, double-edged, double, half.

typical characteristic, representative, generic, stereotypical, special, specific, particular, peculiar, distinctive, defining, definitive.

U

ugly unattractive, hideous, repulsive, graceless, plain, homely, unsightly, unseemly, unshapely, deformed, contorted, mutilated, defaced, disfigured, unlovely, gross (Sl), unprepossessing, ill-favoured, monstrous, misshapen, misbegotten, gruesome, wan, grisly, graceless, inelegant, unaesthetic, unbecoming, unattractive, indelicate, uncouth, ungainly, distasteful, grotty (Sl), coarse, awkward.

ulterior hidden, concealed, secret, covert, underhand, unrevealed.

ultimate last, final, decisive, furthest; utmost, supreme, highest, paramount, top, superlative.

ululant howling, yowling, wailing, wailful, bellowing, full-throated, deep-throated. *See also* singing, humming.

unacceptable undesirable, unwelcome, offensive, displeasing, disagreeable, inadmissible.

unaccompanied alone, solo, unescorted, solitary.

unaccustomed unused, nonobservant, unfamiliar, unwonted, unhabituated, untaught, untrained, uneducated, inexperienced, innocent, naive, new, fresh, raw, callow, green, rusty, unskilful, unseasoned, immature, undomesticated, untamed, unbroken, wild. *See also* not customary.

unadorned plain, simple, unembellished, undecorated, unornamented, untrimmed, ungarnished, unpainted, uncoloured, unvarnished; spartan.

unanimous concordant, concerted, agreed, united, like-minded, harmonious.

unapproachable disdainful, obstinate, starchy, erect, stiff-necked, prickly, touchy, independent, self-sufficient, hardened, unbending, distant, aloof, stand-offish.

unassuming modest, unpretentious, humble, reserved, retiring, diffident.

unatoned unrepented, unregretted, unapologized for.

unauthorized illegal, illicit, unofficial.

unaware uninformed, ignorant, unsuspecting, oblivious, unknowing, incognizant.

unbalanced wobbly, shaky, unstable; asymmetrical, lopsided, unstable, uneven; deranged, irrational, mad, demented, crazy, unhinged; biased, bigoted, partisan, prejudiced, unfair, partial.

unbelievable incredible, counterintuitive, beyond belief, fantastic, miraculous, fabulous, bizarre, weird, ineffable, mysterious, mystical.

unbowed rampant, rearing, upraised, cocked up, pricked up.

uncanny weird, eerie, strange, mysterious, supernatural, ghostly; astonishing, astounding, extraordinary, inspired, remarkable, incredible.

uncertain unsure, unknown, doubtful, dubious, speculative, conjectural, hypothetical, provisional, disputable, contestable, controversial, moot, questionable, suspicious, distrustful, unbelieving, sceptical, agnostic, open-minded. *See also* irresolute, confused, indemonstrable, uncertified, indeterminate, unreliable, capricious.

uncertified undocumented, unchecked, uncorroborated, unverified, unauthenticated, unsigned, unratified, unascertained, unofficial, unproved.

unchaste unvirtuous, wanton, light, loose, frail, fallen, seduced, prostituted, fast, naughty, immodest, unblushing, shameless, flaunting, brazen, amoral, promiscuous, sex-mad, nymphomaniac, scarlet, whorish, tarty, meretricious (Arch).

uncivilized primitive, uncultivated, barbarian, savage, uncultured; coarse, vulgar, uneducated, boorish, uncouth, churlish.

unclaimed remaining, unappropriated, unowned, unpossessed, derelict.

unclean unhallowed, unholy, profane, corrupt, impure, coarse, unrefined, unpurified, septic, festering, poisonous, toxic, unsterilized, insanitary, unhygienic, infectious, contaminated, insalubrious, unhealthy, offensive, foul, nasty, abominable, disgusting, repulsive, nauseating, malodorous, stinking, fetid, sordid, squalid, scruffy, shabby, scurfy, leprous, scabby, mangy, pediculous, crawling, faecal, dungy, stercoraceous, excremental, carious, rotting, tainted, fly-blown, maggoty, grotty (Sl), manky (Sl), yucky (Sl), ponging (Inf), flea-bitten (Inf), lousy (Sl).

uncomfortable unpleasant, disagreeable, cramped, painful, awkward, rough; uneasy, disturbed, troubled, awkward, embarrassed, anxious.

uncommon rare, distinctive, unique, scarce, singular, extraordinary, outstanding; odd, queer, strange, curious, unusual, peculiar.

uncompleted undone, unfinished, unperformed, unprocessed, unfulfilled, unconsummated, unrealized, unattained, unachieved, unaccomplished, unexecuted, never-ending, incomplete, imperfect, fragmentary, missing, short, truncated, neglected, unelaborated, perfunctory, inattentive, neglectful, desultory, procrastinating, delaying, superficial, half-finished, half-baked, underdone, underdeveloped, immature, unripe, lacking, skimpy, scanty, scrappy, sketchy, in outline, sloppy (Inf).

unconcerned aloof, remote, indifferent, detached, cool, unworried.

unconditional unrestricted, unlimited, without strings, catch-as-catch-can (US), anything goes, absolute, discretionary, arbitrary, liberated, lax, excess, immoderate, loose, uninhibited, unbridled, intemperate, incontinent, unruly, abandoned, licentious, wanton, impure, permissive, free-for-all (Inf).

unconscious stunned, concussed, comatose, asleep, out cold, catatonic.

unconventional maverick, independent, freethinking, Bohemian, fringe, beat, hippie, wandering, nomadic, travelling.

uncooked raw, red, pink, rare, bloody, underdone, half-cooked, half-baked, cold, unwarmed, unprepared, undressed, ungarnished, indigestible, inedible, tough.

uncooperative unhelpful, negative, unwilling, obstructive, contrary, perverse, oppugnant, stubborn, obstinate, disobedient, fractious, refractory, recalcitrant, reactionary, resistant, bloody-minded (Inf).

uncovered opened, exposed, bare, naked, nude, divested, undressed, unclothed, stripped, starkers (Inf), nuddy (Inf), debagged (Sl). *See also* shed, bald.

unctuous oily, smarmy, slimy, greasy.

uncut entire, unabridged, unexpurgated, undivided, undiminished, unbroken, intact, unharmed, undamaged, unimpaired, unspoiled,

unadulterated, uncontaminated, untouched, inviolate, virgin, pure, faultless, flawless, perfect.

undaunted heroic, game, unfearing, unshaken, unshrinking, unflinching, unwavering, unhesitant, steadfast, indomitable, unconquered, unbeaten, steeled, armoured.

undeniable indisputable, definite, certain, sure, proven, incontrovertible.

under underground, subterranean, hypogeal, buried, sunk, submerged, immersed, underwater, subaqua, undersea, submarine, suboceanic, deep-sea, deep-water, bathyal, bathypelagic, benthic.

undercover hidden, secret, covert, clandestine, concealed, private.

underestimated undervalued, underrated, misjudged, miscalculated, underpriced, cheap.

underestimating deprecating, detracting, disparaging, scornful, minimizing, conservative, moderate, pessimistic, defeatist, modest, humble. *See also* underestimated.

underfed undernourished, hungry, famished, famine-stricken, starved, voracious, ravenous, fasting, emaciated, macerated, thin, lean, spare, skinny, wasting, anorexic, scraggy, stunted.

underhand secret, sly, deceitful, clandestine, furtive, covert, undercover.

underpriviledged deprived, impoverished, poor, destitute, needy.

understated underemphasized, conservative, minimized, underestimated, unobtrusive, unsubstantial, undervalued, underrated. *See also* subtle, simple, reserved, imperceptible, insipid, deflated, downplayed.

undertaken done, executed, incurred, assumed, self-imposed, assigned, promised, contractual. *See also* enterprising, overambitious.

undervalued underestimated, underrated, disparaged, belittled, denigrated, ignored, disregarded, neglected.

undeserving unworthy, unmeriting.

undesirable unwelcome, unwanted, disliked, unacceptable, inappropriate, unsuitable.

undeviating direct, straight, unswerving.

undirected unguided, random.

undisciplined wild, wayward, unruly, obstreperous, uncontrolled, wilful.

undiscriminating unselective, catholic, omnivorous, unselective, undifferentiating, colour-blind, tone-deaf, uncritical, indifferent, unfussy, unfastidious, unrefined, tasteless, indelicate, insensitive, coarse, vulgar, promiscuous, unrestrained, lax, loose, sloppy, casual, negligent, thoughtless, indiscreet, slipshod, careless, unmeticulous, inaccurate, cursory, perfunctory. *See also* impartial, indiscriminate, wholesale, vague.

undisputed certain, sure, undoubted, accepted, acknowledged, recognized.

undressed unclothed, uncovered, unclad, bared, nude, naked, stripped, strip-searched, disrobed, unattired, undraped, ungarbed, naturistic, gymnosophical, nuddy (Inf), starkers (Inf), bare-bollock (Sl). *See also* in dishabille, exposed, peeling, hairless.

undue unwarranted, unjustified, unnecessary, gratuitous, excessive, immoderate, unexpected, uncalled-for, unlooked-for, undeserved, unmerited, unearned.

uneasy edgy, nervous, agitated, anxious, restless, worried; uncomfortable, awkward, insecure, precarious.

unemphatic unimpassioned, unspirited, unexciting, uninspiring, tame, undramatic, inane, empty, pointless, lame, uninspired, boring, monotonous, stale, prosaic, prosy, commonplace, platitudinous, hackneyed, cliché-ridden, conventional, insipid, wan, colourless, dull, dry, vapid, flat, thin, wersh (Scot), careless, inexact, slovenly, rambling, prolix, disjointed, disconnected, garbled, amorphous, shapeless, smooth, loose, limp, unconvincing, ineffective, feeble, weak, meagre, languid, flaccid, exhausted, spent, vapouring, sloppy (Inf), wishy-washy (Inf), schmaltzy (Sl).

unemployed jobless, redundant, out of work, on the dole.

unentitled unauthorized, unsanc-

tioned, unlicensed, unqualified, unempowered, unfranchised, unchartered, unconstitutional, unlawful, illicit, illegal, illegitimate, unrightful, invalid, false, counterfeit, bogus, spurious, fictitious. *See also* presumptive, undue, undeserving, disentitled.

unequal disparate, different, disproportionate, incongruent, dissimilar, diverse, disagreeing, unlike, uneven, odd, asymmetrical, distorted, irregular, scalene, unique, unequalled, inferior, below par, unequable, variable, variegated, deficient, patchy, inadequate, insufficient, mismatched, ill-matched, ill-sorted, unbalanced, lopsided, unwieldy, listing, leaning, canting, heeling, off balance, overbalanced, top-heavy, overweight, underweight, askew, awry, swinging, swaying, rocking, unstable, untrimmed, unballasted, uncompensated, dizzy, giddy, toppling, falling, skewwhiff (Inf). *See also* unjust.

unequipped untrimmed, unrigged, dismasted, dismantled, undressed, uncovered, unfurnished, ill-provided, deficient, incompetent, incapable, unqualified, unfit.

unexpected unforeseeable, unpredictable, unanticipated, unguessed, unpredicted, unforeseen, fortuitous, rare, accidental, freakish, chance, fluky (Inf).

unexplained unsolvable, unresolved, uncertain.

unfair

unfair unjust, biased, bigoted, partial, partisan, prejudiced; dishonest, wrongful, unreasonable, foul, unsporting.

unfaithful faithless, promiscuous, adulterous, fickle, deceitful, false, cheating, philandering, cruising (Inf).

unfamiliar unknown, unheard of, unprecedented, unused, untried, untested, newfangled, novel, nontraditional, mould-breaking.

unfeeling blind, deaf, insentient, nerveless, senseless, insensitive, clumsy, heavy-handed, unresponsive, impassive, cold-blooded, apathetic, heedless, oblivious, unmindful, forgetful, unwary, impervious, unemotional, hardened, stolid, blockish. *See also* anaesthetized, unconscious, anaesthetic, sleepy.

unfinished incomplete, unpolished, unrefined, shapeless, rudimentary, preliminary, cursory, crude, raw, rough-and-ready, sketchy, vague, approximate.

unfit unsuitable, incompatible, wrong, malapropos, inapposite, inapt, ill-adapted, incapable, ineligible, unqualified, incompetent, inept, unskilful, untimely, inapplicable, inadmissible, inexpedient, inappropriate, inelegant, unbecoming, unseemly, improper, infelicitous, intrusive, outside, alien, fake, sham.

unforgivable unpardonable, unjustifiable, inexcusable, reprehensible, objectionable.

unfriendly cold, aloof, distant, sour, unsociable, uncongenial; hostile, antagonistic, alien, inhospitable.

ungrateful unthankful, unappreciative, ungracious, discourteous, ill-mannered, bad-mannered, forgetful, thoughtless, inconsiderate, unmindful, heedless, rude, selfish. *See also* unthanked, thankless.

ungulate unguligrade, cloven-hoofed, perissodactyl, equine, horsy, asinine, mulish, artiodactylous, piggy, porcine, swinish, ruminant, camelid, cervid, cervine, bovid, bovine, bullish, taurine, ovine, caprine, hircine, cavicorn, hyracoid.

unhappy sad, miserable, depressed, gloomy, crestfallen, disconsolate; unfortunate, ill-fated, luckless, cursed.

unhealthy ill, unfit, unsound, sickly, infirm, decrepit, weak, tired, run down, delicate, invalid, valetudinarian, hypochondriac, mangy, undernourished, anorexic, malnourished, emaciated, peaky, anaemic, jaundiced, bilious. *See also* sick, diseased.

unheard inaudible, toneless, faint, muted, soundproof, ultrasonic, off-air, turned off.

unhearing unaware, oblivious, deaf to, unheeding, unconcerned, indifferent, insensitive, inattentive.

unhurried leisurely, sluggish, languorous, lethargic, inert, slack, slothful, languid, lazy, indolent, sluggardly, listless, idle, apathetic, phlegmatic, methodical, patient, deliberate, circumspect, gradual, Fabian, meticulous, restrained, easy, moderate, gentle, relaxed, stealthy.

unhygienic unhealthy, unwholesome, unsanitary, insalubrious, verminous, dirty, filthy, unclean, squalid, sordid, bad, nasty, noxious, miasmal, dangerous, injurious, harmful, corrupting, polluting, deadly, poisonous, baneful (Arch), rat-infested, flea-bitten, flyblown, undrained, marshy, stagnant, foul, polluted, undrinkable, inedible, indigestible, unnutritious, unsound, stale, bad, off, rotten, decayed, mouldy, unventilated, windowless, airless, musty, fusty, smoke-filled, humid, stuffy, muggy, fuggy, overheated, steaming, freezing. *See also* contagious, toxic.

uniform constant, consistent, regular, harmonious, even, regular, horizontal, plane, level, harrowed, rolled, steamrolled, flattened, blunt, curved, rounded, waterworn, flat, ironed, unwrinkled, uncrumpled, unruffled, unbroken. *See also* conforming, agreeing, monotonous.

unimportant insignificant, immaterial, circumstantial, irrelevant, ineffectual, uninfluential, forgettable, inconsequential, insubstantial, inessential, unnecessary, dispensable, expendable, small, little, negligible, forgivable, venial, nondescript, inappreciable. *See also* obscure, secondary, trivial.

uninhabited deserted, unoccupied, abandoned, vacant, empty.

unintelligent ignorant, stupid, dense, foolish, thoughtless, unthinking, illogical, inane, fatuous, empty-headed, puerile, childish, infantile, immature, unwise, unperceptive, obtuse, stolid, thickheaded, blockheaded, oafish, boorish, doltish, witless, unoriginal, uninventive, unimaginative, imitative, dim-witted (Inf), dim (Inf), thick (Inf), dumb (Inf), dopey (Inf), silly (Inf), daft (Inf), loony (Sl), nutty (Sl), soft (Inf).

unintelligible incomprehensible, meaningless, unclear, obscure, esoteric, inconceivable, inexplicable, unaccountable, gibbering, incoherent, rambling, inarticulate, undiscoverable, unfathomable, inapprehensible, impenetrable, inscrutable, blank, deadpan, impassive, inaudible, muted, garbled, undecipherable, illegible, undiscernible, invisible, hidden, private, arcane, cryptic, mysterious, enigmatic, esoteric, gnostic, sphinxlike, oracular, profound, occult, mystic, transcendental, inexpressible, unpronounceable, unutterable, ineffable, incommunicable, untranslatable, poker-faced (Inf). *See also* unexplained, unrecognizable, difficult, strange, confused.

unintentional unintended, accidental, inadvertent, unconscious, unpremeditated.

uninterested unthinking, uncon-

unique

cerned, heedless, nonchalant, bored, insouciant, indifferent, dull, imperturbable, unresponsive, aloof, insensible, apathetic, complacent, phlegmatic, impassive, uninvolved, unmoved, detached, distant, disengaged, unenthusiastic, unstirred, numb, inactive, slow, stagnating, deadpan, idle, lackadaisical, sluggish, brain-dead (Inf) cool (Sl).

unique exceptional, incomparable, matchless, unrivalled, rare, singular; solitary, lone, single.

united joined, connected, accompanied, partnered, betrothed, promised, engaged, married, wedded, intimate, involved, inextricable, inseparable, intricate, indivisible, associated, symbiotic, incorporated, cooperative, merged, unified, conjoint, composite, combined, coalescent, collected, cohesive, adhesive, concretive, assembled, articulated, seamed, stitched, sewn, patched, darned. See also agreeable, conjunctive, tied.

universal cosmic, galactic, planetary, worldwide, global, international, cosmopolitan, national, nationwide.

unjoined unfastened, adrift, detached, nonaligned, neutral, discrete, distinct, differentiated, separative, excluded, excepted, exempt, abstracted, withdrawn, uninvolved, unmixed, immiscible, unassimilated, unrelated, alien, foreign, external, extrinsic, self-sufficient, insular, isolated, secluded, lonely, alone, left, abandoned, rejected, selective, reclusive.

unjust unfair, discriminatory, prejudicial, partial, partisan, subjective, one-sided, predisposed, preferential, intolerant, biased, prejudiced, jaundiced, warped, twisted, chauvinistic, sectarian, provincial, parochial, insular, xenophobic, racist, colour-prejudiced, anti-Semitic, sexist, ageist, class-prejudiced, homophobic, snobbish, bigoted, fanatical, narrow-minded, hidebound, pedantic, unimaginative, prejudged, preconceived, fixed.

unknown mysterious, strange, unfamiliar, unrecognized, unidentified, anonymous, secret, obscure, unseen, ineffable, unperceived, unexplored, uncharted.

unlawful abnormal, incestuous, sadistic, sado-masochistic, perverted, bestial, animalistic.

unlucky luckless, hapless, accident-prone, unfortunate, ill-fated, star-crossed, accursed, washed-up (Inf).

unmeant unintentional, unintended, involuntary, unimplied, misunderstood, misread, mistranslated, misinterpreted, misrepresented, mistaken, insincere, flattering, tongue-in-cheek.

unmelodious unmusical, tuneless, droning, singsong, untuned, cracked, off-pitch, off-key, off, sharp, flat, toneless, atonal, serial.

unmoved uninspired, wonderless, unamazed, unawed, unimpressed, unadmiring, irreverent, indifferent, blank, serene, tranquil, calm, cool, collected, composed, unsurprised, unexcited, imperturbed, sanguine, unimaginative, nonchalant, insouciant, disinterested, unconcerned, dull, impassive, apathetic, phlegmatic, blasé, unenthusiastic, unimaginative, unaroused, spiritless, cold-hearted, cold-blooded. See also predictable.

unnatural strange, odd, unusual, abnormal, extraordinary, bizarre; affected, forced, insincere, stiff, stilted, self-conscious; inhuman, unfeeling, callous; freakish, uncanny, strange, extraordinary.

unoccupied empty, vacant, available, unfilled, unlived-in, uninhabited, untenanted.

unordered unorganized, ungraded, unsorted, unclassified.

unorthodox unconventional, unusual, abnormal.

unpalatable unappetizing, uninviting, unsavoury, unpleasant, disagreeable, nasty, disgusting, foul-tasting, nauseating, uneatable, inedible, dank, brackish, undrinkable, corked, harsh, stale, rough, rancid, mouldy, rotten, high, bad, off, curdled, fermented, unwholesome, contaminated, poisonous, toxic.

unpleasant displeasing, disagreeable, unacceptable, rebarbative, uncomfortable, painful, discomfiting, discordant, unharmonious, trying, annoying, irksome, invidious, unwelcome, disliked, distasteful, un-

palatable, unsavoury, nasty, horrible, hateful, horrid, disgusting, offensive, odious, repulsive, loathsome, revolting, sickening, nauseating. See also objectionable, unpalatable, painful.

unpopular unattractive, unloved, undesirable, unwelcome, rejected.

unprepared unready, backward, behind, late, slow, disorganized, unarranged, surprised, caught unawares, caught napping, inexpectant, unguarded, exposed, vulnerable, unbuttoned (Inf). See also spontaneous, without preparation, untrained, immature, uncooked, unequipped.

unprofitable unremunerative, uneconomic.

unprosperous badly off, poor, poverty-stricken, penniless, bankrupt, homeless, down-and-out, broke (Inf), hard-up (Inf), stony-broke (Sl), skint (Sl).

unprotected undefended, unguarded, defenceless, ill-equipped, unarmed, unfortified, exposed, pregnable, untenable, dependent, subject, vulnerable, harmless, innocent, meek.

unprovided unsupplied, unfurnished, ill-equipped, absent, vacant, bare, empty, unstocked, unfilled, empty-handed, unsuccessful, unsatisfied, discontented, unfulfilled, unaccommodated, insatiable, greedy, stinted, rationed, skimped, lacking, needing, hard up, poor, undercapitalized, underfinanced, under-

unreal funded, underpaid, understaffed, undermanned, shorthanded.

unreal nonexistent, incorporeal, intangible, impalpable, insubstantial, ethereal, elusive, fleeting, obscure, nebulous, tenuous, vague, flimsy, indeterminate, indefinite, undefined, blurred, shadowy, ghostly, spectral, phantasmal; imaginary, illusory, fanciful, fantastical. *See also* illusory, theoretical, unrealistic, not the real thing.

unrealistic idealistic, utopian, visionary, romantic.

unreasonable unfair, unjust, immoderate, uncalled-for; irrational, foolish, absurd, erratic, headstrong, illogical.

unrecognizable incognizable, indistinguishable, unidentifiable, indistinct, undefined, hidden, indefinite, unknowable.

unrelated irrelevant, inapposite, inapplicable, inapt, inappropriate, unconnected, separate, unilateral, disassociated, extraneous, heterogenous, independent, singular, unallied, unaffiliated, detached, reclusive, discrete, segregated, uninvolved, divorced, foreign, alien, exotic, free, rootless. *See also* illogical, distorted, misconnected.

unreliable fallible, undependable, untrustworthy, treacherous, dishonest, perfidious, insecure, transient, unsound, unstable, unsteady, inconsistent, shaky, precarious, risky, hazardous, dangerous, perilous, ec-centric, erratic, irregular, unpredictable.

unrespected unrevered, unvenerated, trivialized.

unrestrained excessive, inordinate, immoderate, extreme, wild, exaggerated, hyperbolic, magnified, profuse, ostentatious, showy, preposterous, outrageous, fantastical.

unruly disobedient, unmanageable, intractable, rebellious, wilful, disorderly.

unsafe treacherous, untrustworthy, unreliable, doubtful, shaky, slippery, insecure, unsound, precarious, unbalanced, unsteady, unstable, tottering, top-heavy, tumbledown, ramshackle, dilapidated, rickety, frail, crumbling, condemned, jerry-built, shoddy, gimcrack, crazy, weak, leaky, waterlogged, critical, delicate, ticklish, risky, heart-stopping, nerve-racking, last-second, last-minute, dicey, dicky (Inf).

unsaid unspoken, unvoiced, unpronounced, unuttered, unexpressed, unarticulated, unmentioned, untold of, undivulged, unsung, unpromoted, unproclaimed, undeclared, unprofessed, unwritten, unpublished, tacit, half-spoken, understood, implied, inferred, inferential, implicit, meant, indicated, suggested, hinted, intimated, insinuated, implicative, suggestive, allusive, allusory.

unsatisfactory unacceptable, unpraiseworthy, uncommendable, inadequate, insufficient, rejected.

unselfish selfless, altruistic, considerate, kind, compassionate, sympathetic, humble, modest, self-denying, self-effacing, self-abnegating, self-sacrificing, high-minded, honest, noble, munificent, benevolent, charitable, generous, open-handed, big-hearted.

unsexed sterilized, barren, infertile, vasectomized, emasculated, castrated, gelded, neutered, spayed, caponized, unmanned, effete, sexless.

unsociable ungregarious, uncompanionable, uncongenial, uncommunicative, reclusive, reticent, sullen, morose, private, autistic, unforthcoming, unapproachable, withdrawn, domestic, seclusive, retiring, standoffish, aloof, haughty, remote, removed, distant, detached, indifferent, inaccessible, self-contained, forbidding, discourteous, impolite, ungracious, rude, disrespectful, unfriendly, cool, icy, frigid. *See also* shy, lonely, secluded.

unsolved unknown, undiscovered, unexplained, unrevealed, undivulged, unguessed, unsuspected, untold, unspoken, unexplored, untracked, untraced, uninvented, hush-hush (Inf).

unspecified indeterminate, indefinite, unnamed, unmentioned, several, few, many.

unsteady unreliable, teetering, tottering, apathetic, indifferent, suggestible, impressionable, flexible, pliant, easy-going, good-natured.

unsure uncertain, hesitant, doubtful, mistrustful, dubious, sceptical.

unthanked unrewarded, unacknowledged, unrecognized, uncredited, unrequited, forgotten, neglected, ignored.

unthinking thoughtless, unmindful, heedless, inattentive, disregarding, neglectful, careless, selfish, ungrateful, indifferent.

unthought unconsidered, unconceived, unimagined, undreamed-of.

untidy dirty, filthy, unclean, grubby, messy, scruffy, shabby, ragged, unsightly, unkempt, dishevelled, bedraggled, tousled, ruffled, crumpled, sluttish, slovenly, slatternly, careless, slipshod, shoddy, squalid, shambolic (Inf), slobbish (Inf).

untimely mistimed, inopportune, inauspicious, unpropitious, unfavourable, unseasonable, ill-starred, ominous, premature, early, late, unpunctual, inexpedient, inappropriate, unsuited, inapt, unbefitting, inconvenient, intrusive, interrupting, disturbing, disrupting. *See also* anachronistic, busy, mistaken, accidental.

untrained scratch, untaught, untutored, ignorant, uninstructed, undrilled, unexercised, unpractised, inexperienced, unskilled, apprentice, natural, simple, unsophisticated, artless, uncultivated, unrefined, unworked, unprocessed, untilled, fallow.

untrue false, libelous, slanderous,

unused

perjurious, fallacious, erroneous, fictionalized, imagined, distorted, concocted, fabricated, dreamed-up, misrepresented, inaccurate, nonsensical, distorted, perverted, exaggerated, understated. *See also* unreal, lying, misinformed, duplicitous, pretentious, dishonest, unfaithful.

unused inoperational, absent, unusable, unemployable, useless, impractical, unapplied, undisposed of, in hand, in reserve, reserved, preserved, idle, fallow, untried, in abeyance, suspended, deferred, pigeonholed, wasted. *See also* new, not wanted, disused.

unusual uncommon, exceptional, anomalous, incongruous, incoherent, aberrant, erratic, abnormal, eccentric, idiosyncratic, unique, individual, nonconforming, unconventional, unorthodox, odd, peculiar, whimsical, moody.

unwelcome rejected, undesirable, unacceptable, unpopular, unpleasant, excluded.

unwell ill, sick, out of sorts, unhealthy, poorly (Inf), under the weather (Inf).

unwilling disinclined, indisposed, loath, reluctant, demurring, averse. *See also* refusing, cautious, procrastinating, reluctant.

unyielding firm, determined, resolute, dogged, tenacious, persevering, stiff, wooden, rigid, adamant, inelastic, inflexible, unbending, obdurate, case-hardened, uncompromising, intransigent, unmoved, un-

influenced, unrelenting, immovable, irreversible, persistent, incurable, chronic, dour, grim, inexorable, unappeasable, implacable, merciless, pitiless, hard-nosed (Inf), hard-boiled (Inf).

upright perpendicular, erect, vertical, straight; virtuous, righteous, principled, decent, just, fair.

urban interurban, metropolitan, civic, municipal, citified, suburbanized, gentrified, no-go, red-light, suburban, subtopian, oppidan, parochial, countrified, rural, local.

urbane civil, refined, polished, suave, courteous, cultured.

urgent pressing, compelling, imperative, important, instant, crucial; clamorous, persistent, insistent, earnest, persuasive.

usable utilizable, employable, exploitable, convertible, applicable, available, functioning, working, useful, profitable, advantageous, consumable, disposable, reusable, recyclable.

used utilized, employed, exercised, occupied, exhausted, consumed, spent, worn, threadbare, shabby, down-at-heel, dilapidated, second-hand, pre-owned, cast-off, reused, recycled, reclaimed, dog-eared, well-worn, shopsoiled, beaten, hackneyed, stale, pragmatic, practical, utilitarian, everyday, ordinary, convenient, makeshift, provisional, exploited, subservient, instrumental, hand-me-down (Inf). *See also* usable.

various

useful handy, helpful, utilitarian, pragmatic, practical, applied, functional, commodious, convenient, advisable, sensible, suitable, expedient, applicable, versatile, multipurpose, adaptable, disposable, throwaway, available, operative, on-stream. *See also* usable, instrumental, profitable.

useless inutile, futile, unhelpful, unfit, unapt, unsuitable, inapplicable, inconvenient, inexpedient, impractical, unworkable, nonfunctional, ornamental, redundant, superflous, excessive, unnecessary, unwanted, expendable, dispensable, disposable, throwaway, unusable, unserviceable, unemployable, unqualified, unskilled, unable, incompetent, inept, inefficient, feckless, impotent, powerless, inadequate, nonfunctioning, inoperative, spent, effete, invalid, void, null, abrogated, obsolete, outmoded, old-fashioned, antiquated, worthless, valueless, rubbishy, trashy, unsaleable, naff (Sl), screwed-up (Sl), dud (Inf), kaput (Inf). *See also* futile.

V

vacant vacuous, void, devoid, empty, without content.

vacillating wavering, irresolute, unresolved, undecided, uncommitted, equivocal, tergiversating, undetermined, indecisive, unsure, uncertain, hesitating, dithering, stalling, evasive, shifty, wobbly. *See also* changeable, timid, unsteady.

vague indistinct, inexact, desultory, undefined, undifferentiated, undistinguished, interchangeable, standard, average, alike.

vain immodest, overproud, insubstantial, conceited, self-important, stuck-up, snooty, big-headed, megalomaniac. *See also* self-satisfied, self-admiring, cocky, self-interested, boastful, opinionated.

valid genuine, official, legitimate, authentic, bona fide, binding; logical, sound, convincing, cogent, well-founded, powerful.

valuable inestimable, priceless, costly, expensive, rich, irreplaceable, unique, rare, precious, prized, valued, treasured, gilt-edged, bluechip.

variable changeable, inconstant, vacillating, wavering, fickle, capricious.

variegated bicolour, dichroic, trichoic, polychromatic, multicoloured, pied, varicoloured, many-hued, motley, kaleidoscopic, spectral, prismatic, colourful, florid, ornamental, embroidered, chameleonic. *See also* iridescent, checked, striped, mottled.

various divers, sundry, multifarious, multiform, composite, multilateral, polygonal, many-sided, multifaceted, versatile, multipurpose, multirole, polymorphous, multinational, multiracial, multilingual, polyglot.

vast huge, extensive, enormous, immense, gigantic, limitless.

vaulted ribbed, fanned.

vegetating stagnating, inert, torpid, indolent, slothful.

venial vulnerable, imperfect, failing, frail, infirm, feeble, weak, lax, human, defective, deficient, indecorous, indiscreet, unseemly, flagrant, scandalous.

ventilated well-ventilated, fresh, fanned, air-conditioned, cooled, air-cooled.

verdant grassy, leafy, green, fresh, rural.

verifiable certifiable, documented, authentic, recorded, seconded, proved, witnessed. *See also* verificatory, verified.

verificatory demonstrative, illustrative, evidential, determining, validating, assuring, establishing, confirming, testificatory, ratificatory, prima facie, corroborative, supportive, substantial, circumstantial, probative, collative, checking.

verified validated, confirmed, ratified, authenticated, certified, documented, attested, avowed, avouched, avowed, averred, assured, sure, certain, checked, collated.

verminous infested, weevilly, maggoty, grubby, lousy, flea-bitten, moth-eaten.

versatile flexible, variable, adaptable, multifaceted, inconstant.

vertical upright, erect, upended, standing, straight, plumb, sheer, precipitous, plunging. *See also* unbowed, perpendicular.

vetoed banned, embargoed, contraband, injunctive, interdictive, suspended, cancelled, denied, rejected, refused, blackballed, restrictive, forbidden, *verboten* (Ger), impermissible, unauthorized, circumscriptive, exclusive, prohibited, barred, off-limits (US), taboo, repressive, suppressive, preventive, obstructive, inhibited, illicit, illegal. *See also* censored.

vexed annoyed, exasperated, harrassed, perplexed, irate, agitated.

vibrating resonant, pulsating, beating, throbbing, staccato, rhythmic, flickering, quivering, shivering, shaking, agitating, palpitating.

vicious cruel, savage, harsh, severe, sinful, corrupt.

victorious winning, triumphant, prizewinning, the best, world-beating, undefeated, unbeaten, unbowed, unvanquished, invincible, crushing, quelling.

vigilant observant, alert, wakeful, attentive, wary, circumspect.

vile bad, corrupt, degenerate, depraved, disgraceful, debased; loathsome, repulsive, sickening, repugnant, nasty.

villainous wicked, infamous, evil, base, depraved, notorious.

vindicable justifiable, defensible, arguable, refutable, rebuttable, warrantable, admissible, allowable, reasonable, explainable, excusable, pardonable, remissible, forgivable, condonable, venial, exemptible, dispensable.

vindicatory exculpatory, exonerative, justifying, defensive, argumentative, refuting, rejoining, retorting, rebutting, explanatory, excusatory, supportive, corroborative, apologetic, extenuating, mitigative, qualifying, palliative, remissive, justifying. *See also* innocent, vindicable, vindictive.

vindictive vengeful, requiting, retributive, unforgiving, spiteful, venomous, malicious, malevolent, punitive.

violent ferocious, vehement, excessive, outrageous, severe, virulent, intense, extreme, acute, unmitigated, blustering, bluff, rough, harsh, fierce, aggressive, tyrannical, heavy-handed, forceful, powerful, vigorous, energetic, wild, furious, angry, fuming, frenzied, frantic, frenetic, hysterical, kicking, struggling, thrashing, maddened, crazed, enraged, berserk, intemperate, unrestrained, uncontrollable, ungovernable, unruly, untamed, raging, rabid, irrepressible, ebullient, fiery, impassioned, ardent, fervent, eruptive, bursting, convulsive, catastrophic, cataclysmic, devastating, explosive, boiling, agitated, turbulent, tumultuous, tempestuous, stormy, riotous, uproarious, boisterous, rampant, roaring, murderous, barbarous, savage, brutal, bestial, cruel, vicious, bloodthirsty, ravening, hotheaded,

headstrong, bellicose, warlike, threatening.

virginal continent, abstinent, chaste, pure, innocent, maidenly, intact.

virtuous righteous, good, Christian, moral, spiritual, saintly, angelic, sanctified, godly, holy, perfect, unerring, noble, magnanimous, philanthropic, benevolent, generous, altruistic, unselfish, disinterested, idealistic, upright, irreproachable, impeccable, guiltless, blameless, stainless, spotless, immaculate, uncorrupt, innocent, honourable, decent, chivalrous, proper. *See also* ethical, worthy.

virulent deadly, poisonous, toxic, infective, lethal, noxious; hostile, bitter, resentful, acrimonious, malevolent, vindictive.

viscous viscid, inspissate, incrassate, sticky, tacky, adhesive, gluey, waxy, glutinous, colloidal, emulsive, gumbo, gummy, gaumy (Dial), slabby (Arch), thick, stodgy, heavy, mucilaginous, clammy, ropy, stringy, tough. *See also* gelatinous.

visible viewable, observable, distinguishable, discernible, perceptible, perceivable, discoverable, detectable, noticeable, conspicuous, clear, open, overt, plain, evident, manifest, obvious, patent, unconcealed, exposed, apparent, distinct, identifiable, recognizable, unmistakeable, public, available, present, concrete, material, tangible, palpa-

ble, external, outward, superficial,
surface. *See also* clear.

visual optical, ophthalmic, ocular,
binocular, mirror-like, reflecting,
two-dimensional, telescopic, microscopic, stereoscopic, three-dimensional, panoramic, scenic, visional, illusionary, imaginary. *See
also* seeing, bespectacled, visible.

vital important, necessary, key, crucial, requisite, critical; animated, vivacious, energetic, dynamic, forceful, vigorous; alive, live, living, animate.

vituperative abusive, vitriolic, vil-
ifying, reviling, denunciatory, blast-
ing, reproachful, ignominious, opprobrious, slanderous, libellous,
defamatory, calumnious, attacking,
threatening.

vivacious lively, spirited, ebullient, jolly, vital, animated.

vivid bright, colourful, intense,
glowing, dazzling; graphic, distinct,
realistic, powerful, telling, striking.

vocative invocatory, salutatory,
valedictory.

vociferous noisy, loud, vocal,
stentorian, full-throated, thundering,
booming, deafening, shouting,
screaming, yelling, bellowing, roaring, uproarious, clamorous, obstreperous, loudmouthed (Inf). *See
also* cheering, crying, hissing.

voiceless aphonic, dysphonic,
surd, silent, infant. *See also* low-
voiced, speechless, inarticulate.

volatile vapourable, vaporescent,
evaporable.

volcanic eruptive, seismic, pyroclastic, molten, laval.

voluntary unprompted, unforced,
charity, unpaid, philanthropic, humanitarian, altruistic.

vomiting sick, nauseated, seasick,
travel-sick, vomitive.

voracious greedy, gluttonous, ravenous, insatiable, avid, hungry.

vowed pledged, promised, assured,
guaranteed, committed, vouched,
sworn, on oath, depositional, true.

vulgar coarse, gross, cheap, ill-
bred, infra dig, inelegant, ungentlemanly, unladylike, unfeminine,
non-U (Inf), plebeian, plebby (Inf),
loud, showy, meretricious, ostentatious, garish, day-glo, gandy,
tawdry, glitzy. *See also* discourteous, ribald.

vulnerable unprotected, undefended, liable, susceptible, open to,
exposed, naked, bare, uncovered,
unarmoured, unfortified, ex-
pugnable, pregnable, helpless, defenceless, unarmed, isolated, deserted, abandoned, stranded, unsupported, unshielded, unattended, unguarded, unaware, naive, unprepared, unready.

W

wan pale, ashen, colourless, sickly,
pasty, gaunt.

wandering drifting, digressive,
circuitous, devious, divagatory,
rambling, digressing, discursive,

straying, errant, erratic, desultory, abstracted, inattentive, vagrant.

wanting lacking, missing, incomplete, short, sketchy; faulty, defective, imperfect, substandard.

warlike militaristic, bellicose, hawkish, unpacific, Ramboesque, aggressive, belligerent, pugnacious, combative, gung-ho, war-loving, warmongering, bloodthirsty, battle-hungry, war-fevered, fierce, tough, cruel.

warm balmy, temperate, mild, fair, clement, summery, humid, muggy, close, sticky.

warm-hearted cordial, hot-blooded, ebullient, homoiothermic, blushing, pyrexial, fevered, flushed, passionate, ardent, vehement, hot-tempered, burning, torrid, seething, inflaming.

warned cautioned, advised, counselled, cautious, wary, forewarned, forearmed, prepared.

warning cautionary, exemplary, advisable, counsellable, instructive, informative, notifying, hinting, monitory, admonitory, protesting, symptomatic, prognostic, predicting, premonitory, boding, foreboding, ill-omened, ominous, presageful, menacing, minatory, threatening, deterrent, dissuasive, frightening. *See also* warned.

warring fighting, battling, campaigning, belligerent, aggressive, bellicose, militant, mobilized, called-up, conscripted, armed, uniformed, arrayed, embattled, attacking, defending, engaged. *See also* warlike, military.

wary cautious, chary, distrustful, guarded, suspicious, vigilant.

waste superfluous, unwanted, unused, leftover, useless, worthless, throwaway.

wasteful extravagant, unnecessary, uneconomic, improvident, thriftless, prodigal, lavish, spendthrift, time-consuming, energy-consuming. *See also* waste.

watchful alert, attentive, observant, sharp-eyed, vigilant, on guard, careful, wary, circumspect, scrutinizing, surveying, heedful, curious. *See also* diligent, solicitous.

waterproof rainproof, stormproof, flood proof, showerproof, dampproof, watertight, snug, dry-shod.

watery aqueous, aquatic, hydrous, hydrated, hydraulic, hydrodynamic, hydrometric, hydrostatic. *See also* diluted, wet, wetting.

waving undulating, sinusoidal, shaking, tremulous, seismic, succussive, sussultatory, earth-shaking.

wayward fickle, flighty, perverse, headstrong, self-willed, recalcitrant.

weak impotent, powerless, feeble, soft, limp, flaccid, floppy, drooping, sagging, slack, relaxed, gimcrack, shoddy, rickety, wobbly, creaky, seedy, brittle, fragile, delicate, puny, ineffectual, helpless, defenceless, untenable, wonky (Inf). *See also* dilapidated, ill, weakened, weak-willed, insufficient.

weakened debilitated, enervated,

dissipated, sapped, wearied, exhausted, fatigued, tired, weary, failed, impoverished.

weak-sighted visually handicapped, visually impaired, partially sighted, one-eyed, day-blind, night-blind, colour-blind, red-blind, sand-blind, long-sighted, far-sighted (US), hypermetropic, presbyopic, short-sighted, near-sighted (US), myopic, astigmatic, squinting, strabismic, walleyed, cross-eyed, cock-eyed (Inf), boss-eyed (Inf), blinking, winking, nystigmatic, bleary, bleary-eyed, bloodshot, blurry, watery-eyed, red-eyed, seeing double.

weak-willed indecisive, irresolute, wavering, dithering, pusillanimous, vacillating, hesitant, half-hearted, nervous, timid, cowardly, sheepish, effete, mealy-mouthed, spineless, lily-livered, chicken-hearted, namby-pamby, limp-wristed, scared, yellow (Inf), gutless (Inf), chicken (Sl).

wealthy rich, affluent, well-off, well-paid, prosperous, well-to-do, moneyed, propertied, well-situated, well-endowed, comfortable, loaded (Sl), flush (Inf), well-heeled (Inf). *See also* solvent, opulent, lush.

weary exhausted, fatigued, tired, jaded, all in (Inf), dead beat (Inf); irksome, wearing, laborious, tiring, tedious, boring.

welcome desirable, acceptable, pleasant, gratifying, pleasurable.

welcoming inviting, hospitable.

well healthy, fit, able-bodied, hale, hearty, robust; good, satisfactory, lucky, fortunate.

well-behaved obedient, compliant, docile, willing, biddable, dutiful; well-bred, gentlemanly, ladylike, dignified, well-mannered, gracious, courteous, polite, good, ethical, virtuous, law-abiding.

well-known celebrated, renowned, famous, popular, infamous, notorious, flagrant, blatant, glaring, sensational, manifest.

well-made well-crafted, professional, workmanlike, shipshape, finished, stylish, elegant, artistic, Daedalian, clever, craftily contrived.

well-off well-to-do, solvent, affluent, prosperous, rich, wealthy, worth millions, well-heeled (Inf), flush (Inf), loaded (Sl).

well-ordered well-organized, methodical, meticulous, punctilious, systematic, scientific, businesslike, formal, accurate, straight, regular, uniform.

well-rounded curvy, curvaceous, pear-shaped, shapely, fleshy, fat, overweight, obese, corpulent, stout, plump, portly, paunchy, podgy, tubby, chubby.

wet soaked, drenched, sodden, wringing, sopping, soused, waterlogged, streaming, dripping, awash, soggy, bathed, steeped, flooded, awash, swamped, drowned, submerged, dipped, ducked, dunked.

wetting watering, moistening,

damping, humectant, irrigational, irriguous (Arch), hydrotherapeutic.

white pure-white, snow-white, lily-white, milky, lactescent, whitish, albescent, off-white, pearly, ivory, alabaster, marble, chalky, creamy, magnolia, ecru, unbleached, undyed, greige, silver, argent, fair-skinned, albinotic, Caucasian. *See also* whitened, white-haired, pale, pure.

white-haired fair, blond(e), platinum-blond(e), flaxen-haired, tow-headed, Nordic, canescent, hoary, grizzled, pepper-and-salt.

whitened bleached, blanched, decolorized, faded, colourless, achromatic, semitransparent, white-washed, snow-capped, hoary, frosty, foaming, spumy, white-hot.

whole integral, total, holistic, general, universal, entire, complete, full, integrated, unified, all, every, any, each, individual, single, one, all-inclusive, comprehensive, gross, all-embracing, across-the-board, global, worldwide, international. *See also* uncut, sound.

wholesale broad, wide, general, all-embracing, wide-ranging, all-inclusive, comprehensive, catholic, widespread, world-wide, global, universal, blanket (Inf), carpet (Inf).

wicked bad, sinful, evil, wrong, erring, iniquitous, nefarious, flagitious, unrighteous, misbehaving, improper, disreputable, disgraceful, fallen, knavish, roguish, rascally, slipping, sliding, recidivous, deteriorating, naughty, disobedient, dishonest, transgressing, trespassing, delinquent, criminal, corrupt, rotten, shameless, unprincipled, worthless, unscrupulous, conscienceless, despicable, reprehensible, vile, base, foul, beastly, heinous, vicious, cruel, brutal, hellish, maleficent, malevolent, hard-hearted, callous, villainous, miscreant, inhuman, infamous, flagrant, outrageous, abominable, atrocious, irredeemable, unforgivable, unpardonable, irremissible, inexpiable, unatonable. *See also* immoral, venial, impious, criminal.

wide extensive, expansive, ample, broad, immense, vast, large; distant, remote, away; dilated, outspread, expanded, outstretched; capacious, spacious, roomy, ample, commodious.

widespread extensive, rife, rampant, pervasive, ubiquitous, omnipresent, endemic, epidemic, pandemic.

widowed husbandless, widowered, wifeless, widowish, widow-like.

wieldy manageable, manoeuvrable, tractable, flexible, pliable, malleable, ductile, yielding, handy, convenient, foolproof, untroublesome, practical, adaptable, smooth-running, easy-running (US), easy-flowing (US), well-oiled.

wilful self-willed, headstrong, wayward, stubborn, dogged, obstinate, obdurate, intransigent, pigheaded,

willed

bullheaded, mulish, bloody-minded (Inf).

willed volitional, intentional, deliberate, willing, disposed, conative. *See also* iron-willed, wilful, autocratic, free.

willing agreeable, content, disposed, inclined, prone, ready, game, receptive, assenting, consenting, prepared. *See also* eager, amenable, helpful, voluntary.

windy breezy, blowy, gusty, blustery, squally, biting, freezing, bitter, icy, gale-force, northerly, boreal, anemological.

winter hibernal, midwinter, hiemal, brumal.

wintry chilly, cold, cheerless, bleak, frosty, icy, desolate.

wise sagacious, sapient, thoughtful, thinking, reflecting, reasoning, rational, sensible, profound, deep, intellectual, highbrow, knowledgeable, erudite, learned, perspicacious, perceptive, oracular, level-headed, prudent, judicious, balanced, objective, impartial, just, fair-minded, broad-minded, circumspect, unprejudiced, statesmanlike, diplomatic, discreet, tactful, politic, well-advised. *See also* intelligent.

wistful thoughtful, meditative, forlorn, pensive, reflective, melancholy.

wonderful marvellous, miraculous, astounding, aweful, amazing, beguiling, fantastic, imaginary, impossible, surprising, unexpected, improbable, unbelievable, incredible, inconceivable, unimaginable, indescribable, unutterable, unspeakable, ineffable, inexpressible, mind-boggling, mind-blowing, striking, overwhelming, awe-inspiring, breathtaking, impressive, admirable, exquisite, excellent, exceptional, extraordinary, unprecedented, unusual, remarkable, noteworthy, dramatic, sensational, shocking, exotic, outlandish, strange, odd, outré, weird, bizarre, peculiar, unaccountable, mysterious, enigmatic, puzzling, shattering, bewildering, thaumaturgic, magic, phenomenal, stupendous, fearful, frightening.

wondering astonished, astounded, amazed, awestruck, fascinated, admiring, impressed, surprised, inexpectant, marvelling, spellbound, rapt, dazzled, blinded, dumbfounded, flabbergasted, shocked, scandalized, thunderstruck, dazed, stupefied, bewildered, puzzled, aghast, gob-smacked (Sl). *See also* wide-eyed, wonderful.

woodcrafted carved, woodcarved, wood-turned, woodsculpted, whittled, woodburned, woodcut, black-line, white-line, wood-engraved, wood-blocked, woodprinted, xylographic(al), xylopyrographic(al), pyrographic(al).

wooded forested, forestal, timbered, afforested, reafforested, treecovered, arboreous, woodland, sylvan, sylvatic, sylvestral, bosky, copsy, braky.

woody ligneous, ligniform, hard-grained, soft-grained, wooden, treen, oaken, beechen, ashen.

wordy verbose, loquacious, long-winded, garrulous, rambling, diffuse.

workable operable, doable, manageable, manipulatable, manoeuvrable, negotiable, practicable, useful, viable.

working labouring, busy, industrious, employed, horny-handed, drudging, sweating, grinding, slogging, hard-working, plodding, persevering, tireless, energetic, active, painstaking, thorough, attentive, diligent, assiduous, exercising, practising, athletic. *See also* laborious.

worldly earthly, terrestrial, mundane, physical, carnal, profane; greedy, materialistic, avaricious, covetous, selfish; urbane, sophisticated, blasé, experienced, cosmopolitan.

wormlike vermicular, helminthic, fluky, cestoid, annelid, segmented, polychaetous, oligochaetous, lumbricoid, hirudinean, leechlike, helminthological.

worn frayed, tattered, ragged, threadbare, shabby; haggard, exhausted, fatigued, wearied, drawn, tired.

worried troubled, concerned, solicitous, caring, anxious, fretting, harassed, plagued, haunted, tormented.

worshipful reverential, venerational, adoring, praising, hero-worshipping, anthropolatrous, devoted, devotional, prostrate, humbled, supplicatory, penitent, prayerful, dutiful, meditative, contemplative, ascetic. *See also* idolatrous, worshipped.

worshipped honoured, revered, venerated, blessed, esteemed, adored, glorified, extolled, praised, admired, lionized, idolized.

worshipping reverent, devout, pious, observant, religious, devotional, prayerful, dutiful, solemn, congregational, parochial.

worthless valueless, unimportant, insignificant, paltry, futile. *See also* inferior, bad, poor, harmful, damnable.

worthwhile profitable, useful, advantageous, beneficial, wholesome, healthy, salutary, sound, good (for), salubrious, refreshing, edifying, favourable, kind, propitious.

worthy laudable, meritorious, deserving, admired, esteemed, respected, valued, admirable, estimable, creditable, approved, braw (Scot), noble, exemplary, good, virtuous, preferable, better, superior, first-rate, capital, prime, quality, superfine, rare, vintage, classic, outstanding, superlative, top-flight, flawless, perfect, choice, select, handpicked, exquisite, recherche, chosen, selected, tested, exclusive, famous, great, notable, eminent, distinguished, glorious, dazzling, splendid, brilliant, magnificent, marvellous, sensational, terrific, wonderful, superb, grand, fantastic, fabulous, amazing, prodigious, gorgeous, fab (Inf), super (Inf), dynamite (Sl), magic (Inf), top-notch (Inf), ace (Inf), A1 (Inf), stunning (Inf), smashing (Inf), corking (Sl), spiffing (Sl), topping (Sl), swell (Sl), dandy (Inf), classy (Sl), hunkydory (Inf), groovy (Sl), brill (Sl), cosmic (Sl), wizard (Inf), bang-on (Inf), scrumptious (Inf), jammy (Sl). *See also* best, valuable, worthwhile, not bad.

wretched distressed, downcast, miserable, pitiful, contemptible, base.

wrinkly crinkly, creased, puckered, lined, seamed, knitted.

wrong unjust, biased, prejudiced, discriminatory, favouring, partial, partisan, uneven, out-of-line (Inf). *See also* incorrect, improper, abnormal, immoral, in the wrong, unforgivable, gone wrong.

wry askew, crooked, distorted, twisted, deformed, lopsided; dry, witty, ironic, mocking, droll.

aureate, or, amber, honey-coloured, old-gold, mustard, buff, tawny. *See also* yellowish, yellow-haired, yellow-faced, cowardly.

yellow-faced sallow, jaundiced, bilious.

yellow-haired fair-haired, flaxenhaired, golden-haired, tow-haired, blond.

yellowish xanthous, luteous, fulvous, flavescent, sulphurous.

yielding productive, fruitful, fertile, prolific, bumper, harvested; submissive, compliant, biddable, accommodating, obedient, acquiescent; pliable, elastic, supple, pliant, flexible, resilient.

young juvenile, childlike, boyish, girlish, maidenly, virginal, innocent, underage, minor, preschool, junior, teenage, adolescent, pubescent, infantile, babyish, unfledged, kneehigh. *See also* immature, maturing.

young new, early, recent, fresh, raw; infant, junior, adolescent, juvenile, immature, green, callow.

youthful boyish, girlish, puerile, juvenile, immature, fresh.

Y

yearly annually, per annum, every year.

yellow creamy, beige, fallow, champagne, citron, chartreuse, primrose-yellow, citrine, gold, gilt,

Z

zealous fervent, ardent, enthusiastic, eager, intense, fanatical.

zero nil, no, infinitesimal. *See also* null.